W9-AOW-317

THE AMAZING STORY OF LISE MEITNER

Escaping the Nazis and Becoming the World's Greatest Physicist

To
Ruth Lewin Sime
in gratitude

THE AMAZING STORY OF LISE MEITNER

Escaping the Nazis and Becoming the World's Greatest Physicist

ANDREW NORMAN

AN IMPRINT OF PEN & SWORD BOOKS LTD.
YORKSHIRE – PHILADELPHIA

First published in Great Britain in 2021 by
PEN AND SWORD HISTORY
An imprint of
Pen & Sword Books Ltd
Yorkshire – Philadelphia

ISBN 978 1 39900 629 3

A CIP catalogue record for this book is available from the British Library.

Typeset in Times New Roman 11.5/14 by
SJmagic DESIGN SERVICES, India.
Printed and bound in the UK by CPI Group (UK) Ltd.

Pen & Sword Books Limited incorporates the imprints of Atlas, Archaeology, Aviation, Discovery, Family History, Fiction, History, Maritime, Military, Military Classics, Politics, Select, Transport, True Crime, Air World, Frontline Publishing, Leo Cooper, Remember When, Seaforth Publishing, The Praetorian Press, Wharncliffe Local History, Wharncliffe Transport, Wharncliffe True Crime and White Owl.

For a complete list of Pen & Sword titles please contact
PEN & SWORD BOOKS LIMITED
47 Church Street, Barnsley, South Yorkshire, S70 2AS, England
E-mail: enquiries@pen-and-sword.co.uk
Website: www.pen-and-sword.co.uk

Or
PEN AND SWORD BOOKS
1950 Lawrence Rd, Havertown, PA 19083, USA
E-mail: Uspen-and-sword@casematepublishers.com
Website: www.penandswordbooks.com

Contents

Acknowledgements

I am especially grateful to Ruth Lewin Sime for her kindness, generosity, and expertise; Philip and Anne Meitner for welcoming me into their home, sharing memories, and permitting me to use material from the Churchill College Archives; Bernard C. Burgess for help with translations and research; Anthea J. Coster and Arina R. Klokke for providing information about their grandfather Dirk Coster, and to Arina's husband Eelco M. Havik; Karl Grandin; Helen Fry; and Anthony Barrett.

I am grateful to Robert Pugh, Barry L. King, Tom Topol, the Reverend John Lenton, Allen Packwood, and Susanne Uebele.

I also thank Churchill College Archives, Cambridge, UK; University of Chicago Library; Rijksmuseum Boerhaave Museum Archives, Leiden, Netherlands; and the Archive of the Max Planck Society, Berlin-Dahlem.

Letters quoted in the text were, in the main, translated by Ulla McDaniel, Eleonore Watrous, Bernard C. Burgess, Rachel Norman, and Eelco Havik.

I am deeply grateful to my beloved wife, Rachel, for all her help and support.

Introduction

In May 1993, US physics historian Margaret W. Rossiter coined the term the 'Matilda effect'.[1] This was a reference to Matilda Joslyn Gage (1826–1898), whose article entitled 'Woman as an Inventor' had been published a century earlier in the *North American Review*.[2]

'Although woman's scientific education has been grossly neglected', said Matilda, 'yet some of the most important inventions of the world are due to her'. A woman, she said, 'has to face contempt of her sex, open and covert scorn of womanhood', and 'deprecatory allusions to her intellectual powers'. In the case of inventions by women, and Matilda listed some of the more major ones, 'she would hold no right, title, or power over this work of her own brain'.

Sixty-three years later, on 10 December 1946, a woman physicist, whom German-born theoretical physicist Professor Albert Einstein (1879–1955) described as even 'more talented than Marie Curie herself', would find herself a victim of such discrimination when her one-time colleague, Otto Hahn, was awarded the Nobel Prize for Physics. The third member of the team of Berlin researchers who Fritz Strassmann, the second member of the team, described as 'the intellectual leader of our team', was ignored. Her name was Lise Meitner.

Foreword

Lise Meitner was born in Vienna, Austria on 7 November 1878. She was petite in stature and, from a young age, passionately interested in science. Subsequently, she was determined to make this her career, but events were stacked against her from the start. For girls, unlike boys, state education ended at the age of 14, and, in any event, women were debarred from university education.

The breakthrough came when the Austrian government relaxed its regulations and permitted women to enrol as undergraduates. For Lise, this came only just in time, and she managed to master the preparatory school curriculum by cramming seven years of study into two and passing the qualifying examination – or *Matura* – to enter the university. However, having obtained her degree from the University of Vienna, she found it impossible to obtain a professional post and, accordingly, moved to Berlin where she worked as an unpaid laboratory assistant. Finally, in 1917 at the Kaiser Wilhelm Institute for Chemistry (KWIC) in Berlin's borough of Dahlem, her talents were recognised, and she was appointed head of physics with her own physics department. (This is not to be confused with the Kaiser Wilhelm Institute for Physics (KWIP), Dahlem, which shared the same campus.)

In 1938 there came another setback when Lise, on account of her being an ethnic Jew, was forced to leave Nazi Germany. Lise was not a practising Jew, for she and her siblings had been left to choose their own faith, and in 1908 she had become a Protestant (in a Catholic country), although she was not particularly religious. She, therefore, relocated to Sweden. However, she kept in contact with her fellow researchers in Berlin.

The heaviest known element at the time was uranium, and Lise was fascinated by the results that others had achieved by bombarding (i.e. irradiating) it with neutrons. In 1934, she persuaded Otto Hahn, the head of the KWIC, to join her in a 'uranium investigation'. The outcome was that her team of three, comprising herself and two chemists, Hahn and Strassmann, came up with some extraordinary results which they were at a loss to explain.

Lise, in collaboration with her nephew, who was also a physicist, was finally able to explain their results to them. In fact, they had unknowingly achieved nuclear fission – the theoretical explanation that became the foundation for various new fields of activity: nuclear power, medical-scanning technology, radiotherapy, electronics, and, of course, the atomic bomb – the creation of which filled Lise with horror.

The following is an account of the crucial part that Lise played in our understanding of the world of atoms, and how deliberate and strenuous attempts were made to deny her contribution, to belittle her achievements, and to write her out of the history books.

Chapter 1

The Journey Begins

I am at my home in Poole, Dorset, on the south coast of England, when the telephone rings. It's Robert ('Bob'), a friend of mine from just up the road. 'How do you fancy a day trip, to a very special place?' he enquires.

'And where might that be?'

'You'll see!'

Bob, myself, and another friend, Barry, are in the habit of going out together for day excursions, often to visit the home of some famous historical figure or other. But today begins mysteriously!

As we motor along, Bob driving, Barry asks him if he enjoyed his recent visit to Stockholm.

'It was great! Lovely to meet up with old colleagues.'

'And the Nobel Prize ceremony?' I ask, knowing that Bob was in the habit of attending this annual event. Chemistry is Bob's subject. In fact, he is a distinguished professor and still 'in harness'; whereas Barry, an educationalist, and I, a doctor, are both retired. 'Remind me, how long were you in Stockholm for?' I enquire.

'A decade or so.'

'Good facilities?' asks Barry.

'Excellent. The labs were excellent.'

'No regrets about settling back in the UK?'

'Only the wet weather, but I must admit, it's a bit warmer!'

I notice that we are driving along the A31 and about to join the M27. Bob is still being very secretive about our destination. Is it something connected with the city of Winchester, I wonder? Is it something to do with Jane Austen, who lived hereabouts? Ah, now we have joined the M3. Yes, Winchester, that will be it. We're going to Winchester!

No, I'm wrong! We've turned off to Basingstoke, and we're now on a minor road to heaven knows where. I hope Bob knows where he's going. He must do, I suppose, after all, he's got the SatNav switched on. Perhaps I can get a sly glimpse of it! Destination Bramley, Hampshire. The plot thickens! Now he's slowing down, and we park outside a church, the Church of St James. I know, he wants us to see something inside the church! But no, he's walking through the graveyard.

'And there it is!' says Bob.

'Bob's brought us all this way just to look at a gravestone?' says Barry.

The gravestone is modest and unpretentious, and partially covered with yellow lichen. It is therefore difficult to read the inscription, but fortunately the rays of the late morning sun are picking out some of the lettering nicely. And there is the name:

LISE MEITNER

1878–1968

'I must confess, I'm none the wiser!' say I.

'Me neither, I'm afraid,' says Barry. 'So, who was she?'

'Lise Meitner worked in Stockholm, in the same building as I did; her laboratory had been on the floor below me. She was there before my time, so I never met her, to my great regret! How I would love to have talked with her. Atomic physics, that was her speciality. In my opinion,' says Bob, 'Lise was perhaps the most underrated and undervalued scientist of all time.'

Chapter 5

The Friedrich Wilhelm University, Berlin

In September 1907, Lise commenced at the Friedrich Wilhelm University of Berlin, founded in 1809–1810 during the reign of Friedrich Wilhelm II, King of Prussia. Here, she would attend lectures by Professor Max Planck, who she would come to admire enormously.

Planck's assistant in the physics department was Max von Laue, one year her junior, who would also play an important part in her life.

Up until now, Planck had not been an advocate of women's education, but in Lise's case he was prepared to make an exception. In short, he was impressed by her ability, by her knowledge, and by her achievements to date. In fact, Planck extended the same warmth and hospitality to Lise as he did to his male staff. At weekends, for example, he would invite to his home not only the noteworthy scientists of the day, but also his research students and his assistants. His wife Marga and twin daughters Emma and Grete, who were a decade younger than Lise, were also present. What fun and games were to be had in his garden! 'Come on, Miss Meitner, surely you can run faster than that!' cries the breathless professor, as everyone joins in a game of 'catch as catch can'! Little does Planck realise that, in encouraging Lise, he is paving the way for her, one day, to play a part in one of the greatest discoveries in science.

Lise would describe Planck in almost reverential terms and refer to his 'unusually pure disposition and inner rectitude', 'lack of pretension', and selflessness.[1]

At the Friedrich Wilhelm University, Lise met biology student Gerta von Ubisch, to whom she was to owe a debt of gratitude. Years later, Lise told Gerta:

> Please believe me when I tell you that I have never forgotten what a help you were to me when I came to Berlin as a relatively young girl; knowing nobody and very shy in a

> way (as you really noticed) that bordered on human fear. I have very fond memories of the beautiful weekends in your delightful family mill.

This was almost certainly a reference to the Ubisch family home. For as scholar of German literature Professor James Reed pointed out, the Brandenburg region, which surrounds the national capital Berlin, is famously known as the 'mill country'.[2]

Continued Lise, 'It was a beautiful, carefree time in which we luckily had no idea of what was coming.'[3]

Gerta was to pay Lise the following compliment.

> Nobody, who has seen your early beginning could have doubted that that would lead to something great one day. The extent to which coincidence was involved in bringing you into this field of science may be disregarded. I presume that you would have achieved the same success in any other field of theoretical and practical physics. My small part in world history has been to help you over the first months of shyness with your colleagues, to whom you would otherwise have come a little later. The prejudice against women was unjustified and soon overcome, but as a man you would have made faster progress.[4]

It was autumn 1907 and Lise was approaching her 29th birthday. She was approached by Dr Otto Hahn, a chemist, who was her junior by four months. Hahn was interested in radioactivity, and he suggested that he and she collaborate. This liaison would prove to be fruitful in many ways but would one day end in a most unsatisfactory manner, as will be seen.

Meanwhile, a familiar problem had arisen. Hahn worked for Professor of Chemistry, Emil Fischer (1852–1919), who would not permit women even to set foot in his Institute.

'Don't worry, Miss Meitner, I have found a way around it,' said Hahn. He told her that in the basement of the university's Chemistry Institute is a former carpenter's workshop, which he had fitted out as a laboratory when he had first arrived here the previous year. Furthermore, it had a separate entrance, so this is where the two of them could perform their studies of radiation together. As Lise said, Hahn soon had the room 'fitted out' for measuring radioactivity.[5]

But Lise had to understand that it was strictly forbidden for her to enter any other part of the Chemistry Institute, including Hahn's own laboratory on the first floor. She would therefore be unable to participate in any way in the collegiate atmosphere of the place, and enjoy the company of other like-minded researchers, and the opportunities to exchange ideas.

After Lise had settled in Berlin there was a pattern of regular Christmas visits to Vienna, presumably to see her widowed mother, springtime excursions to the countryside, and summer holidays in the mountains. Lise's nephew Philip Meitner recalled how, when Lise was working in Berlin, she always stayed with his family when she returned home to Vienna.

In 1908, Elisabeth Schiemann (born in Estonia 1881), a resident of Berlin since 1887, commenced as a student at the Friedrich Wilhelm University, being awarded her doctorate in 1912. She and Lise met, and this was the start of a lifelong friendship. Elisabeth became a geneticist and pioneer crop researcher, about whom more will be said shortly.

In September 1909, Lise attended the 81st Convention of German Scientists and Physicians held at Salzburg, in her Austrian homeland. Here she met 30-year-old physicist Professor Albert Einstein of the University of Bern in Switzerland. Einstein proceeded to explain to his audience, Lise included, his Theory of Relativity: Energy equals Mass multiplied by the Square of the Velocity of Light – or $E=mc^2$. This concept, of the interchangeable nature of mass and energy, he had first proposed on 27 September 1905 in a paper entitled, 'Does the Inertia of a Body depend upon its Energy Content?' The paper was published in the German scientific journal, *Annallen der Physik*. One day, Lise would employ Einstein's theory to unravel one of the great mysteries of science!

Meanwhile, it was all so thrilling! And she herself had reported to the conference on two experiments that she had carried out with Otto Hahn. The shy and retiring Lise was gradually growing in confidence!

Philipp Meitner, the father to whom Lise owed so much, died on 9 December 1910.

Chapter 6

Atomic Theory: Elements, Atoms, Radioactivity

Countless people, but principally physicists and chemists, played their part in elucidating the structure of the atom and the way atomic forces operate. These are just a few of them.

Greek philosophers Democritus (c.460–c.370 BCE) and Leucippus (fifth century BCE) theorised that the world was made up of tiny particles, which we now call 'atoms', 'atomos' being Greek for 'indivisible'.

In 1672, British scientist Sir Isaac Newton (1643–1727) proposed, in his Theory of Light, that light itself is made up of particles.

In 1803, British chemist John Dalton (1766–1844) proposed that the atoms of a given element are exactly alike in terms of their weight, and atoms of different elements are different.

An element is a substance that cannot be decomposed into a simpler substance or substances by chemical means. Elements such as carbon, lead, copper, mercury, and silver have been known since ancient times.

In February 1920, US science writer and educator Anne Marie Helmenstine summarised the position in regard to naturally existing and artificial (man-made) elements.

> Of the 118 elements that have been discovered, there are 90 elements that occur in nature in appreciable amounts. Depending on whom you ask, there are another 4 or 8 elements that occur in nature as a result of radioactive decay of heavier elements. So, the grand total of natural elements is 94 or 98. As new decay schemes are discovered, it's likely the number of natural elements will grow. However, these elements will likely be present in trace amounts.
>
> There are 80 elements that have at least one stable isotope. The other 38 elements exist only as radioactive

> isotopes. Several of the radioisotopes instantly decay into a different element.
>
> It used to be believed that of the first 92 elements on the Periodic Table [from hydrogen Z=1 to uranium Z=92] that 90 elements occur naturally. (Technetium [Z=43] and promethium [Z=61] were synthesized by man before they were identified in nature.)

Periodic Table: a table of the chemical elements arranged in order of atomic number.

> Assuming 98 elements can be found, however briefly, in nature, there are 10 found in extremely minute amounts.

They are technetium (Z=43), promethium (Z=61), astatine (Z=85), francium (Z=87), neptunium (Z=93), plutonium (Z=94), americium (Z=95), curium (Z=96), berkelium (Z=97), and californium (Z=98).[1]

What was known about elements, atoms, and radioactivity in the first decade of the twentieth century?

In 1869, Russian chemist Dmitri I. Mendeleev (1834–1907) had published a Periodic Table of the known elements, in which they were listed in order of their atomic weight. (Atomic weight: The ratio of the average mass per atom of the naturally occurring form of an element to 1/12 of the mass of carbon-12 atom.) There were, however, gaps in the record as many elements were, as yet, undiscovered.

The Periodic Table has eighteen vertical columns (known as 'Groups') and seven horizontal rows (known as 'Periods'). Elements in the same group have similar properties. In each period, elements change in nature from metals on the left-hand side to non-metals on the right-hand side, with metalloids (possessing some of the properties of each) in the middle. Mendeleev also noticed that elements with similar atomic structure tend to recur at intervals in the table – hence 'Periodic'.

In 1896, French physicist and engineer (Antoine) Henri Becquerel (1852–1908) discovered (natural) radioactivity (which he called 'invisible phosphorescence') in salts of uranium. The uranium had emitted rays which registered on a photographic plate. Three years later, he showed that this consisted of charged particles that were deflected by a magnetic field.

Uranium is a white, radioactive, metallic element (number 92 in the Periodic Table). It was discovered by German chemist Martin H. Klaproth (1743–1817) in 1789. One day, the study of uranium by Lise and Hahn would stir up an enormous controversy and change the shape of the modern world.

In 1897, British physicist, Joseph J. Thomson (1856–1940) discovered the electron, a small atomic particle with a negative charge (-1).

In 1898, Polish-born French physicist and chemist Marie Curie (née Sklodowska, 1867–1934) and her husband, French physicist Pierre Curie (1859–1906), discovered the existence of the radioactive elements radium (Z=88) and polonium (Z=84). They theorised that radioactive particles cause atoms to break down, releasing radiation that takes the form of energy and subatomic particles. The Curies' discovery gripped the imagination of scientists, Lise and Hahn included, and 'world attention crystallized around "radioactivity" and its strange and fascinating properties'.[2]

Subatomic particles: particles smaller than or occurring within an atom.[3] They include protons, neutrons, and electrons.

In 1899, New Zealand-born British physicist Ernest Rutherford (1871–1937) was appointed Professor of Physics at McGill University, Montreal, Canada. In that year, he discovered two new kinds of radiation (emanation) emitted from uranium. He named them alpha (α) rays and beta (β) rays. These are now known not to be rays, but particles.

The alpha particle consists of two protons and two neutrons bound together (into a particle that is identical to a helium nucleus). The beta particle is an electron.

Proton: a subatomic particle with a positive charge (+1).

Neutron: a subatomic particle of similar mass to a proton but with zero electric charge (charge 0).

Electron: A subatomic particle with a negative charge, with mass about 1,800 times less than a proton. Electrons are present in all atoms in groupings called 'shells' around the nucleus.

Further attempts to understand the atom and atomic theory would provide one of the greatest intellectual challenges of the twentieth century.

In 1900, Max K.E.L. Planck (1858–1947) proposed his quantum theory, which postulates that atoms can neither emit nor absorb electromagnetic radiation in a continuous manner, but only in discrete amounts, which he called 'quanta'. Hence, 'Quantum Theory'.

Quantum: A discrete quantity of energy proportional in magnitude to the frequency of the radiation it represents.[4]

A quantum has the characteristics of both particles and waves. The quantum theory enabled scientists to describe the relationship between energy and matter at the atomic and subatomic levels.

It was Planck who had recognised Lise's talents and helped her on her way.

In the same year, 1900, Becquerel postulated that the electron and the beta particle were one and the same. Also in 1900, an unknown type of emission from radium (Z=88) was discovered by French chemist and physicist, Paul Villard.

In 1902, Rutherford, and British radiochemist Frederick Soddy at McGill University, Montreal, Canada, published a paper entitled 'Law of Radioactive Change'. Until now, atoms had been regarded as indivisible. But Rutherford and Soddy demonstrated that radioactivity involved the spontaneous disintegration of atoms into other, as yet unidentified, substances.

In 1903, Rutherford named the emission discovered by Villard 'gamma rays', which differed from the alpha and beta rays that he himself had previously discovered.

In 1905, Einstein (who took Swiss nationality in 1901) published his Theory of Special Relativity. This included the famous equation $E=mc^2$, indicating that energy and matter are interchangeable. Einstein theorised that the quantum theory applied not just to the emission or absorption of energy, but to the radiation itself. Thus, quanta of electromagnetic radiation, such as light, are called 'photons'.

Photon: A particle with zero mass consisting of a quantum of electromagnetic radiation.

One day, Lise Meitner would receive the greatest praise from Einstein. She would also make use of his equation to solve a supremely important question in nuclear physics.

In 1907, Rutherford, together with German physicist Hans W. Geiger and British-born New Zealand physicist Ernest Marsden, devised the alpha particle scattering experiment that led, in 1911, to the discovery of the atomic nucleus.

These great men and women of science, and in particular those who had experimented with bombarding atoms with subatomic particles, paved the way for one of the most significant discoveries in the history of scientific research; one in which Lise was to play a pivotal role.

Chapter 7

The Collaboration Between Otto Hahn and Lise Meitner

A fruitful period of collaboration between Lise and Otto Hahn occurred between late 1907 and 1934, when an event occurred in Rome which would change both of their lives.

Prior to 1907, Lise had produced four scientific papers. All that was now about to change and between 1907 and 1934 she published forty or so scientific papers jointly with Hahn, and another sixty-three scientific papers either alone, or as a co-author with others.[1]

Hahn's story is as follows. He was born on 8 March 1897 in Frankfurt am Main in the state of Prussia, then part of the German Empire. His father Heinrich was a prosperous glazier, married to Charlotte (née Giese).

Hahn studied chemistry and mineralogy at the University of Marburg and at the University of Munich. In 1901, he received his doctorate in chemistry for a dissertation entitled, 'On Bromine [Z=35] Derivatives of Isoeugenol'. Having completed his one-year military service, he returned to Marburg to work for two years under the leadership of German chemist Professor Theodor Zincke.

In 1904, Hahn worked at University College, London under the leadership of British chemist Sir William Ramsey, who discovered the inert gases. Hahn's subject was the new field of radiochemistry. Hahn stated that it was Ramsay 'who advised me to give up organic chemistry and work on radioactivity'.[2] This brought immediate dividends, and Hahn's first important discovery was announced to the Royal Society in London on 16 March 1905.[3] Ramsay, he said,

> handed to me … a large porcelain dish containing more than a hundred grams of white barium salt. I was to extract the ten milligrams of radium it contained, according to Madam Curie's method, which was fractional crystallisation, and to establish the atomic weight of that element.

In fractional crystallisation, small amounts of radioactive substances preferentially precipitate with larger quantities of known compounds. Upon repetition the concentration of radioactive substance is increased.

However, Hahn continued,

> It very soon turned out that the preparation that had been thought to be radium must in fact contain another one or more radioactive substances. What happens is that during fractional crystallisation the radium becomes enriched in the first fractions, and by means of many repetitions of the process one finally gets it in the pure state. In my preparations, however, I still found some considerable activity in the more easily soluble fractions; in fact, besides the long-lived radium emanation there was a strongly radiating substance that was given off by the short-lived thorium [Z=90]. Its activity was considerably stronger than that of normal thorium. So, it was bound to be a new radioactive element, which obviously must have arisen out of the parent element, thorium.[4]

In other words, having extracted and separated the radium from the barium salt, Hahn did not simply dismiss the presence of strong radioactivity in the leftover residue, but kept an open mind. One day, in a matter of much greater importance, he would fail to exhibit this quality, as will be seen. Because 'the new radio-element could not be chemically distinguished from thorium, but was, however, much more strongly radioactive … Hahn called it radio-thorium for short'.[5]

Hahn believed that in radiothorium he had discovered a new chemical element, radioactive and with a characteristic half-life (the time required for exactly half of a parent nuclide to decay into a daughter nuclide). It was, in fact, an isotope of an existing element, as would later become clear, thanks to the work of Frederick Soddy, as will shortly be seen.

Nuclide: a nucleus defined by its number of protons (atomic number) and its number of neutrons.

Isotope: One of two or more atoms of the same element that have the same number of protons in their nucleus but different numbers of neutrons. Isotopes of an element have different atomic masses, even though their chemical properties are identical.

From autumn 1905 to summer 1906, Hahn worked at the Physical Institute of McGill University in Montreal, Canada with Professor Ernest Rutherford. Here, in 1906, he discovered what he called radioactinium. Said Rutherford, 'Hahn has a special nose for discovering new elements'. In fact, radioactinium was not a new element but an isotope of actinium (Z=89). Said Hahn of Rutherford, his 'enthusiasm for the new field of radioactivity aroused my own enthusiasm'.[6]

In 1906, Hahn returned to Germany and took up his new position with Emil Fischer at the Chemical Institute of the University of Berlin. In June 1907, he obtained his 'Habilitation'. This had involved the following. Having been awarded a doctorate, a candidate applied for an assistantship at the institute of a professor in his or her field. After a maximum period of six years, during which time the person undertook research and some teaching, a scholarly dissertation was submitted. Once 'habilitated', the candidate was deemed eligible to commence lecturing immediately (such a lecturer being called a 'Privatdozent') and to apply for the post of full professor (instead of an adjunct, or assistant professor) at any German university.

Hahn was now qualified to teach at the University of Berlin. In that year, he discovered what he called mesothorium – an isotope of radium (Z=88).

Meanwhile, said Lise, the physics department, where informal colloquia (academic conferences or seminars) were held on Wednesdays, became 'an exceptional center of intellectual activity'.[7] This was the type of environment in which she thrived.

In the wider world, further discoveries were being made. In 1907, Rutherford discovered the principle of the 'half-life'.

In 1908, Geiger (1882–1945) and Rutherford (now Professor of Physics at Victoria University, Manchester, UK) invented a radiation counter as a means of detecting ionising radiation.

Ion: An atom or group of atoms that has either lost one or more electrons, making it positively charged (a cation), or gained one or more electrons, making it negatively charged (an anion).

Ionisation: The process of producing ions.

Ionising radiation: Radiation of sufficiently high energy to cause ionisation in the medium through which it passes. It may consist of a stream of high-energy particles (e.g. electrons, protons, alpha particles) or short-wavelength electromagnetic radiation (ultraviolet, X-rays, gamma rays).

In 1908, US experimental physicist Robert A. Millikan (1868–1953) measured the charge (-1) and mass of the electron. (The proton charge is +1.)

In that year, 1908, Hahn identified another radioactive substance (an isotope of bismuth Z=83), which he called actinium C. This followed chemical separation and the measurement of alpha and beta ray decay curves.

In that same year, when university education for women 'was at last officially permitted and regulated, Emil Fischer at once gave Lise permission to enter the Chemistry Institute laboratories during working hours'.[8]

In 1909, Rutherford and British solar physicist, Thomas Royds, demonstrated that alpha particles were doubly ionised helium atoms.

In 1909, Hahn discovered radioactive recoil: when an atomic nucleus emits an alpha particle, the nucleus will recoil physically. Lise swiftly employed the 'recoil method' as a means of separating the elements.

In 1909, US experimental physicist Robert Millikan and US physicist Harvey Fletcher ascertained the charge of an electron, which is considered to be the fundamental basic unit of electric charge.

In 1910, Hahn was appointed Professor of Chemistry at the Friedrich Wilhelm University of Berlin.

In 1911, Geiger and Marsden, under the direction of Rutherford, observed that, when alpha particles are used to bombard the atom, about one particle in 8,000 is deflected sideways or backwards. This finding led Rutherford to propose that the mass of the atom is concentrated at its centre. Thus, the atomic nucleus was discovered. Rutherford also deduced that the nucleus was positively charged, and that electrons were located outside of the nucleus.

In 1911, the Kaiser Wilhelm Gesellschaft (Society-KWG) was founded, in order to promote the natural sciences in Germany.

Chapter 8

The Kaiser Wilhelm Institute for Chemistry, Berlin

In October 1912, Hahn and Lise relocated to the newly constructed Kaiser Wilhelm Institute for Chemistry (KWIC), which was located at Dahlem on the outskirts of Berlin. The institute was officially opened on the 12th of that month and Lise, who was now to join the institute, had been invited to the opening ceremony, where she met German Emperor and King of Prussia, His Imperial Majesty Kaiser Wilhelm II. Hahn now became director of the Radioactivity Research Department. Meanwhile, Lise would continue to collaborate with Otto Hahn, but only as a guest. However, the facilities here at the KWIC were truly excellent![1]

In late 1912, Planck appointed Lise as his assistant. This was her first paid position. Up until then, 'a meagre stipend from her father was her sole source of financial support'.[2]

Swedish physicist Eva von Bahr came to the University of Berlin in January 1913 and studied for a short time under Professor of Experimental Physics, Heinrich Rubens. It was during this time that she met Lise, and this was the start of another lifelong friendship. On 22 March 1913, Otto Hahn married Edith Junghans, an art student from Vienna.

In 1913, Frederick Soddy (1877–1956) showed that a radioactive element may exist in a number of different forms – what he called 'isotopes'.

Most elements in nature are represented by several isotopes. However, of all the elements in the Periodic Table, twenty-one exist with only one naturally occurring nuclide (i.e. they are not naturally isotopic). Some elements have many isotopes: for example, mercury has seven. There are only twenty elements in which isotopes have been produced artificially; most of them being heavy elements at the top of the Periodic Table.

Thanks to Soddy, the three new radioactive substances discovered by Hahn in 1905 (radiothorium), 1906 (radioactinium), and 1908 (mesothorium) were subsequently identified as isotopes of thorium and actinium: namely, thorium-228, thorium-227, and actinium-228 respectively. (The numbers 227 and 228 are the approximate atomic weights of each element, defined as mass of each of that element's respective atoms.)

In 1913, Thomson discovered that the gas neon was composed of atoms of two different atomic masses (neon-20 and neon-22). This was the first physical evidence for the presence of isotopes in an element.

In 1913, Danish theoretical physicist Niels Bohr, son of schoolmaster (Henrik Georg) Christian Bohr and Ellen (née Adler who was Jewish), used Planck's quantum theory of physics to propose his quantum model of the atom, whereby electrons could only travel in certain select orbits around the nucleus. These orbits, otherwise known as 'shells', or 'energy levels', are located at fixed distances from the nucleus. The orbit of least energy – the so-called 'ground state' – was the most stable.

A 'shell' is made up of several orbitals. Electrons could move between energy levels, but only by absorbing or emitting energy. The shell energy defines the amount of energy required to displace an electron from its orbital.

One day Bohr would become Lise's colleague, friend, supporter, and staunch admirer.

As already mentioned, in 1869 in his Periodic Table, Mendeleev listed the elements according to their relative atomic weights. However, in 1913, British physicist Henry G.J. Moseley (1887–1915) stated that the position of an element in the Periodic Table is governed *not* by its atomic weight, but by its atomic number (or 'Z' number, which is equal to the number of protons in its atomic nucleus). The Periodic Table was now reorganised, based on atomic number and not atomic weight.

The time would come when Hahn would fail to recognise this well established fact, confuse atomic weight with atomic number, and, as a result, come to erroneous conclusions on matters of the utmost importance.

Lise was now in her element, if the pun may be forgiven, and when she was invited to attend Sunday piano and violin concerts with Einstein and Planck, she knew she had definitely arrived on the scene!

Austrian physicist and mathematician Philipp Frank (1884–1966) studied at the University of Vienna under Ludwig Boltzmann (Lise's former teacher). He succeeded Einstein as professor at the Charles University of Prague (1912–1938). Frank described Lise as 'a Viennese girl, who had made such great discoveries in the field of radioactive phenomena that Einstein liked to call her "our Madame Curie", and in private sometimes expressed the opinion that she was a more talented physicist than Madame Curie herself'.[3]

Hahn, however, gave the impression that he preferred to remain aloof in his relationship with Lise. Said he:

> There was no question of any closer relationship between us outside the laboratory. Lise Meitner had had a strict lady-like upbringing and was very reserved, even shy. I used to lunch with my colleague, Franz Fischer almost every day, and go to the café with him on Wednesdays, but for many years I never had a meal with Lise Meitner except on official occasions. Nor did we ever go for a walk together. Apart from the physics colloquia that we attended, we met only in the carpenter's shop. There we generally worked until nearly 8 in the evening, so that one or other of us would have to go out to buy salami or cheese before the shops shut at that hour. We never ate our cold supper together there. Lise Meitner went home alone, and so did I. And yet we were really close friends.[4]

This may not be everyone's idea of a close friendship! Hahn implies that he and Lise did not socialise, but a photograph gives the lie to this assertion. It shows a group including Lise and Hahn, and one of Max Planck's daughters, having a picnic. Whether this daughter was Emma or Greta is not known, as they were identical twins, and it was probably the other twin who took the photo. It was also the case that Lise was to become godmother to Hahn's son Johann – 'Hanno' – born 1922, and also to Hahn's grandson (Johannes) Dietrich Hahn, born in 1946.

Hahn did go so far as to admit that Lise 'took a hand in my musical education. During the long hours when we were taking readings she would, to the best of her ability, hum to me many a song by Brahms, Wolf, Schumann and other composers'.[5]

Chapter 9

War and After

The First World War commenced on 28 July 1914: Germany and Austria were now pitted against Britain and France. On 1 August 1914, Hahn was conscripted into a territorial reserve unit of the German army.

On 1 October 1914, the Kaiser Wilhelm Institute for Physics (KWIP), Berlin-Dahlem was officially founded, with Einstein as its first director.

In 1915, Lise asked herself, 'How can I in all conscience remain here in the laboratory when our soldiers are suffering at the Front?' She therefore resolved to embark on a course of training in order to become an X-ray technician with the Austrian army. But in 1916, having served in this capacity with the Austrian army, she returned to her laboratory, but not without a deep sense of guilt, for the war continued to drag on.

Meanwhile, in January 1915, Hahn was transferred to a gas combat unit, involved in chemical warfare research. In other words, the creation and production of poison gas, to be used on both the western and the eastern fronts. The unit was led by German chemist Professor Fritz Haber.

Hahn was undoubtedly aware that the use of poison gas was contrary to the Hague Convention. However, the French had been the first to use it, followed by the British. Did he have any reservations about it, even when he witnessed the suffering of the victims of gassing at first hand? No, for he subsequently confessed that, 'our minds were so numbed that we no longer had any scruples about the whole thing'.[1] Lise, who probably never witnessed a gas attack, declared, 'Above all, any means which might help shorten this horrible war are justified'.[2] There would come a time, however, when Lise would utterly condemn the use of a far more powerful weapon, one which she, inadvertently, had a hand in creating.

In December 1916, Hahn was transferred to Supreme Headquarters (GHQ) in Berlin, where he resumed his radiochemical research.

On 19 June 1917, Eva von Bahr, who was now a teacher at the Brunnsvik Folk High School, Dalarna, Sweden, married fellow-teacher

Niklas Bergius. She was henceforth known as Eva von Bahr-Bergius. In that year, Lise was invited to Sweden to stay with the couple for several weeks.

In that same year, Lise was given the task of creating a department of radioactive physics at the KWIC. The department for radioactivity was subsequently divided into 'Chemical-radioactive' (Hahn) and 'Physical-radioactive' (Meitner).[3]

In 1917, German physicist James Franck was invited by Haber to join his Kaiser Wilhelm Institute for Physical Chemistry and Electrochemistry (KWIPCE).

Franck was born in Hamburg, Germany in 1882. He was the son of Jacob, a Jewish banker, and Rebecka, who was also Jewish. In 1907, Franck had married Ingrid (née Josephson), who bore him two daughters, Dagmar and Elisabeth ('Lisa'). He was one of Lise's closest friends and confidants. In 1918, Franck became head of the physics department at Haber's institute.

In 1918, Hahn and Lise published a paper entitled 'The Mother of Actinium: A New Radioelement of Long Half-life'. This was to announce a spectacular success. Following chemical separation, they had measured the alpha activity of a uranium sample and discovered a new element (Z=91 on the Periodic Table). They named it 'protactinium'. This was a joint discovery and Hahn recognised it as such. But in his future dealings with Lise, in relation to another and this time hugely important discovery, this would not unfortunately be the case.

The war ended on 11 November 1918 with the surrender of Germany and the signing of the armistice. During the course of the First World War, Lise and Hahn had jointly published a total of eight scientific papers.

In 1919, Lise was appointed head of the physics department at the KWIC. Meanwhile, von Laue was appointed Professor of Theoretical Physics at the University of Berlin.

In that year, Rutherford bombarded nitrogen atoms with alpha particles, during the process of which, nitrogen was transformed into an isotope (non-radioactive) of oxygen. Also, subatomic particles were emitted, which Rutherford suggested might be the nuclei of hydrogen atoms. In 1920, Rutherford named these particles 'protons', and he and his team were thus the first in history to initiate an artificial nuclear reaction. Rutherford also demonstrated that protons are present in the nuclei of all atoms.

Chapter 10

The Years 1920 to 1934

By the year 1920, the Hahn-Meitner department at the KWIC had become two independent departments. Professor Otto Hahn would now concentrate on radiochemistry; Lise would concentrate on nuclear physics.

In 1920, Franck left the KWIPCE for Göttingen, Germany, to take up the post of Professor of Experimental Physics at the University.

In 1921, Hahn discovered 'Uranium Z', a nucleus whose charge and mass were equal to Protactinium-234, but which differed in its radioactivity. He thus became the first person to discover nuclear isomerism. Not for the first time, or the last, Hahn would rely on a physicist to provide a theoretical explanation for this phenomenon, which German theoretical physicist and philosopher Carl Friedrich von Weizsäcker did in 1936.

Isomerism: the existence of atomic nuclei that have the same atomic number and the same atomic weight, but different energy states.

In spring 1921, at the invitation of Swedish physicist Manne Siegbahn, Lise spent several weeks in Sweden, as visiting professor at the University of Lund. Here, she studied X-ray spectroscopy, which was a means of identifying elements by measuring the wavelengths of their X-ray spectra. In 1924, Siegbahn would be awarded the Nobel Prize for Physics, 'for his discoveries and research in the field of X-ray spectroscopy'. Years later, Lise would encounter Siegbahn once again, in entirely different circumstances.

In 1922, Lise discovered what came to be called the 'Auger Effect', whereby an atom that has been ionised by the removal of an electron from an inner shell loses energy by emitting an electron from an outer shell. Lise's discovery was published in the *Zeitschrif für Physik*. However, the details were contained in a long scientific paper that included other observations, and this is perhaps why it went unnoticed at first. In the event, however, credit for this was given to the French physicist

Pierre V. Auger, who made the same discovery and described it more clearly the following year.

In that year of 1922, Lise obtained her *Habilitation*, a rare and extraordinary feat for a woman at that time. She was now eligible to teach at the University of Berlin, and to apply to become a full professor. In the same year, von Laue was appointed deputy director of the KWIP.

In 1924, French physicist Louis de Broglie (1892–1987) suggested that electrons had wave-like properties in addition to their particle properties. The principle was later applied to protons and neutrons. Meanwhile, Lise co-authored the Institute of Chemistry's *Yearbook*.

In 1925, British experimental physicist Patrick Blackett (1897–1974), a research fellow working under Rutherford's direction at the Cavendish Laboratory in Cambridge, bombarded nitrogen with alpha particles. He became the first to prove that radioactivity could cause the transmutation of one element (in this case nitrogen) into another (oxygen).

Between 1922 and 1925, Lise published sixteen articles on atomic structure and on beta and gamma radiation.

In 1926, Lise was appointed Germany's first female Professor of Physics at the University of Berlin. She now counted amongst her associates a glittering array of other notable physicists, including German-born Jewish theoretical physicist Albert Einstein; New Zealand-born British physicist Ernest Rutherford; British physicist James Chadwick; German-US physicist Otto Stern; German theoretical physicist Max Planck; Niels Bohr; Austrian-Dutch theoretical physicist Paul Ehrenfest; and Max Born.

In 1927, German theoretical physicist Werner K. Heisenberg proposed the quantum uncertainty principle which states that the position and momentum of a particle in a quantum system cannot be measured with absolute precision.

On 26 October 1927, Lise described how Hahn had written to her, and she had thanked him for his advice 'on how to adjust the slit' of the beta spectrometer.[1]

In 1928, Hahn was appointed Director of the KWIC. In that year, German physicist Friedrich Hund (1896–1997) and US physicist Robert Millikan (1868–1953) proposed the concept of the molecular orbital, a mathematical function describing the wave-like behaviour of an electron. Also in that year, the Geiger counter was improved and was known as the Geiger-Müller counter.

In 1930, Austrian physicist Erwin Schrödinger (1887–1961) introduced his 'cloud model' of the atom, based on quantum theory. Electrons do not travel in fixed orbital 'shells' around the nucleus, he said, but they are to be found in 'electron clouds', the denser parts of the cloud being where the greatest density of electrons is located. Furthermore, electrons have wave-like properties, as well as behaving like particles of matter. It is impossible to specify the location of an electron, only to estimate the mathematical probability of it being in a certain place at a certain time. Schrödinger's 'cloud model' was subsequently extended to include protons and neutrons, which are viewed not as definite solid particles, but as statistically determined 'clouds'.

In 1929, Soviet-US theoretical physicist George Gamow (1904–1968) proposed his 'liquid-drop' model of the atomic nucleus. This described the collective behaviour of nucleons in the nucleus as a whole. The liquid-drop model predicts that splitting of the atomic nucleus involves deformation of its structure, resulting in the formation of two (and possibly three) droplets of similar but not exactly equal size. One day almost a decade later, this would have enormous implications for Lise and her nephew, Otto Frisch.

In 1930, Gamow proposed his theory of alpha particle decay. The nucleus contained alpha particles, which were able to escape from it via its 'skin'.

But nuclear fragments that were any larger than the alpha particle would find it very difficult to escape. This is due to the 'Coulomb Energy Barrier', named after French physicist Charles-Augustin de Coulomb (1736–1806).

An alpha particle has a charge of two units. A fragment with a charge of six units, said Gamow, could *never* escape.

Said US physics historian Spencer R. Weart,

> this picture was firmly embedded in the minds of nuclear physicists including in particular, the Berlin group [Hahn, Lise, and Strassmann]. It was one reason they assumed that a uranium nucleus could never find a way to transform in one step, into a substantially lighter nucleus. How could a substantial fragment escape?[2]

The adoption of this notion of Gamow's by Lise and the Berlin team was to have adverse consequences for them, as will be seen.

In 1932, James Chadwick (1891–1974), Rutherford's assistant director of research at the Cavendish Laboratory (of which Rutherford had been director since 1919), discovered that, when beryllium was bombarded by alpha particles, an unknown radiation was emitted. Chadwick concluded that the radiation was composed of particles with mass similar to that of protons but without electrical charge. Chadwick had discovered the neutron.

Chadwick subsequently showed that the presence of neutrons pushes the protons apart, thereby helping to reduce the electrostatic repulsive forces between them, and thus increasing the stability of the nucleus.

This is according to Coulomb's law, formulated by Charles-Augustin de Coulomb, which states that in the case of two electrically charged objects, like charges repel and unlike charges attract. This is known as the 'Coulomb force' (electrostatic force).

Chadwick also showed that neutrons always reside in the nucleus and are about the same size as protons.

In April 1932, at the Cavendish Laboratory in Cambridge, British physicist Sir John D. Cockcroft (1897–1967) and British-Irish physicist Ernest T. S. Walton (1903–1995), working under Rutherford's leadership, used a linear accelerator (whereby subatomic particles could be accelerated in straight lines) to bombard lithium nuclei with high-energy protons, whereupon alpha particles were emitted. This was the first artificially induced disintegration of an atomic nucleus.

A linear particle accelerator accelerates charged subatomic particles or ions to a high speed by subjecting them to a series of oscillating electric potentials along a linear beam line. The principles for such machines were proposed by Swedish physicist Gustav Ising in 1924, and the first working machine was constructed by Norwegian physicist Rolf Widerøe in 1928.

In 1932, Heisenberg proposed the proton-neutron model of the nucleus i.e. that an atom is composed of a positively charged nucleus with negatively charged electrons surrounding it, bound together by electrostatic force. He used this to explain isotopes.

Chapter 11

Radioactivity: Tools Available to Lise and the Berlin Team in Their Investigation of Uranium

Natural radioactivity

As already mentioned, natural radioactivity was first discovered by Henri Becquerel in 1896.

A radioactive atom will attempt to reach stability by ejecting nucleons (protons or neutrons), as well as other particles, or by releasing energy in other forms.

What determines whether or not an isotope is radioactive or not?

It is the balance of protons and neutrons in the nucleus that determines whether a nucleus is stable (non-radioactive) or unstable (radioactive). An excess of either neutrons or protons causes instability.

In the lower section of the Periodic Table, say up to atomic number 20 (or 'Z' number, which equals the number of protons in the nucleus of an atom), the nuclei of the lighter elements have equal or roughly equal numbers of protons and neutrons. These elements are therefore stable, and not radioactive. It is also the case that when a nucleus contains an even number of protons, this gives it greater stability. But, on moving upwards in the Periodic Table towards the heavier elements, the number of neutrons progressively exceeds the number of protons; finally reaching a ratio of about 1.3 to 1. When the imbalance reaches a certain level, the instability becomes so great that the element becomes radioactive.

All nuclides with an atomic number above 83 and atomic mass number above 209 are radioactive. (But there are also some lighter nuclides that are radioactive, for example the two isotopes of carbon.)

There are eleven naturally occurring radioactive elements: elements 84 (polonium) to 92 (uranium), together with technetium (element 43) and promethium (element 61).

Radioactive decay

Radioactive decay may be seen as an attempt by the atoms of a radioactive isotope to achieve a lower energy state and thereby achieve stability. In the process, a radioactive nuclide spontaneously transforms into a daughter nuclide, which may or may not be radioactive, with the emission of one or more subatomic particles or photons. This daughter nuclide will usually contain a different number of protons and therefore, by definition, be a different chemical element to the parent. If the daughter nuclide is also unstable (radioactive), the process is repeated until stability occurs.

In the case of natural radioactivity, the decay is a slow process. Uranium-235, for example (which consists of 92 protons, 92 electrons, and 143 neutrons), has a half-life of 700 million years (and is only weakly radioactive).

Types of radioactive decay

Alpha decay

Put simply, an alpha particle (helium nucleus) is emitted from the nucleus. Alpha decay typically occurs in the heaviest nuclei.

Beta (negative) decay

Put simply, this involves the conversion of a neutron into a proton and a beta particle (electron). This electron is emitted from the atomic nucleus (and is not one of the electrons surrounding the nucleus). In the process, a new element is formed, the daughter isotope having a different number of protons from the parent.

Gamma decay

The nucleus emits radiation (short-wavelength electromagnetic waves) without changing its composition.

The decay curve

The radioactivity of a material refers to the rate at which it emits radiation. Radiation is the energy or particles that are released during radioactive decay.

Radioactive decay occurs each time a nucleus ejects particles or energy, and each radioactive isotope decays at its own unique rate, i.e. each radioactive nuclide has its own characteristic half-life. By measuring the number of disintegrations per unit of time, a decay curve may be constructed. This is useful when it comes to the identification of isotopes. The time required for half the original nuclide to decay is called the half-life of the nuclide.

Artificial (or induced) radioactivity

Elements are stable if they have the same number of protons and neutrons. Nuclei with too many (or too few) neutrons are unstable and will decay by emitting radiation. In beta decay, following neutron bombardment and the capture of a neutron by the nucleus, the new neutron will turn into a proton and emit an electron (from within the nucleus itself and not from outside the atom). Beta decay, therefore, causes the atomic number of the nucleus (then number of protons) to increase by one, while the mass number remains the same.

In terms of quantum mechanics, an ‘excited state’, such as occurs when a neutron is captured by an atomic nucleus, describes a system that has a higher energy level than the ‘ground state’ (i.e. more energy than the absolute minimum). A system in an excited state tends to return quickly to the ground state. Therefore, excited nucleus states are usually very short-lived and decay occurs almost immediately.

Available instrumentation

The photographic plate

This is a glass plate to which an emulsion of silver salts is applied. The absorption of radiation by the salts causes the film to turn from transparent to dark and non-transparent.

The Gold Leaf Electroscope (GLE)

This was invented by British clergyman and physicist Abraham Bennet in 1786. It consists of a glass jar fitted with the non-conducting cork through which passes a metal conducting rod. To the lower end of this rod are attached two gold leaves side by side in parallel. When a positively charged object is placed in contact with the top of the conducting rod, the positive charges within the rod are repelled and pass downwards into the gold leaves, which now each become positively charged. Once again, like charges repel and the leaves separate, like a pair of butterfly wings. This is according to Coulomb's law.

The number of electrons in an atom equals the number of protons, so atoms are electrically neutral. But if an atom loses or gains an electron, it becomes negatively or positively charged, respectively. Such charged particles are called ions.

If a source of radioactivity is placed adjacent to the GLE, it serves to ionise the air within the jar.

This enables the charge on each gold leaf gradually to leak away, whereupon the gold leaves come back together. The rate at which this occurs depends on the strength of the radioactivity. The stronger the radiation, the quicker the leaves will close up. Clearly, the virtue of the GLE is twofold. Firstly, it enables radioactivity to be detected: secondly, with the aid of a stopwatch and a measuring scale, the rate of radioactive decay can be plotted in the form of a decay curve.

Lise's workbench for the discovery of fission, about which more will be said shortly, survives to this day, as do the instruments that she used in her research. They include a neutron source (a mixture of radium and beryllium), with which to bombard uranium. This

> was sealed in brass tubes and placed in a paraffin block, which slowed down the neutrons. To measure radioactivity and the extremely small quantities of radioactive substances produced, the measuring room was equipped with home-made Geiger-Müller radioactivity counters to determine the decay of the extremely small quantities of radioactive substances produced. The Geiger-Müller counters used to detect the radiation produced were powered by large, high-voltage batteries and transferred impulses to mechanical counters through amplifiers and auxiliary apparatus.[1]

The batteries were kept on the shelf below.

The Geiger-Müller counter

An excellent description of that vital tool in the armoury of Lise and all who study radiation was given by science and technology writer Chris Woodford.

> A Geiger counter is a metal cylinder filled with low-pressure gas sealed in a plastic or ceramic window at one end. Running down the center of the tube there is a thin metal wire made of tungsten. The wire is connected to a high, positive voltage so there's a strong electric field between it and the outside tube.
>
> When radiation enters the tube, it causes ionization, splitting gas molecules into ions and electrons. The electrons, being negatively charged, are instantly attracted by the high-voltage positive wire and as they zoom through the tube, collide with more gas molecules and produce further ionization. The result is that lots of electrons suddenly arrive at the wire, producing a pulse of electricity that can be measured on a meter and (if the counter is connected to an amplifier and loudspeaker) heard as a 'click'. The ions and electrons are quickly absorbed among the billions of gas molecules in the tube, so the counter effectively resets itself in a fraction of a second, ready to detect more radiation.

Geiger counters can detect alpha, beta, and gamma (electromagnetic) radiation.[2]

The cloud chamber

This is

> an apparatus for tracking ionized particles. It consists of a vessel fitted with a piston and filled with air or other gas, saturated with water vapour. When the volume of the vessel is suddenly expanded by moving the piston outwards, the vapour cools and a cloud of tiny droplets forms on any nuclei, dust, or ions present. As fast-moving ionizing particles collide with the air or gas molecules, they show as visible tracks.[3]

Chapter 12

Enrico Fermi and Uranium

In 1934, Italian-US physicist Enrico Fermi (1901–1954) was Professor of Experimental Physics at Sapienza University in Rome. In that year he discovered how to produce slow (thermal) neutrons.

'Fermi recognized in neutrons a powerful new tool for probing the nucleus, since the uncharged particles could enter nuclei unhindered by the Coulomb barrier, which normally repels incoming particles.' Fermi's source of neutrons was radon gas (a decay product of radium) mixed with powdered beryllium.

In October 1934, 'Fermi decided to put a piece of paraffin in front of his neutron source. Much to everyone's astonishment, neutrons passing through this paraffin produced an extraordinarily enhanced activity in the nuclei they interacted with.' Fermi deduced that the paraffin had slowed the neutrons down.[1] Fermi had discovered that slow neutrons are more readily captured by the target nuclei than are fast neutrons.

Slow neutrons: Neutrons that have had their energies reduced by a 'moderator', a substance that slows down the speed of energetic neutrons.

In regard to the 'problem of transmuting chemical elements into each other', said Fermi, 'it is well known that the first and most important step towards its solution was made only nineteen years ago by the late Lord Rutherford, who started the method of the nuclear bombardments'. That was in the year 1919. Rutherford demonstrated, said Fermi,

> that, when the nucleus of a light element is struck by a fast alpha-particle, some disintegration process of the struck nucleus occurs, as a consequence of which the α-particle remains captured inside the nucleus and a different particle, in many cases a proton, is emitted in its place. What remains at the end of the process is a nucleus different from the original one; different in general both in electric charge and in atomic weight.

In other words, a different element had been created. Sometimes, said Fermi, this one disintegration will result in a stable nucleus. Very often, however, the 'product nucleus' is unstable, and it therefore disintegrates further until stability is achieved. After the first 'practically instantaneous disintegration', said Fermi, 'the emission of electrons' follows after 'a lag in time'. This is the 'so-called artificial radioactivity' which 'was discovered by Joliot and Irene Curie at the end of the year 1933'.

It was Fermi's opinion that there might be an alternative to alpha particles as a means of producing artificial radioactivity. 'I decided therefore to investigate … the effects of the bombardment with neutrons'. A problem was, he said, that

> the available neutron sources emit only a comparatively small number of neutrons. This drawback is, however, compensated by the fact that neutrons, having no electric charge, can reach the nuclei of all atoms, without having to overcome the potential barrier, due to the Coulomb field that surrounds the nucleus.[2]

Fermi commenced his experiments in March 1934, and in May 1934 he bombarded the final element, uranium. Of the forty-seven elements that he and his team bombarded with neutrons, Fermi discovered that elements 'of any atomic weight could be activated' in a process whereby

> the absorption of the bombarding neutron produces an excess in the number of neutrons present inside the nucleus; a stable state is therefore reached, generally through transformation of a neutron into a proton which is connected to the emission of a β (beta)-particle.

What Fermi is describing here is the process of 'beta decay'.

> Fermi showed that although lighter elements, when bombarded with neutrons, were transmuted to still lighter elements by the chipping off of either a proton or an alpha particle, heavier elements act in the opposite way.

> Their stronger electrical barriers captured the incoming neutron, making them heavier. However, being now unstable, they decayed to an element with one more unit of atomic number.[3]

In collaboration with Italian physicist Franco D. Rasetti and Italian chemist Oscar D'Agostino, Fermi discovered that 'the heavy radioactive elements thorium and uranium' could be 'strongly activated by neutron bombardment'. In the case of uranium, 'the existence of periods [in other words, decay products with half-lives] of about 10 sec, 40 sec, 13 min, plus at least two more periods from 40 minutes' was 'well established'. But what Fermi was unable to confirm was 'whether these periods represent successive or alternative processes of disintegration'.

Fermi now concentrated on the 'beta-active element with the period [half-life] of 13 min'.[4] He now 'excluded the possibility that the 13 min-activity is due to isotopes of uranium (Z=92), protactinium (Z=91), thorium (Z=90), actinium (Z=89), radium (Z=88), bismuth (Z=83), lead (Z=82). Its behavior excludes also ekacaesium (Z=87) and emanation (Z=86)'.

This 'negative evidence' suggested to him the possibility that thirteen-minute activity derived an element with an atomic number 'greater than 92'. In other words, heavier than uranium, the heaviest known element at that time.[5]

Unfortunately for Fermi, however, his conclusions were based on false assumptions and no such 'transuranic' elements (transuranic: 'beyond uranium') had in fact been produced! Had Fermi checked the remainder of the elements with lower atomic numbers, he would have discovered the source of the radioactivity, and therefore not ascribed it to 'transuranes'.

But why did Fermi not check the remaining elements for beta activity? Because it was unimaginable to him and to most physicists of the day that such a large 'chunk' could be split off the heavy uranium nucleus by neutron bombardment.

Lise and her nephew Frisch stated that 'In making chemical assignments, it was always assumed that these radioactive bodies had atomic numbers near to that of the element bombarded, since only particles with one or two charges were known to be emitted from nuclei'.[6]

In other words, it was considered impossible, at that time, for something as small as a neutron to make anything more than minor changes to a large atom such as that of uranium. Furthermore, such dramatic changes had never previously been observed. So, if any transmutations had been made, they were likely to show up as radioactive isotopes of elements adjacent to uranium in the Periodic Table.

News of Fermi's scientific investigations was to set Lise on a path towards playing a key role in one of science's most significant discoveries ever.

Four years later, in 1938, Fermi was awarded the Nobel Prize for Physics 'for his demonstration of the existence of new radioactive elements produced by neutron bombardment, and for his related discovery of nuclear reactions brought about by slow neutrons'.

Professor H. Pleijel, chairman of the Nobel Prize Committee for physics, went so far as to congratulate Fermi for his discovery for the first time in history, of '"transuranic" elements number 93 and number 94', to which Fermi had assigned the names 'Ausonium' and 'Hesperium'.[7]

This, however, was not the end of the story. For Fermi had created not transuranic elements but lighter, known elements formed by the splitting – or 'fission' – of uranium.

Meanwhile, in September 1934, Lise and Hahn travelled to Moscow and Leningrad as participants in the Mendeleev Congress.[8]

Chapter 13

A Word of Caution From Ida Noddack

German chemist and physicist Ida Noddack (née Tacke, 1896–1978) was educated at the Technical University of Berlin. After graduating in 1918 with a degree in chemical and metallurgical engineering (as one of the first German women to study chemistry), she worked in the chemistry department of a Berlin turbine factory.

In 1926, Ida married fellow chemist Walter Noddack. The previous year, they had published a joint paper in which they claimed to have discovered two new elements, numbers Z=43 and Z=75. Only one, element Z=75, was confirmed, and named by them 'Rhenium', after the River Rhine, which Ida had known as a child.

In September 1934, a paper by Ida was published in the journal *Zeitschrift für Angewandte Chemie*, entitled 'On Element 93'. In it, she discussed Fermi's findings. 'We are interested only in the one example dealing with the supposed production of element 93', she declared.

Ida described how Fermi had first removed all radioactive daughter products of his uranium prior to bombarding it with neutrons. Whereupon, he had produced no less than

> five different radioactive half-lives [i.e. indicative of five different radioactive isotopes]. Fermi was able to make a chemical separation of one of the new radio-elements which had a half-life of 13 minutes. Fermi next tried to show that the radio-element which is responsible for this beta activity was not an isotope of any element near uranium [i.e. in the Periodic Table].

And having eliminated elements 91, 90, 89, 88, 83, and 82 (lead), and also elements 87 and 86, Fermi concluded 'that it might be the unknown element 93 (or perhaps 94 or 95)'.

Ida dismissed Fermi's conclusion out of hand. 'This method of proof is not valid', she said. 'It is not clear why he did not investigate the element polonium (84), which is also between uranium (92) and lead (82), and why he chose to stop at lead'. In other words, why did Fermi not seek the source for the radioactivity in elements below (i.e. lighter than) lead in the Periodic Table? 'Therefore, the proof that the new (13 minute) radio-element of atomic number 93 is in no sense successful, since Fermi's method of eliminating other possibilities has not been carried through to completion.'

Ida now made a novel and revolutionary suggestion. 'When heavy nuclei are bombarded by neutrons, it is conceivable that the nucleus breaks up into several larger fragments, which would of course be isotopes of known elements but would not be neighbours of the irradiated element.'[1] Ida's proposal was dismissed by the Berlin team – something that its members would later come to regret. Had the team given Ida's suggestion proper consideration, this might well have dissuaded them from embarking on what was to be a four-year-long 'wild goose chase' in search of Fermi's alleged 'transuranes'.

Chapter 14

Lise is Fascinated by Fermi's Findings

Referring to Enrico Fermi's bombardment of uranium with neutrons in spring 1934 and his 'discovery' of so-called 'transuranic elements', said Lise,

> I found these experiments so fascinating that, immediately after the reports on them appeared in [the scientific periodicals] *Nuovo Cimento* and *Nature* [published 16 June 1934], I persuaded Otto Hahn to renew our direct collaboration (which had been interrupted for several years) with a view to investigating these problems.[1]

Here, it should be stressed, as Lise made perfectly clear, that it was *she* and not Hahn who initiated the 'uranium investigation'. This is a point of great significance.

Fermi's research, said Lise, was 'of consuming interest to me and it was at the same time clear to me that one could not get ahead in this field in physics alone. The help of an outstanding chemist like Otto Hahn was needed to get results'.[2] The uranium investigation thus became a joint venture by Lise the physicist and Hahn the radiochemist: a fact that one day Hahn would vehemently deny.

Hahn was reluctant to collaborate with Lise in this matter until a paper by his former co-worker German nuclear chemist, Aristide von Grosse appeared in *Physical Review* on 1 August 1934. In it, von Grosse suggested that Fermi's alleged 'element 93' was more likely to be element 91 – protactinium – which Lise and Hahn himself had discovered in 1918.

'So it was that in 1934, after an interval of more than 12 years, we started working again together', said Lise, and by October 1934, she and Hahn had begun their own experiments in bombarding uranium with neutrons.[3] In the course of this, said Lise, 'We were of course not entirely uninfluenced by Fermi's assumption that in the case of uranium only higher elements were being formed.'[4]

However, it should be remembered that Fermi had made only a cautious suggestion in this regard, i.e. that he had created 'transuranic elements', and the Berlin team would have been well advised to keep an open mind on the subject. This, however, proved not to be the case.

The Periodic Table is so-called because certain groups of elements behave in more or less similar ways. For example:

- Non-metals consist of sixteen elements, mostly solids or gases, that occupy the upper right including the whole of column 18.
- Metals consist of ninety-one elements; almost all are solids (mercury is an exception) and occupy the left and centre of the Periodic Table.
- Semi-metals have a mixture of the properties of metals and non-metals and occupy a position intermediate between the metals and the non-metals.

Elements Z=58 to Z=71 are called the lanthanides (or rare Earth metals). Elements Z=90 to Z=103 are called the actinides (or transuranium elements). Elements in columns 3 to 12 are known as the transition metals.

Fermi was guided by the notion that, because elements Ac, Th, Pa, and U (Actinium Z=89; Thorium Z=90; Protactinium Z=91; Uranium Z=92) chemically resemble (i.e. are homologues of) the transition elements La, Hf, Ta, and W (Lanthanum Z=57; Hafnium Z=72; Tantalum Z=73; Tungsten Z=74), then elements beyond uranium would resemble transition elements beyond W – i.e. Re, Os, Ir, and Pt (Rhenium Z=75; Osmium Z=76; Iridium Z=77; Platinum Z=78).

Therefore, said Fermi, if he had indeed created element 93, 'it would be chemically homologous with [similar to] manganese [Z=25] and rhenium [Z=75]'.[5]

This assumption was not correct, and the transuranium elements in fact, 'resemble lanthanides far more than any transition element',[6] as Bohr had originally proposed in the early 1930s.

On 6 March 1936, in their paper entitled 'New Conversion Processes in the Case of Irradiation of Uranium: Elements Beyond Uranium', the Berlin team reflected this notion in the following nomenclature, which they used for the proposed elements beyond uranium (i.e. of atomic numbers 93–96 inclusive):

Eka-Re; Eka-Os; Eka-Ir; Eka-Pt[7]

(The prefix 'Eka' was first used by Mendeleev himself.)

Meanwhile, in spring 1935 chemist Fritz Strassmann, who had entered the KWIC in 1929 on a scholarship and was an expert in chemical analysis, joined the Berlin team. In 1933, Strassmann had resigned from the Society of German Chemists when it was taken over by the Nazis. Both he and his wife Maria refused to join any Nazi-affiliated organisation. Strassmann was consequently blacklisted from working in industry or as an independent researcher, and it was Lise who had persuaded Hahn to find an assistantship for him at half-pay.[8] The outcome was that, from 1935 to 1938, the Berlin team published no less than ten scientific papers on transuranes.

In 1935, Chadwick left the Cavendish Laboratory to become Professor of Physics at Liverpool University. Here, he installed a cyclotron. The cyclotron was invented in 1929–1930 by Ernest O. Lawrence at the University of California, Berkeley, USA. It accelerates charged particles outwards from the centre along a spiral path and, in its time, it was the best source of high-energy particles for experiments in nuclear physics.

Also in 1935, Lise and Max Delbrück (1906–1981) published *Der Aufbau der Atomkerne: Natürliche und Künstliche Kernumwandlungen* (The Structure of Atomic Nuclei: Natural and Artificial Nuclear Conversions).[9]

German-US biophysicist and Nobel Laureate Max Ludwig Henning Delbrück was born in Berlin on 4 September 1906. He had been an assistant to Lise at the KWIC in 1932. In 1937 he left Germany for the USA.

Delbrück's brother Justus was a lawyer. His sister Emmi married professor of psychiatry and neurology Klaus Bonhoeffer (elder brother of evangelical pastor and theologian, Dietrich Bonhoeffer). In 1945, Klaus, Dietrich, and Justus were charged with being implicated in the July Plot. The two brothers were executed. Justus was imprisoned. He survived the war but died of diphtheria whilst in Soviet custody in late October the same year.

In their paper of 6 March 1936, Hahn stated boldly that 'the chemical characteristics' of the decay products 'leave no doubt that they are element 93'. He also stated that

> for the representatives of the elements 94-96 we are certain from their general chemical properties to which groups they belong. By the bombardment of U [uranium] with slow neutrons and various chemical separations of the products together with a study of the radiation emitted, the evidence indicates that new radioactive isotopes of elements 92-94 are obtained according to the scheme.[10]

It now fell to Lise to calculate the nuclear reactions that would account for the creation of these five new 'transuranes' (Z=93 to Z=96). Three nuclear reactions were proposed, each involving neutron capture, the three processes being referred to as Process 1, Process 2, and Process 3.

In 1936, Strassmann bombarded uranium with thermal (slow) neutrons, and reported that he had found barium as a decay product. But, said Fritz Krafft, who interviewed Strassmann personally on the subject, 'Lise Meitner's sceptical remark of the next morning, that that must be nonsense, had been sufficient for him to throw his records into the wastepaper basket without any regrets'.[11] So, once again, valuable evidence had been dismissed, this time by Lise. As for Hahn, he was unaware of Strassmann's finding.

Also in 1936, Bohr proposed his 'Compound Nucleus' theory:

> **Formation of the compound nucleus.** When a high-energy projectile such as a neutron collides with a nucleus, a compound nucleus is formed, wherein the neutron is absorbed by the initial nucleus.[12]

In that same year, Carl F. von Weizsäcker in Leipzig, Germany, and Hans Bethe and Robert Bacher at Cornell University, Ithaca, New York expanded on Gamow's concept of the 'Liquid-Drop' model of the atomic nucleus. This accounts for the drop-like shape of most nuclei and makes an approximate prediction of the 'binding energy' – the energy required to separate subatomic particles in atomic nuclei and electrons bound to nuclei in atoms. This, and the application of the concept of surface tension to the liquid-drop model of the nucleus, was to have profound implications for Lise, at the time of the great discovery that awaited her, as will be seen.

Thirteenth April 1937 found Lise speculating 'about the importance of radioactive substances on earth and stars'.[13]

On 14 May 1937, the Berlin team with Lise as principal author submitted a paper entitled 'About the Transformation of Uranium by Neutron Irradiation'.[14] However, said Lise, 'The result is very difficult to reconcile with current concepts of the nucleus'. The problems, some of which she herself voiced, were as follows:

1. The decay chains proposed in Processes 1 and 2 were longer than expected.
2. Three decay chains running in parallel was an unexplained result, as it implied that the neutrons had produced three different effects on the uranium atoms simultaneously.
3. The dozen or so decay products (half-lives) found were far more than would have been expected.
4. Isomers could not be theoretically explained.
5. How could a slow neutron possibly cause such great alterations in a uranium nucleus? Nothing like this had been seen before.

On 15 May 1937, Hahn as principal author submitted a paper entitled 'About the Transurane and its Chemical Behaviour' to the German language scientific journal *Chemische Berichte*, in which he displayed his confidence in his team's discovery. 'In general, the chemical behaviour of the transuranes … is such that their position in the periodic system is no longer in doubt. *Above all, their chemical distinction from all previously known elements needs no further discussion*.'[15]

Meanwhile in Paris in late 1937, Irène Joliot-Curie and Pavel Savitch (Pavle Savić) had discovered a 3.5-hour beta activity after bombarding uranium with neutrons, which they believed to be a transuranic element.[16]

On 9 May 1938, Lise accepted an invitation by Bohr to join him in Copenhagen, albeit on a temporary basis.[17] However, because her Austrian passport was no longer valid since the Anschluss (the annexation of Austria into Nazi Germany on 12 March 1938), she was refused a travel visa.[18]

Finally, in May 1938, the Paris team decided that the 3.5-hour activity indicated an element chemically similar to lanthanum (Z=57). This finding was dismissed out of hand by the Berlin team, 'the idea that Z could change by 35 units' being 'unthinkable at the time'. However, 'it later transpired that the activity really did correspond to an isotope of lanthanum'.[19] The chemistry was unclear, and the findings were therefore disregarded by the Berlin team.

Frisch summarised the position in regard to the 'transuranes' as follows. Lise, he said, 'saw how difficult it was to account for the large number of different substances formed [by neutron bombardment of uranium], and things got even more complicated when some were found (in Paris) that were apparently lighter than uranium'.[20] The truth was that the Paris team had split the atom, without realising it. So had everyone else, from Fermi onwards, and the supposed 'transuranes' were, in fact, fission fragments.

Chapter 15

The Nazi Menace

In the wider world, matters had not stood still. The events leading up to Lise's exile from Germany and her beloved Kaiser Wilhelm Institute began when, on 30 January 1933, a homicidal maniac named Adolf Hitler came to power as Chancellor.[1] And by dint of rhetoric, this madman convinced the German people, full of hope and expectation as they were, to follow slavishly their 'saviour' as he led Germany, with no compunction whatsoever, to utter destruction.

Despite the growing anti-Semitism of the Nazi regime, Lise was determined to remain at her post, something she would later come to regret. And because she was an Austrian citizen and because the KWIC was a privately run and not a state-run institution, she would be safe, for the time being at least.

At the time of Hitler's coming to power, Einstein, who was of Jewish heritage, was visiting the USA. He did not return to Germany and subsequently became a US citizen. Whereupon, in April 1933, von Laue became interim director of the KWIP.

Meanwhile, in March 1933, the first concentration camps were created in Germany: the first being located at Dachau near Munich in Bavaria. This was originally intended for the detention of political prisoners. However, such camps came to contain what the Nazis termed 'undesirables' – Jews, Romanis/Sintis (a Romanic people of central Europe), Serbs, Soviet prisoners of war and civilians, Poles, homosexuals, political and religious opponents, and the disabled. For a Jew, it mattered not whether he or she practised their faith or not, or whether, like Lise, he or she had converted to Christianity, for this was all about 'ethnic cleansing'.

On 17 April 1933, Franck resigned as Professor of Physics at Göttingen, appalled at the mistreatment of his Jewish colleagues by the Nazis. After a year spent at the Institute for Theoretical Physics in Copenhagen, Denmark (officially renamed the Niels Bohr Institute on 7 October 1965), Franck relocated to the USA, where he worked at Johns Hopkins University, Baltimore, Maryland, and subsequently at the University of Chicago.

In the same year, Hahn became visiting professor at Cornell University, Ithaca, New York (from 30 January to June).

In a letter to the Francks dated 22 April 1933, Hahn's wife Edith showed herself to be an honourable and decent-minded person when she declared that she was almost envious of James and his family 'for being Jews and thus having justice entirely on your side, while we bear the disgrace and inextinguishable, irreparable shame for all time'. This was another damning indictment of Nazism, with which Lise herself was now threatened.[2]

On 27 August 1933, Hahn made strenuous efforts to prevent Lise's 'lectureship privileges and long-term position at the University of Berlin from being withdrawn', when he wrote to the Prussian Minister for Science, Art, and Popular Education Bernhard Rust as follows.

> Professor Meitner is not of pure Aryan descent. Nevertheless, I believe that the discharge provisions of the April 7, 1933 law pertaining to (tenured) [i.e. permanent] professional positions cannot be applied here for the following reasons. The provisions for carrying out this law … state that anyone who had fulfilled all requirements for obtaining his [or her] first regular position by August 1, 1914 can be considered equivalent to a regular (tenured) employee.[3]

Lise fulfilled these requirements, said Hahn. But his efforts were in vain.

On 17 October 1933, Einstein went to the USA.

In the German parliamentary elections of 12 November 1933, the National Socialist German Workers' Party ('Nazi Party') received 92.11% of the votes cast.

In January 1934, French chemist, physicist, and politician, Irène Joliot-Curie (daughter of Marie and Pierre Curie) and her husband Frédéric Joliot bombarded light elements such as aluminium and boron with alpha particles, whereupon they emitted radiation. Thus, for the first time, a previously stable (non-radioactive) material was made radioactive by exposure to specific radiation.[4] This was the first example of artificially induced radioactivity.

In that year, Hahn and Lise resumed their collaboration, with momentous results, as will now be seen! Also in that year, Dutch physicist, Peter Debye was installed as director of the KWIP.

According to the census of 1934, there were 191,481 Jews living in Austria. Of these, 176,034 lived in Vienna. They included many famous writers, film and theatre directors, actors and producers, set designers, architects, doctors and lawyers, businessmen and bankers, artists and journalists, comedians, musicians, and composers.

The US Holocaust Memorial Museum has documented about 42,500 camps and ghettos that existed in Germany and the occupied territories between 1933 and 1945. These included slave labour camps, Jewish ghettos, concentration camps, prisoner of war camps, brothels containing sex slaves, and euthanasia camps for the elimination of the elderly and infirm. However, 'It is almost impossible to count the number of camps that the Nazis started – there were hundreds and possibly thousands. Many camps had sub-camps: a sub-camp could be as big as many other camps or just a couple of prisoners in some farm or building.'[5] An estimated 15–20 million people may have perished in these various camps and ghettos,[6] and about 6 million were Jews. The genocide of European Jews is known as the Holocaust.

German leader Adolf Hitler was a person who, by his own admission and by the observations of at least two other notable people, heard voices. The likelihood is that it was in these voices that his hatred of Jews and others originated and manifested itself, and that it was the 'command hallucinations' that he heard which ordered him to take, or not to take, specific actions such as those described above. In other words, Germany was in the hands of a paranoid schizophrenic.[7]

Nonetheless, a measure of the Führer's popularity is that whereas in 1939 membership of the Nazi Party was 5.3 million, of a population of about 70 million, by 1945, this number had risen to 8 million. How tens of millions of Germans could have become fanatical supporters of a ranting maniac, and enthusiastically endorsed and actively participated in his murderous policies, beggars belief.

Is it possible that ordinary German citizens were unaware of the presence of the ghettos in their towns and cities, where Jews were imprisoned and starved to death; or of those whom the Nazis termed 'undesirable' being marched through the towns or transported by lorry to the railway station; or trains – i.e. cattle trucks – embarking for destinations with names such as Buchenwald, Oranienburg, and Sachsenhausen? And did Germans not notice that people were disappearing from their midst, or that virtually nobody ever emerged from these camps; of the foul aromas – i.e. the stench of burning human flesh – that emanated from tall chimneys within these camps?

Did no one observe that people were informing on their neighbours if they suspected them of harbouring such undesirables or of expressing sympathy for them; or that such neighbours swiftly disappeared from view, as if they had never existed?

The truth is, of course, that almost every German in the land, unless he or she was in a permanent vegetative state, knew *exactly* what was going on. Some, by their passivity, were complicit in these crimes; others were active and enthusiastic participants in them, and a few brave souls opposed them, and in so doing risked paying the ultimate price.

These notable exceptions included Oskar Schindler (who survived, having saved many Jews); Count Claus von Stauffenberg (executed by firing squad, 21 July 1944, for attempting to assassinate Hitler); Sophie Scholl (executed by guillotine, 22 February 1943 for being a member of the 'White Rose Society', a non-violent, intellectual resistance group); and Dietrich Bonhoeffer (executed by hanging, Flossenbürg concentration camp, 8 April 1945, accused of being associated with the failed July Plot). In late October 1944, Lise had learned that Max Planck's eldest son, Erwin, had been tortured to death by the Gestapo for his part in the failed July Plot.[8]

This, then, was the price of resistance, the price of opposing a thug who stood with a gun to your head or threatened you with the gas chambers.

In 1936, Debye became Professor of Physics at the Friedrich Wilhelm University, Berlin. One day, Lise would owe her life to him, and to other loyal colleagues.

On 12 March 1938, Lise's homeland, Austria, was annexed by German troops, and Germany was incorporated into the Third Reich, an event known as the 'Anschluss'.

In Vienna, immediately after the Anschluss,

> Jews were being harassed. They were driven through the streets … their homes and shops were plundered and the process of 'Aryanization' began. The Nuremberg Laws

> applied in Austria from May 1938, so that people with one Jewish grandparent were deemed to be Jewish, even if they or their parents had converted to another faith. 201,000 to 214,000 people were caught by these anti-Jewish laws.[9]

The Nuremberg Laws 'were reinforced with innumerable anti-Semitic decrees. Jews were gradually robbed of their freedoms; were blocked from almost all professions; were shut out of schools and universities, and were forced to wear the yellow badge [in the shape of a star]'.[10]

> After the *Anschluss* (12 March 1938), all Jews were effectively forced to emigrate from Austria, but the process was made extremely difficult. The emigration center was in Vienna, and the people leaving were required to have numerous documents, approving their departure, from different departments. They were not allowed to take cash or stocks or valuable items like jewellery or gold, and most antiques or artworks were declared 'important to the state' and could not be exported, and were often simply seized; essentially only clothes and household items could be taken, so nearly everything of value was left behind. To leave the country, a departure 'tax' had to be paid, which was a large percentage of their entire property. Emigrants hurried to collect only their most important personal belongings, pay the departure fees, and had to leave behind them everything else. Departure was only possible with a visa to enter another country, which was hard to obtain, especially for the poor and elderly, so even the wealthy sometimes had to leave behind their parents or grandparents. The last Jews left legally in 1941. Almost all Jews who remained after this time were murdered in the Holocaust.

However, some foreign officials assisted by issuing far more visas than they were officially allowed to, as will be seen.[11]

Jews seeking exit visas and other documentation necessary for emigration, however, 'were required to stand in long lines, night and day, in front of municipal, police, and passport offices' in Vienna. 'Would-be emigrants were forced to pay an exit fee and to register all of their immovable and most of their movable property, which was confiscated concurrent with their departure from the country.'[12]

'Jewish citizens were humiliated as they were commanded to perform different menial tasks, without any consideration of age, social position or sex.'[13]

US President Franklin D. Roosevelt 'took the initiative of calling a conference at Évian-les-Bains, a French resort town on the shores of Lake Geneva. Representatives of thirty-two countries attended the conference', held from 6–15 July 1938, in order to address the question of German and Austrian refugees wishing to flee persecution from Nazi Germany.

'All of them paid lip service to the refugees. The desperate Jews attempted to reach any possible destination, with thousands of Jews immigrating during this period to Shanghai, China, at a time when the gates of most countries had been locked before them.'[14]

Today, the investigation of the atom continues apace. For example, it is now known that protons and neutrons are made up of even smaller particles, called 'quarks'. Meanwhile, the attention shifts to Rome.

Chapter 16

Lise Escapes the Clutches of the Nazis

Just as the long and complex saga of the elusive 'transuranes' was coming to a climax, so Lise was obliged to leave Germany for her own safety. For her, this would be a nightmare. Yet, paradoxically, had she remained in Berlin the circumstances may well not have arisen that provided her with the opportunity to provide the theoretical framework for a discovery that would change the world.

On 14 March 1938, Swiss physicist Paul Scherrer invited Lise to lecture in Switzerland, as a means of her leaving Germany.[1] But this was impossible, as she possessed no valid travel documents.[2]

Otto Hahn, to his credit, appealed in person on 17 March 1938 to chemist Heinrich Hörlein, treasurer of the Emil Fischer Society (Gesellschaft), the organisation that sponsored the KWIC, that Lise should be permitted to remain at her post. However, Hörlein declared that Lise must go.

In April 1938, Lise accepted an invitation from Bohr to visit his Institute for Theoretic Physics in Copenhagen. But when she approached the Danish consulate in Vienna on 10 May 1938, she was refused a travel visa to Denmark as, since the Anschluss, her Austrian passport was no longer valid.[3]

Carl Bosch, President of the KWG (from 1937), was insistent that Lise be permitted to remain at the KWIC.[4] But when permission was declined, Bosch wrote on 22 May 1938 to Reich Minister of Education, Wilhelm Frick, requesting permission for Lise to leave Germany for a neutral foreign country.[5]

On 2 June 1938, James Franck, who had relocated to the USA in 1934, put in train an application for Lise to be admitted to the USA.[6]

Lise's enemies at the KWIC included Professor Kurt Hess, head of a 'guest department' situated on the third floor. Hess referred openly to Lise as 'The Jewess who endangers the Institute',[7] and just prior to her flight he attempted to betray her to the authorities. However, it was her friends who won the day, and the support that she had from them in her time of need attests to the love and admiration that they had for her.

Various friends and colleagues of Lise collaborated in order to facilitate her escape, and fortunately, several first-hand accounts survive of the operation. They included Niels Bohr; Dirk Coster (Dutch spectroscopist and Professor of Experimental Physics at the Royal University of Groningen, Netherlands); Hendrik ('Hans') A. Kramers (theoretical physicist, Leiden, Netherlands); Peter Debye (Dutch Director of the KWIP in Berlin); Adriaan D. Fokker (Research Director of the Teylers Museum at Haarlem, and also Professor of Physics at the University of Leiden, Netherlands, and musician); Paul Rosbaud (Austrian physicist); and Hahn himself. As for the escape, it reads better than a spy drama!

On 6 June 1938, Bohr and his wife Margrethe visited Berlin, where they met Lise. On his return to Copenhagen, Bohr 'began seeking a position for Meitner in the Scandinavian countries and asked Kramers to notify Dutch physicists that she was in urgent need of help. Kramers immediately contacted Coster in Groningen and Adriaan Fokker in Haarlem'.[8]

One of those petitioned by Bohr was Siegbahn, who was requested to find a position for Lise at his soon-to-be opened Physics Department of the Nobel Institute of the Royal Swedish Academy of Sciences in Stockholm. Bohr repeated his request several times.[9]

Said Coster's granddaughter, Anthea J. Coster, 'And then there were two offers – one from Sweden and one from Holland. She decided on Sweden. Then I think things became critical for Lise and Debye contacted my grandfather'.

In mid-June 1938, when new restrictions were about to be placed on those wishing to emigrate from Germany, Bosch appealed to the Ministry of the Interior for Lise to be given permission to leave the country, but the request was refused.[10]

Coster and Fokker attempted to raise sufficient funds to enable Lise to take up a post at Groningen University's physics department.[11] But despite their best efforts, no permanent position could be found for Lise in Holland.

On 16 June 1938, Debye appealed to Bohr to offer Lise a position urgently.[12] Bohr, who had previously assisted many refugee scientists, had urged Lise to relocate to Denmark, and had offered her a place at his own Institute for Theoretical Physics in Copenhagen, where he would have welcomed her with open arms. However, on 21 June, he informed Fokker that, to his regret, circumstances beyond his control meant that his offer was to be withdrawn.[13]

Meanwhile, Hahn asked Rosbaud (who unbeknown to him was liaising with British Intelligence) to try to obtain a false passport for Lise, but evidently without success.[14]

On 24 June 1938, Coster petitioned the Dutch Ministry of Justice in the Hague to permit Lise to work as a physicist in the Netherlands.[15] But Coster was only able to raise sufficient funds to make this possible for a period of one year.

On 27 June 1938, Coster sent Debye a coded message to say that he intended to visit Berlin to seek an 'Assistant' (code word for 'Lise') 'to fill a one-year appointment'.[16]

On 4 July 1938, Bosch informed Lise that 'the policy prohibiting scientists from leaving Germany would soon be strictly enforced', and therefore she was in danger.[17] Lise and Debye agreed that it was now imperative that she leave as soon as possible.[18]

Lise subsequently stated that 'when she heard from von Laue that professors, whether Jewish or not, were no longer allowed to leave Germany it was clear to her that she should leave Germany, and she wrote to Coster. Coster, together with Fokker and de Haas, got the permit to allow her into Holland without a visa. Coster came to Berlin to accompany her'.[19]

This was a reference to Lise's friend, Dutch physicist and mathematician Wander J. de Haas of Leiden.

On 6 July 1938, Debye sent Coster another coded message in respect of 'the assistant we talked about'. He ended, 'if you were to come [to Berlin] rather soon – as if you received an SOS [urgent appeal for help] – that would give my wife and me even greater pleasure'.[20] Said Anthea, 'Peter Debye knew my grandfather would read through the lines', in other words realise that Lise's situation had become desperate.

On Saturday, 9 July 1938, Fokker contacted the Dutch Ministry of Justice and the office of the Dutch Border Guards. On Monday, 11 July, Fokker was informed by the Ministry that 'provisional admission' would be granted, and that written confirmation of this would be provided.[21] On that same day, after a desperately anxious wait, permission was given for Lise to enter Holland.[22] Whereupon, Coster boarded a train to Berlin, and was welcomed to the Debye family home.[23]

A measure of the great lengths to which Coster was prepared to go in order to secure an academic position for Lise in the Netherlands is revealed by the following letter that he sent to Adriaan Fokker – 'Aad' – on 11 July 1938.

> Dear Aad,
> Hans Kramers informed me that Lise Meitner will probably be fired in Berlin-Dahlem. It would be great if she could work in Holland for a while. Hans wrote to me, that he would support a grant from the Lorentz-fund.

(The Lorentz fund finances research in the field of physics. It is named after the Dutch physicist Hendrik Lorentz.)

> Could you tell me what the other members of the fund think and how large the grant could be? Maybe it would be possible to ask colleagues for a regular contribution. I'm prepared to commit myself for 5 years, for an amount between fl [florin – or guilder] 50,- and fl 100,- a year. If Lise Meitner could work in Groningen, I probably could obtain a sum of approx. fl. 500,- a year from funds from Groningen.
>
> She would have excellent employment here, for in the near future we will have a 400,000 Volt neutron generator, i.e. more than 100 grams of RA + Be-equivalent.

The explanation for this is as follows.

> The 400,000 volt neutron generator was a particle accelerator (most likely a linear accelerator) that could be used to generate neutrons.
>
> The early neutron source that Fermi, Meitner and others usually used was a sealed glass tube filled with a mixture of radon gas (a decay product of radium) and powdered beryllium. The radon emits alpha particles which react with beryllium to produce carbon-12 and neutrons.
>
> Coster apparently was building a neutron generator which emitted neutrons at hundreds of times the rate of a

> radon-beryllium mixture, probably similar to the one in Meitner's lab which was nearing completion when she fled Germany.[24]

Coster continued,

> Of course, I would desire this very much, but I am prepared not to have my personal contribution depend on this.
>
> Could you be so good as to write me what you think of a contribution from the Lorentz fund? I have committed myself to inform Bohr within a week if I get the impression that in Holland it is impossible to achieve anything for LM, so that he could look for help in Denmark and Sweden. It would, however, cause me regret if we could not get her to Holland. Kind regards, Yours, Dirk[25]

On 16 June 1938, Coster wrote again to Fokker to say that he had approached Hugo R. Kruyt, Professor of Chemistry at Utrecht University, to see if funding for Lise might be forthcoming from Dutch industrialists. 'I have always thought that one should have as many irons in the fire as possible', he said. Coster had also enquired as to whether 'the Amsterdam University could offer Lise Meitner a position'.

Finally, said Coster, since Fokker had 'initially drawn my attention to LM's precarious position ... following your message I sent her a letter to invite her to stay with us for the summer. Then I still thought that it would be easy for her to find a position in England or America'.[26]

Said Coster's granddaughter Arina R. Klokke, 'My grandfather arranged beforehand, with his neighbour, that her passport would not be checked. He asked help from his neighbour, Netherlands politician Edzo Hommo Ebels, a member of the Provincial Executive of Groningen'.

The escape route

The Dutch city of Groningen in northern Holland, where the Coster family lived and where Dirk was Professor of Physics and Meteorology at the university, is 350 miles or so due west of Berlin. The little railway station of Nieuwe Schans marked the border. Here, the Dutch railway network to the west was connected with the German railway network to the east. The plan was for Lise to take the train from Berlin to Groningen. The journey would take about seven hours.

Continued Arina,

> Ebels drove with Dirk to Nieuwe Schans on 11 July. Ebels, son of a large farmer from the region and former mayor of nearby Beerta, had great prestige there. They asked (probably: ordered) the Dutch border officials to use friendly persuasion in order that their German colleagues would allow Lise Meitner travel to the Netherlands on the basis of the visa granted by the Dutch government.[27]

On 12 July 1938, the day before Lise's escape, Coster wrote as follows to Sam Goudsmit:

> I received an S.O.S. letter from Debye so that I will be going to Berlin today. I will most probably return on Wednesday, with or without L.M. I have requested [Dutch physicist Hessel] de Vries to write to you as soon as the case is okay. The high voltage apparatus is now in function, but the problem now concerns the Geigertellers [Geiger counters].
>
> As soon as I have returned with or without Lise M., I will report on my findings in Berlin. I hope you will in any case come to Groningen then, when she, too, will be there, and you will then be able to discuss with her if there will be possibilities for her in America. Dear greetings, Yours Dirk[28]

On that final evening in Berlin, Tuesday, 12 July 1938, Lise worked late at the Institute. This was to avoid suspicion as she was almost certainly under constant surveillance. Prior to her departure next day, Hahn gave her a diamond ring as a security 'for urgent emergencies'.[29] This was a 'beautiful diamond ring', said Hahn, 'that I had inherited from my mother and which I had never worn myself but always treasured'.[30] Also, to his credit, Hahn had attempted to persuade the authorities to grant Lise a pension, but to no avail.[31] One day, however, Hahn would fail to acknowledge the contribution to his Berlin team made by Lise, over a matter of supreme scientific importance and instead, claim all the credit for himself, as will be seen.

Rosbaud also became involved, and it was he who drove Lise to the railway station. (Hahn did not possess a motor car at that time.)[32]

According to Hans, the Costers' eldest son, in order to help Lise 'feel unobtrusive, his father asked her to remove the diamond ring and [he] slipped it into his waistcoat pocket'.[33]

Lise herself

Lise kept both a pocket diary and a larger notebook. On that day, Wednesday, 13 July 1938, in her pocket diary, Lise simply wrote: 'Journey to Groningen'.[34]

In her notebook for that day, Lise's entries for 12 and 13 July read:

> 12/vii To the Institute early – Hahn told me about the plans of Coster and Debye.
>
> Met Coster during the morning – worked with Hahn until 8 p.m.
>
> Then there was a squabble about not closing the damp bedroom.
>
> Hahn very nervous, too much going on.
>
> Rosbaud came at 10.30 p.m. and we drove to Hahn's house.
>
> 13.VII Said goodbye early to Hahn. Ring [a reference to the ring that Hahn gave her]. All quiet. Met Coster at the railway station. At Nieuwe Schans the customs officers had been briefed. 6 p.m. Groningen.[35]

Almost a decade later, on 1 July 1947, in a letter to her friend Gerta von Ubisch, Lise described her escape, and the preamble to it, in more detail:

> You know that I was in Germany until mid-1938. Today, I know that I was wrong. I should have left in '33, when Rockefeller [the Rockefeller Foundation, USA] had offered me money for a job abroad, but Planck and Hahn persuaded me not to leave and I was very attached to our Institute.

It has been pointed out that, had Lise accepted Rockefeller's offer, a whole new world – 'The New World' – would have opened up for her, for in the USA were a plethora of well-funded universities. Furthermore, as a distinguished physicist, she would undoubtedly have received a warm welcome, but nothing compared to the welcome she was to receive when she visited that country in early 1946.[36]

Continued Lise,

> I had set up the Physics Department from the very first; it was, so to say, my life's work and it seemed so difficult for me to separate myself from it. So I was only too happy to be persuaded to stay by Planck and Hahn, yet it was very wrong of me, not only from a practical point of view, but also on moral grounds. Unfortunately, I only realized that after I left Germany. Personally, I had no difficulties until I left, but it was very difficult for many years.
>
> One was always wavering between the need to do nothing or something that went against the security of its employees and responsibility for the Institute. But when I heard from friends in May '38 that a secret decree had come to the universities, that no university professor, regardless of whether 'Aryan' or 'non-Aryan', was allowed to leave Germany anymore, it seemed to be high time to go. The big difficulty was not only that the borders were already being watched; I had an Austrian passport, and after the occupation of Austria by Hitler, no country would admit anyone bearing such a document. The story of my escape was like something from a novel. Dutch friends obtained permission from their government and letters of transit for a long-standing Dutch friend [Dirk Coster] to come secretly to Berlin, to escort me to the border and enter Holland at a remote crossing-place.
>
> So as not to arouse suspicion during my last day in Germany, I stayed at the Institute until 8pm correcting the work of one of my younger colleagues. Then I had about ninety minutes to pack some essential items into two small cases and leave Germany for ever with 10 marks in my purse. So I came, in mid-July, to Holland without any promise of an appointment; I was almost sixty years of age.[37]

The date was Wednesday, 13 July 1938, and Lise, now aged 59 and exhausted, had arrived safely in the Netherlands, where the Costers welcomed her to their home in Göttingen and helped her to regain her strength. In the light of subsequent events, Lise had escaped in the nick of time.

One may imagine this petite lady, alighting from the train, trembling with fright as she passed through the German-Dutch checkpoint. Lise's escape was a moment of great significance, not only for her, but for her family; for those who had helped her, and for her scientific colleagues everywhere. But it was even more significant in the sense that as soon as she alighted from the train, set foot on Dutch soil, breathed the free Dutch air, and passed through the German-Dutch security, from that moment, final victory for the Allies in the war was assured, for reasons of which Lise would not have approved and could never have imagined.

Coster's wife Miep 'thought the German border guards may have let Meitner through because they assumed the "Frau Professor" was a professor's wife'.[38] Miep was known to remark how Lise had been 'cast out into the void'. Those who expressed delight at Lise's escape included Bohr and Wolfgang Pauli. Hahn, on a postcard to Coster, sent his 'heartiest congratulation'.[39]

Anthea J. Coster[40] was born in 1953, by which time both her paternal grandparents, Dirk Coster and his wife Lina M. Coster ('Miep', née Wijsman), were deceased. (Dirk had died in February 1950 and Miep three years later.)

Anthea was able to shed more light on Lise's escape. When Lise arrived at the Costers' home in Göttingen,

> My uncle Herman has a memory of a petite woman, somewhat stunned and dazed, saying over and over again 'The Pope! The Pope!' He interpreted this to mean that Lise hoped that the Pope would come out with a strong statement against Germany and the persecution of Jews. However, someone else said Niels Bohr was referred to as 'The Pope'.

In other words, Lise was expressing her gratitude to her 'saviour'. (Dirk and Miep Coster had four children: Hendrik, Ada, Els, and the youngest, Herman.)

Continued Anthea,

> My grandfather Dirk was upset because he had access to only enough funds for a post-doc [postdoctoral research fellowship] for Lise. Once they learned that she was going to Sweden, they cancelled plans until they received a letter from Peter Debye which was worded in such a way as to say, 'Come to Berlin and look at an assistant I have for you, but you need to hurry as if you received an SOS'.

In other words, should the Nazi authorities have intercepted this letter, it would have given them no indication whatsoever that the 'Assistant' in question was Lise.

> They then had to convene a special meeting of the Dutch National Academy of Sciences to get paperwork for the government to approve her coming into Holland.
>
> When my grandfather went to Berlin, he stayed overnight at Peter Debye's house. He did not see Lise Meitner until the train station. When they got in, he casually sat down across from her. Right before they crossed the German border, he took the diamond ring that Otto Hahn had given her for safekeeping. There was NO incident at the border. The German guards saw her and knew that the Dutch would let her in. According to my grandmother [Miep], they probably thought she was a wife of somebody – not a famous scientist. Once they reached Groningen, my grandfather cabled Otto Hahn to say that 'the baby' had safely arrived.[41]

Finally, although Lise

> had the Dutch government's permission, she did not have a valid passport. So my grandfather went with his neighbor (someone high up in Dutch local government) to the border that the train would cross to let the Dutch guards know that this would be happening, and so the Dutch guards could warn the German guards on the other side that they would take this person in [i.e. admit her to the Netherlands]. The thought was that the Dutch guards were on friendly terms with the German guards.

I asked Anthea why her grandfather had taken such risks to rescue Lise Meitner. Lise had first met Dirk Coster and his wife Miep in the spring of 1921 in Sweden when he was at Lund University under Swedish physicist Professor Manne Siegbahn. Here, Coster was able to teach Lise about spectroscopy. He himself was conducting research on the X-ray spectroscopy of different elements. Said Anthea, 'My grandfather and Lise Meitner were friends from a long time back'.

> I think the entire physics community initiated the rescue. My grandfather probably volunteered to go because we lived in Groningen, and maybe the border crossings there were less strictly monitored than those nearer to Amsterdam. My grandfather was also pretty politically active. He hated Hitler. He helped find positions for a number of Jewish physicists starting in the 1930s. He was definitely good friends with Lise Meitner. So the bottom line is, I think it was in his nature.

Anthea's words are borne out by a photograph which exists of the Coster family at their home in March 1935. It also includes a Jewish woman and child who they were sheltering. (Neither Dirk nor Miep was Jewish.)

Whilst staying with the Costers, Lise signed the visitors' book. And immediately above her signature was that of Goudsmit and the date 'July 1938'. This suggests that Coster was exploring the possibility of Lise obtaining a post in the USA.[42]

Dirk Coster received a telegram from Austrian theoretical physicist Wolfgang Pauli, said Anthea, to say that 'he would become as famous for escorting Lise Meitner out of Germany as he would be from his co-discovery of hafnium'. This was a reference to the element Z=72, which Coster and Hungarian radiochemist, George de Hevesy had isolated in 1923, thus filling a gap in the Periodic Table.

Chapter 17

Into Exile

On Saturday, 16 July 1938, Fokker wrote to Bohr as follows:

> Dear Bohr,
> [On] Thursday [last] Coster wired you to tell that Lise Meitner was [safely] in Groningen. On the Saturday before, Coster received a letter from Debye stating that the necessity of [her] leaving Germany was very urgent. We could only get [be] sure of the official permission to enter the Netherlands on Monday morning and Coster left at once for Berlin. On Wednesday he came back, and Lise Meitner came with him.

'The attention of the authorities had already been drawn to her case', said Fokker. Furthermore,

> At the time it had become known among the university professors that the government had adopted the policy of denying an exit to the German scientists. So, the German frontiers will very soon be closed from the inside. Everything was arranged very cleverly so as not to arouse any suspicion, and Coster was not allowed to show himself during the time he was in Dahlem. Happily, all went smoothly.

What of the future?

> For a fortnight Lise Meitner will stay in Coster's house in Groningen. Of course, she will write you all about that. I think that after July 28th, when Coster and his family will be off for a holiday to France, Lise Meitner will stay with us, and my address from August 1st will be: Solleweg 50, Beckbergen, unless I give you another statement.

> I hope that we shall have some news from Sweden and that she is permitted to enter in. With kind regards[1]

During the period when Lise was staying with the Coster family, Dirk Coster's wife Miep wrote to Fokker to say that both she and her husband were 'very angry' with him:

> What have you done so suddenly? Lise Meitner explicitly says that she could not bring herself to write a letter to Bohr. You should understand that, as she has to jump into a vacuum at her 59th [i.e at the age of 59]. Under the circumstances she has to hear from you that she is not here on behalf of some impersonal fund but financed by personal acquaintances. Of course, that very evening she said that she only wants to accept that money as a loan, not as a gift. Now she will want to pay us back the money, instead of saving everything she can for her pension in Sweden.[2]

This letter demonstrates that Miep too was involved, and also that she too cared deeply for Lise. It also demonstrates just how fiercely independent Lise was, and how she abhorred the thought of being subsidised by her friends and was determined to stand on her own feet at all costs. In the event, it was on 21 July 1938 that Lise relocated to Fokker's home in Haarlem. However, in the absence of positive news from Sweden she returned, shortly afterwards, to the Costers.

Finally, on 26 July 1938, after strenuous attempts by Fokker and Siegbahn, news came that Lise's Swedish visa had been granted.[3] Bohr had brought his influence to bear, and a position had been found for her at Siegbahn's Nobel Institute in Stockholm. Also, it was Siegbahn who had obtained permission for Lise to enter the country.

On 28 July 1938, Lise flew to Copenhagen, her air fare from Groningen having been paid by Coster.[4] Here, the Bohrs welcomed her to their home, prior to her commencing work in Sweden.[5] In retrospect, had Lise chosen to remain in Holland, with the German invasion of the Netherlands on 10 May 1940, her life would once again have been in danger.

Years later, Lise expressed to Gerta von Ubisch just how apprehensive she had been in respect of her escape. 'From Holland, using borrowed money, I flew in an aeroplane to Sweden by way of Copenhagen, haunted by fear for my fate if a forced landing had to be made in Germany.'[6]

At about this time, Bragg informed Lise (via Siegbahn) that Girton College, Cambridge was prepared to offer her a post, but as this was only guaranteed for one year, she felt that she could not take the chance.[7]

Sweden was an enlightened country, in the sense that women had been permitted to study at Swedish universities since 1873 and to pursue academic careers since 1925. However, for Lise life there was not altogether what she would have wished, as will be seen. Nonetheless, during her time in Sweden she published some two dozen scientific papers, including two with Otto Frisch (February and March 1939).[8] Also, as Sweden was a neutral country, Lise was able to correspond with her former colleagues, Hahn and Strassmann, in Germany. In fact, from 13 July 1938 when she left Germany until Christmas 1938 when she and her nephew Frisch made a discovery which changed the course of world history, as will be seen, Lise wrote to Hahn no less than twenty-one times, and he to her twenty times.[9] And they were to exchange letters many times thereafter.

As regards Lise's family, however, they were far away, and of her close friends, Eva von Bahr-Bergius and her husband Nicklas were 300 miles distant in Kungälv; Elisabeth Schiemann was 675 miles distant in Berlin; and the Bohrs were 400 miles distant in Copenhagen.

Lise was hardly of the age to uproot. The only money that she possessed was the sum of ten German marks. Under her leadership, the physics department at the KWIC, where she had worked for twenty-six years, had achieved worldwide recognition and acclaim. And now she had been forced to abandon the unfinished uranium investigation, of which she had been, in Strassmann's words, the 'intellectual leader' for four years. The shock to her system can hardly be imagined.

Annie W. Ellerman, of the wealthy Ellerman Shipping Company, was born in Margate, Kent, England in 1894. She married writer Kenneth Macpherson and in 1933 the couple set up home in Switzerland, where their house became a 'receiving station' for refugees from the Nazis. Said she, 'It was considered too dangerous for me to enter Germany, but I went several times to Vienna and Prague to interview applicants and bring out documents that they needed for their visas. We helped a total of a hundred and five'.[10]

Annie gave a poignant description of what it was like to be a refugee.

> You were a citizen of good standing. Then overnight you were declared an enemy, beaten up [Lise was fortunately spared such terrors] your possessions seized and if you were very, very lucky, allowed to leave with your family and a suitcase apiece for an alien land where your professional qualifications were useless. I had to meet the people to whom such things had happened, some still scarred from the beatings they had received. Yet, it was the intangible things that they mourned rather than their former security: comradeship, childhood memories and above all, their language.[11]

Furthermore, Lise's relatives, as ethnic Jews, also fled Germany to avoid their otherwise inevitable fate. As for Lise herself, her academic books and papers had been impounded in Germany. She felt that, in Stockholm, the equipment with which she was initially provided was minimal, and she bitterly bewailed the fact that she had no assistant. The final straw was the feeling she had of being unwelcome, and that Siegbahn had only accepted her on sufferance.

In May 1938 in Paris, Irène Joliot-Curie and Serbian physicist and chemist Pavel Savitch announced that they had discovered a lanthanium-like substance, following the bombardment of uranium by neutrons. Whereupon Hahn, in late summer 1938, declared that, 'My co-worker Strassmann and I – by then Lise Meitner was no longer with us – put that assertion from Paris to the test'.

Hahn continued,

> In fact we did get a substance similar to lanthanum, which we took to be radium [Z=88]. It even seemed that what we had was several isotopes of this radium. When we tried to identify them more exactly, we were faced by something distinctly odd. We had been adding barium, as a carrier [i.e. a substance which aids the precipitation of another] to what we were calling radium, and now we could no longer separate our radium from the barium.[12]

On 27 October 1938, 'Nazi Germany carried out the brutal eviction of Jews with Polish citizenship. This was the first mass deportation of Jews'.[13]

On 1 November 1938, Lise received a great compliment when German physicist Arnold Berliner (1862–1942) wrote to her as follows. 'Now it makes me happy to think that I was able to be at your service now and then, and that I did it with pleasure … I would do it again and with some disposition, if only … yes, if only.'[14] In summer 1912, Berliner had founded the German scientific journal *Die Naturwissenschaften* ('The Science of Nature'), published by *Springer Verlag*, of which he had been editor ever since. Lise had known him since the 1920s and shared with him not only an interest in physics, but also in music.

On 2 November 1938, Hahn wrote to Lise to say, in respect of the bombardment of uranium with neutrons, 'We are now *almost* convinced that we are dealing with several – 2 or 3 – radium isotopes, which decay to actinium [Z=89], etc'. The finding of radium, he said, 'is really so interesting and improbable that we should like to publish it before Curie gets to it, and before she hears it from anyone else'. Hahn therefore asked Lise to keep the radium finding confidential. He continued, 'Naturally we would like it very much if you would think about the situation, how an alpha transformation can come about, probably also with slow neutrons, and at the same time produce several [radium] isomers'.[15] To this, Lise responded on 4 November by urging Hahn to send her 'more factual details'.[16] On 7 November 1938, she celebrated her 60th birthday.

Impatient lest the Paris team should steal his thunder, Hahn submitted his findings to *Die Naturwissenschaften* on 8 November, describing the production of three radium and three actinium isomers. 'Here, surely for the first time', he declared, 'is a case of *alpha-particles being split off by slow neutrons*'.[17]

On 9–10 November 1938, in Germany and Austria, there occurred an event known as 'Kristallnacht' – 'The Night of Broken Glass'. This was a pogrom (organised massacre of a particular ethnic group)[18] against the Jews of Germany and Austria carried out by the SA paramilitary forces and civilians.

> During the pogrom 91 Jews were murdered, more than 1,400 synagogues across Germany and Austria were torched, and Jewish-owned shops and businesses were plundered and destroyed. In addition, the Jews were forced to pay 'compensation' for the damage that had been caused and approximately 30,000 Jews were arrested and sent to concentration camps.[19]

Many Jews were beaten, and many Jewish homes destroyed.

> German police officials arrested some 6,000 Austrian Jews who were deported to the Dachau and Buchenwald concentration camps. Only those who promised to emigrate immediately, leaving their property behind, were released. Twenty-seven Austrian Jews were murdered in the course of the pogrom.[20]

On the evening of 9 November 1938, day one of Kristallnacht, Hahn dined with Auguste ('Gusti') and Justinian ('Jutz') Frisch (parents of Lise's nephew Otto Robert Frisch) and Gisela and Karl Lion, her only remaining relations in Vienna.[21] The following day, Jutz was arrested and imprisoned, prior to being sent to the Dachau concentration camp.

'Kindertransport' was an organised rescue effort from November 1938 to September 1939, whereby Jewish children were rescued from Nazi Germany, Austria, and Czechoslovakia and taken to the UK, the Netherlands, Belgium, and France: countries which waived their immigration requirements for the purpose.

Following *Kristallnacht*, 'Jewish and Quaker community leaders met with the British government to explore ways in which children could be saved from the actions of the Nazi regime'. Annie Ellerman described the role of British Quakers in assisting refugees as 'magnificent'.[22]

Quaker: a member of the Religious Society of Friends, a Christian movement devoted to peaceful principles and rejecting both formal ministry and all set forms of worship.[23]

> The British government allowed for the immigration without visas of Jewish children, but without their parents, through the Children's Transport program called Kindertransport. Between December 1938 and the start of World War II on Sept 1, 1939 when the program was forced to end, nearly 10,000 Kindertransport children had been rescued and had arrived in England.
>
> Because it was not safe for Jews to travel to Germany, six volunteers from the Friends Service Council travelled to Berlin. The gathering of the children, paperwork, and travel plans were coordinated between Quakers in Vienna

> and Berlin and Jewish organizations. Their care and travel were also coordinated in Britain by the group, Movement for the Care of Children. Then, the children were placed in boarding schools, including Quaker schools, often due to scholarships offered by the schools; in foster homes; or in hostels.[24]

The fact that the Quakers were involved in assisting Jewish children in their plight was to have a particular significance in respect of Lise's nephew, Philip Meitner, as will be seen.

Meanwhile, in early November 1938, Lise travelled from Sweden to Copenhagen, Denmark and on 13 November she arrived at the Institute for Theoretical Physics, of which Bohr was Director. Bohr had been appointed Professor of Theoretical Physics at the University of Copenhagen in 1916. In 1921, he had founded the Institute, to which Lise had now been invited by Bohr himself and his wife, Margrethe (née Nørlund).

Here, they were joined by Otto Hahn, who had travelled from Berlin. For Hahn, however, his reunion with Lise must have come as something as a shock to him, because she objected forcefully to the Berlin team's findings on several grounds. For example, how could neutron capture by uranium result in the creation of so many isotopes and isomers? According to author, educator, and scientific researcher Professor Ruth Lewin Sime, no less than sixteen such 'species' had been identified by the team as originating from uranium at the 'latest count'![25]

Said Ruth,

> The multiple isomerism and especially the *inherited* multiple isomerism of radium and its decay products were as inexplicable for radium as it had been for the transuranes. But the most serious difficulty with radium was the mechanism of its formation. For uranium (Z=92) to be transformed into radium (Z=88), a uranium nucleus would have to expel two alpha particles (helium nuclei); this could not happen, according to theory, unless the neutron that initiated the reaction was highly energetic [i.e. a fast neutron]. Had the neutrons been any slower, [and the Berlin team had used slow neutrons] they would simply have been captured instead.[26]

To summarise, the reason why Lise advised the Berlin team to check that it was actually radium that they had produced was because, at that point, it was considered theoretically impossible for a neutron to split off two alpha particles from uranium to form radium.

The outcome was, said Strassmann, that Lise 'urgently requested that these experiments be scrutinized very carefully and intensively one more time. Fortunately, L. Meitner's opinion and judgment carried so much weight with us in Berlin that the necessary control experiments were immediately undertaken'. It was Lise's 'critical demand that motivated us to test our findings once again, after which the result came to us'.[27] If ever confirmation of Lise's crucial and ongoing role in the Berlin team's research (even in her absence) was required, this was it!

In December 1938, the Nobel Prize for Physics was awarded to Enrico Fermi, 'for his demonstrations of the existence of new radioactive elements produced by neutron irradiation, and for his related discovery of nuclear reactions brought about by slow neutrons'. In his Nobel lecture, given on 12 December, Fermi referred to elements 93 and 94 ('transuranes') as if their existence was an established fact. He had even given them names: ausonium and hesperium respectively. Furthermore, in the decay products of uranium, he said, 'we were able to trace among them elements up to the number 96 [i.e. four transuranes]'.

On 19 December 1938, Hahn wrote to Lise as follows.

> Actually, there is something about the 'radium isotopes' that is so remarkable that for now we are telling only you. The half-lives of the three isotopes have been determined quite exactly, they can be separated from *all* elements except barium, [and therefore] all reactions are consistent [with radium]. Only one is not – unless there are very unusual coincidences: the fractionation doesn't work. Our Ra [radium] isotopes act like *Ba* [barium].

Prior to Lise having suggested to Hahn that he re-examine his team's finding of radium, Hahn, in his own words stated that, 'We [he and Strassmann] did not dream that our "radium" was in fact barium'.[28]

Hahn continued,

> We are coming steadily closer to the frightful conclusion: our Ra isotopes do not act like Ra but like Ba … All other elements, transuranes, U, Th, Ac, Pa, Pb, Bi, Po [uranium, thorium, actinium, protactinium, lead, bismuth, polonium] are out of the question. I have agreed with Strassmann that for now we shall tell only *you*. Perhaps you can come up with some sort of fantastic explanation. We know ourselves that it [uranium] *can't* actually burst apart into Ba.

The team therefore proposed to do further work. 'All very complicated experiments!' said Hahn, 'but we must clear it up'.

Before the institute closed for Christmas, continued Hahn, 'we do want to write something for [*Die*] *Naturwissenschaften* about the so-called Ra-isotopes, because we have very nice [decay] curves. So please think about whether there is any possibility – perhaps a Ba-isotope with much higher atomic weight than 137?' Was Hahn still hoping that despite all, he had discovered a transurane? 'If there is anything you could propose that you could publish, then it would still in a way be work by the three of us', he said.[29]

These words indicate that, despite Lise's absence, Hahn still saw her as an integral member of the team. He was in regular contact with her, he confided in her, sometimes to the exclusion of his colleagues, and he virtually begged her to assist him in matters of theoretical physics, which he simply did not understand. In fact, during her time at the KWIC, she had often said to Hahn in exasperation, 'Hahnschen ['Little Hahn'], go upstairs and do some chemistry, you understand nothing of physics!'[30] Many a true word spoken in jest!

However, the words of Hahn, 'in a way', reflected the fact that he did not intend to include Lise's name as co-author of his forthcoming scientific paper.

Hahn's words also reveal that he was thinking of elements in terms of their atomic weight and forgetting that what defines an element is not its atomic weight but its atomic number (or 'Z' number, which equals the number of protons in its atomic nucleus). This was a fundamental mistake to make, and there was no excuse for it because, as already mentioned, this definition had been established a quarter of a century previously in 1913, by British physicist, Henry G.J. Moseley.

On 21 December 1938, Hahn wrote to Lise to say,

> How beautiful and exciting it would be just now if we could have done our work together as before. What we conclude from our Radium evidence is that as 'chemists' we must draw the conclusion that the three isotopes that have been so thoroughly studied are not radium at all but, from the chemist point of view, Barium.

Nevertheless, 'We cannot suppress our results, even if they are perhaps physically absurd. You see, you'll be doing a good deed if you can find a way out of this'.[31]

Hahn was exercising all his charm, and again virtually begging Lise for help. In return, she would provide him with an answer, and when she did, he would respond by completely abandoning and disowning her. This was done with no compunction whatsoever, at a time when the Nazis were gone and no longer pointing a proverbial gun at his head.

On 22 December 1938, the Berlin team duly submitted its paper, entitled 'Concerning the Existence of Alkaline Earth Metals resulting from Neutron Irradiation of Uranium', to *Die Naturwissenschaften*. It was published on 6 January 1939. Eighty-five per cent of the paper, of which Hahn was principal author, was devoted to the earlier mistaken assumption, by the Berlin team, that radium was a product of the neutron irradiation of uranium! Said the authors, 'when uranium is irradiated by neutrons, there are several new radioisotopes produced, other than the transuranic elements – from 93 to 96, previously described by Meitner, Hahn, and Strassman'. (For once, since Lise's departure from Germany, Hahn had acknowledged her in a scientific paper.) The team identified these as three isotopes of radium. Their final conclusion, however, was 'that the new products are not radium, but rather barium itself'. Yet nowhere is there mention of the fact that it was Lise who had insisted that the Berlin team check the radium findings, the validity of which she had mistrusted.

Hahn continued,

> As chemists we really ought to revise the decay scheme given above [for the mistakenly identified radium isotopes]

> and insert the symbols Ba, La, Ce [barium, lanthanum, cerium] in place of Ra, Ac, Th [radium, actinium, thorium]. However, as 'nuclear chemists' working very close to the field of physics [which in Hahn's case was something of an exaggeration!], we cannot bring ourselves yet to take such a drastic step [which would imply a major splitting of the uranium atom] which goes against all previous experience in nuclear physics. There could perhaps be a series of unusual coincidences which has given us false indications.[32]

Reading between the lines, Hahn's thoughts can be imagined. He had rushed to print on several occasions, when his findings made no theoretical sense and now, unless he could find some explanation, he was in danger of having to admit that four years of work had been in vain.

The intention of Hahn and Strassmann had been to create transuranic elements. The possibility that they had (inadvertently) 'split the atom' was something that they could not bring themselves to believe. Not only that, the finding of barium as a fission product was just as surprising to Lise as it was to Hahn, to whom she responded as follows. 'Your radium results are very startling. A reaction with slow neutrons that supposedly leads to barium!' And in respect of the uranium nucleus and Hahn's talk of 'bursting', she declared, 'At the moment the assumption of such a thoroughgoing breakup [splitting of the atom] seems very difficult to me, but in nuclear physics we have experienced so many surprises, that one cannot unconditionally say, "it is impossible".'[33]

The seed had been sown in Lise's mind, by the existence of the barium, that instead of subatomic particles being 'chipped off' the atomic nucleus of uranium in several small steps, the whole nucleus could simply burst, i.e. break into pieces.

Meanwhile, Lise proceeded to acquaint Hahn of just how dire her position as a physicist in Stockholm was. Said she, 'I have gradually put together a single needle electrometer, a few usable counters, an amplifier, [and] a very poor automatic counter, absolutely no help'.[34]

Chapter 18

Eureka! Lise and Her Nephew Otto Frisch Strike Gold!

On 23 December 1938, Lise travelled the 300 miles to Kungälv, on the west coast of Sweden, to spend Christmas at the home of Eva von Bahr-Bergius and her husband Nicklas and family. Otto Frisch was also invited. This was to be a momentous visit.

Frisch was born in Vienna on 1 October 1904. His father was the aforementioned Justinian, a painter of delightful watercolours of Germany, the Netherlands, England, and the Middle East, who Frisch described as a 'polyhistor' (a person of wide-ranging knowledge or learning).[1] His mother was Auguste (née Meitner), Lise's older sister and a concert pianist.

It was in 1907 that Lise relocated to Berlin, and Frisch remembered how, when he was a child, his aunt, who was twenty-six years his senior, 'came home for occasional short visits. She did come and talk physics to me, and I asked her questions, and it certainly helped to have someone who obviously was competent and known in the subject'.[2]

In 1922, Frisch enrolled at the University of Vienna and in 1926 he was awarded a doctorate in physics. The following year, he obtained a research post at the National Physical Laboratory in Berlin, and in 1930, he became assistant to Professor Otto Stern.

Frisch described how, when he himself relocated to Berlin in 1927 and lived in lodgings, he was in the 'close vicinity' of his aunt Lise,

> so I saw her practically every day, and I didn't feel at all cut off from my family. In fact, I saw a certain amount of her work. I learned later that she had been asked by her own collaborator, [Otto] Hahn, why not take me into her lab? She didn't want to do that because she didn't want to be put in a position of conflict if I should not prove satisfactory. In fact, she had always steadfastly refused to give me any kind of support or testimony.[3]

Following the seizure of power by the Nazis in March 1933, discrimination against the Jews of Germany commenced immediately, and was followed by a series of anti-Jewish laws, designed to make the lives of Jews unbearable. Frisch was thus obliged, in that year, to relocate to England, where he joined Professor Patrick Blackett at Birkbeck College to study radioactivity. In 1934, Niels Bohr invited Frisch to join him at his Institute in Copenhagen, where he remained for five years. Bohr had been appointed Professor of Physics at the university in 1916, and the institute had been founded in 1921.

In his autobiography entitled *What Little I Remember*, Frisch gave a chapter and verse description of the conversation between himself and Lise, which took place at Kungälv, Sweden, just prior to Christmas Day, 1938. And, as this would prove to be one of the most significant conversations in all of scientific history, it will bear repeating in detail. But first, how does an atomic nucleus hold itself together?

Within the nucleus, an electromagnetic force tends to force the positively charged protons apart (Coulomb's law). However, a so-called 'strong force' serves to attract protons to neutrons, but this force acts only over relatively short distances. Finally, a 'weak force', which is responsible for radioactive decay, tends to make the nucleus break apart. Beyond a certain size of nucleus (as with the heavier elements), the relatively large proportion of neutrons serves to increase the spaces between the protons. The strong nuclear force is therefore less and less able to hold the nucleus together, and the atom becomes increasingly less stable and likely to undergo radioactive decay.

'When I came out of my hotel room after my first night in Kungälv', said Frisch, 'I found Lise Meitner studying a letter from Hahn and obviously worried by it'. The letter was to inform Lise that the three substances that Hahn and Strassmann had discovered and which 'they had found it impossible to separate ... from the barium which, routinely, they had added in order to facilitate the chemical separations', were, in fact, 'isotopes of barium'. Frisch described this news as 'startling'.

> Was it just a mistake? No, said Lise Meitner; Hahn was too good a chemist for that. But how could barium be formed from uranium? No larger fragments than protons or helium nuclei (alpha particles) had ever been chipped away from nuclei, and to chip off a large number not nearly enough

> energy was available. Nor was it possible that the uranium nucleus could have been cleaved right across. A nucleus was not like a brittle solid that that can be cleaved or broken; George Gamow had suggested early on, and Bohr had given good arguments that a nucleus was much more like a liquid-drop. Perhaps a drop could divide itself into two smaller drops in a more gradual manner, by first becoming elongated, then constricted, and finally being torn rather than broken in two? We knew that they were strong forces that would resist such a process, just as the surface tension of an ordinary liquid-drop tends to resist its division into two smaller ones. But the nuclei differed from ordinary drops in one important way: they were electrically charged, and that was known to counteract the surface tension.
>
> At that point we both sat down on a tree trunk (all that discussion had taken place while we walked through the wood in the snow, I with my skis on, Lise Meitner making good her claim that she could walk just as fast without), and started to calculate on scraps of paper. The charge of a uranium nucleus, we found, was indeed large enough to overcome the effect of the surface tension almost completely; so the uranium nucleus might indeed resemble a very wobbly, unstable drop, ready to divide itself at the slightest provocation, such as the impact of a single neutron.
>
> But there was another problem. After separation, the two drops would be driven apart by their mutual electric repulsion and would acquire high speed and hence a very large energy, about 200 MeV [200 million electron volts to be released per atom] in all; where could that energy come from? Fortunately, Lise Meitner remembered the empirical formula for computing the masses of nuclei and worked out that the two nuclei formed by the division of a uranium nucleus together would be lighter than the original uranium nucleus by about one-fifth the mass of a proton.[4]

The Nazis may have deprived Lise of her professorial position, laboratory, books, and scientific papers. What they could not deprive her of was the knowledge contained in her amazing brain!

Frisch continued, 'Now whenever mass disappears energy is created, according to Einstein's formula $E=mc^2$, and one-fifth of a proton mass was just equivalent 200 MeV. So, here was the source for that energy; it all fitted!'[5] In other words, Lise and Frisch were the first to put two and two together and realise the implication of fission in respect of its potential for releasing colossal amounts of energy. Meanwhile, one can imagine Lise and her nephew playing a joyful duet together on the pianoforte when they returned home.

Continued Frisch,

> A couple of days later I travelled back to Copenhagen in considerable excitement. I was keen to submit our speculations – it wasn't really more at the time – to Bohr, who was just about to leave for the USA. He had only a few minutes for me; but I had hardly begun to tell him when he smacked his forehead with his hand and exclaimed: 'Oh what idiots we have all been! Oh, but this is wonderful! This is just as it must be!'

Frisch told Bohr that he and Lise intended to write a paper about their new theory, and Bohr 'promised not to talk about it before the paper was out'.

'The paper was composed', said Frisch, during the course of 'several long-distance telephone calls' with his aunt, 'Lise Meitner having returned to Stockholm in the meantime. I asked an American biologist who was working with [George de] Hevesy what they call the process by which single cells divide in two: "fission", he said, so I used the term "nuclear fission" in that paper'. The biologist in question was William A. Arnold.

It was at the suggestion of Czech physicist George Placzek, said Frisch, that he performed experiments 'to show the existence of those fast-moving fragments of the uranium nucleus. I quickly set to work, and the experiment was done in two days, and a short note about it was sent off to *Nature*, together with the other note I had composed over the telephone with Lise Meitner'.

Lise concluded, said Frisch,

> that probably most of the radioactive substances which had been thought to lie beyond uranium – those 'transuranic'

> substances which Hahn thought they [the Berlin team] had discovered – were also fission products; a month or two later she came to Copenhagen and we proved that point by using a technique of 'radioactive recoil' which she had been the first to use, about thirty years previously. Yet transuranic elements were also formed [by uranium bombardment with neutrons]; that was proved in California by [US physicist] Ed [Edwin] M. McMillan [in 1940], with techniques much more sensitive than those available to Hahn and Meitner.[6]

So, in a twist of fate, it *was* possible after all to create transuranes by the neutron bombardment of uranium. In fact, the Berlin team had created one such transurane in 1936, as indicated by Lise's decay curve, 'Process 3', as she subsequently realised and acknowledged. The wheels had turned full circle!

It has been shown that, in general, major advances in science are made by small groups of scientists, not by large congregations of them. Sometimes the 'group' may be as small as one – viz. Alexander Fleming and his discovery of penicillin in 1928. In this present case, the group had only two members, a 60-year-old scientist, Lise, and her nephew Otto Frisch, aged 34.

The Berlin team had embarked on their experiments with the aim of creating elements beyond uranium – 'transuranes'. The possibility of splitting probably did not occur to any of the three scientists who believed in any case that this was theoretically impossible. But as French scientist Louis Pasteur said, 'Chance favours the prepared mind'. At first the mind of Lise was equally unprepared, but having acknowledged that such an eventuality *was* possible, she and Frisch set about providing an explanation for it which, building on the work on Gamow, Bohr, von Weizsäcker, and others, they did.

Chapter 19

Aftermath

Another of Lise's nephews, Philip Meitner, had escaped from Austria and arrived in England on 16 June 1938. This was the month prior to Lise's escape from Germany. The escape of Lise's other siblings and their families will be discussed shortly. Meanwhile, Philip's parents, Walter and Lotte Meitner, remained trapped in Vienna. But, of course, she could not communicate with them for fear of attracting the attention of the Nazis. Lise was aware, however, that her sister Auguste's husband, Justinian Frisch, was still languishing in Dachau concentration camp.

As regards what happened next, vis-à-vis Lise and the Berlin team, the timeline is relevant.

On 28 December 1938, Otto Hahn wrote to Lise Meitner: 'Dear Colleague! I want to quickly write a few more things about my Ba [barium] fantasies, etc. Perhaps Otto Robert [Frisch] is with you in Kungälv and you can discuss it a bit. Would it be possible that the uranium-239 [^{238}U plus a neutron] breaks up into a Ba and a Ma?'

'Ma' was a reference to masurium, a predicted but as yet unconfirmed element which was subsequently given the name 'technetium' (Z=43).

Hahn continued, 'The exact mass number is not important. It could also be 136 + 103 or something like that. Of course, the atomic numbers don't add up. Some neutrons would have to change into protons so that the charges would work out, Is that energetically possible? I do not know; I only know that our radium has the characteristics of Ba …'[1]

Once again, Hahn was confusing atomic weights with atomic numbers, and failing to understand that in radioactive decay, the sum of the atomic numbers (i.e. the sum of the protons, or 'Z' number) of the fission products must equal the atomic number of the parent nucleus.

On 29 December 1938, Lise wrote to Hahn: 'Dear Otto, Your Ra-Ba results are very exciting.' However, she told Hahn that the promised manuscript, i.e. his and Strassmann's forthcoming paper, had not yet arrived for her to consider.[2]

On 1 January 1939, by which time the manuscript had arrived, Lise wrote to Hahn to say, 'We have read and considered your paper very carefully; *perhaps* it is energetically possible for such a heavy nucleus to break up. However, your hypothesis that Ba and Mo [by which Lise meant 'Ma'] would result is impossible for several reasons.'

The principal reason was, of course, that the sum of the atomic numbers simply did not add up.

Lise now voiced her fears that the 'transuranes' hypothesis was wrong, and if this was so 'all the work of the last 3 years [in fact four years] had been incorrect'. In that case, 'as a joint retraction [by the three of them, herself, Hahn, and Strassmann] is surely not feasible' (because the Nazi authorities would have objected to any association of Hahn and his colleagues with Lise, an ethnic Jew), then in Lise's opinion 'we should consider *simultaneous* statements, one from the two of you and one from me'.[3] In other words, Lise was anxious in case it should be thought that she herself still believed in the so-called 'transuranes', when in fact she had long entertained doubts about reconciling their existence with atomic theory: doubts which she had repeatedly expressed to her two colleagues.

On 2 January 1939, Fermi arrived in New York City, having accepted a post at Columbia University. By March, he had performed experiments that indicated that a chain reaction (a self-sustaining nuclear fission process spread by neutrons)[4] was possible.

On 3 January 1939 Lise wrote to Hahn:

> Dear Otto! I am now almost *certain* that the two of you do have a splitting [of the uranium atom] to Ba and I find that to be a truly beautiful result, for which I most heartily congratulate you and Strassmann. Both of you now have a beautiful, wide field of work ahead of you. And believe me, even though I stand here with very empty hands, I am nevertheless happy for these wondrous findings.[5]

In this poignant letter, Lise expressed her great sadness at being separated from the Berlin team, at this crucial stage.

On the same day, 3 January 1939, Frisch wrote to Lise as follows.

> Dear Tanter [Viennese for 'Aunt'], I was able to speak with Bohr only today about the splitting of uranium. The conversation

> lasted only five minutes as Bohr agreed with us immediately about everything. He just couldn't imagine why he hadn't thought of this before, as it is such a direct consequence of the current concept of nuclear structure. He agreed with us completely that this splitting of a heavy nucleus into two big pieces is practically a classical phenomenon, which does not occur at all below a certain energy but goes readily above it. (That is also consistent with the very great stability of normal uranium and the very large instability of the compound nucleus) [i.e. of uranium plus one neutron].'[6]

To have the blessing of as great an authority as Niels Bohr was indeed a supreme accolade for Lise and her nephew!

On 6 January 1939, Hahn and Strassmann's paper 'On the Detection and Behaviour of Alkaline Earth Metals produced by Neutron Irradiation of Uranium' was duly published in *Naturewissenschaften*.

On 7 January 1939, Hahn wrote to Lise: 'It seems almost certain that the transuranes stay'.[7] This statement by Hahn is of great significance because it indicates that he still had not grasped the fact that the transuranes were fission fragments.

In an undated letter written at about this time, Lise informed Frisch that 'Hahn and Strassmann have just tried another Ba-Ra separation, with the same result, so I do not doubt that [uranium] splits into two nuclei'. However, 'For now I do not want to tell Hahn about my … hypothesis'. This was because if Hahn

> verifies it experimentally, then for political reasons he cannot refer to a written communication from me. When it [i.e. Lise and Frisch's forthcoming paper] is published, however, he can cite it. Normally, I am really not so concerned about publishing – on the contrary. But in my current bad situation I must, unfortunately, think of such things, to show people that I am not completely dim-witted.[8]

Here, Lise indicates her fear that Hahn would act true to form and claim all the credit for the theoretical explanation of nuclear fission, which she and her nephew Frisch had provided. The truth was, of course, that he was incapable of providing such an explanation himself.

On 8 January 1939, Frisch wrote to Lise: 'What do you think about trying to find the "recoil" nuclei [fragments] with a proportional amplifier?' I.e. by measuring the 'incredible number of ions' i.e. the large ionisation pulses that the uranium fragments would create, thereby confirming their presence. Frisch also stated that two days previously, Bohr had asked how he had arrived at his 'estimate of surface tension' of the nucleus and had 'agreed completely' with Frisch's explanation of it.[9]

On 13 January 1939, Frisch performed the proposed experiment and swiftly detected the fission fragments. He would now write a paper on the subject.

On 14 January 1939, Lise and Frisch learned that, through Lise's efforts, Frisch's father Jutz and his mother Gusti had been granted Swedish visas. Jutz would therefore be released from Dachau concentration camp and the couple would join Lise in Stockholm.[10]

Meanwhile, in New York, Bohr confided the fission discovery to US physicist Léon Rosenfeld, forgetting to say that he had done so in confidence. The secret was now out![11]

On 16 January 1939, two papers were submitted to *Nature*. The first, by Lise and Frisch, entitled 'Disintegration of Uranium by Neutrons: A New Type of Nuclear Reaction', was a masterpiece of clarity and erudition. It dealt with the following topics.

The supposed 'impossibility' of neutron bombardment causing large changes to the uranium nucleus and its atomic number

The authors stated as follows. 'In making chemical assignments, it was always assumed that these radioactive bodies [the so-called 'transuranes'] had atomic numbers near that of the element bombarded, since only particles with one or two charges were known to be emitted from nuclei.'

When the Berlin team discovered barium as a fission fragment,

> at first sight, this result seems very hard to understand. The formation of elements much below uranium [i.e. much lighter elements] has been considered before, but was always rejected for physical reasons, so long as the chemical evidence was not entirely clear cut. The emission, within a short time,

> of a large number of charged particles may be regarded as excluded by the small penetrability of the 'Coulomb barrier', indicated by Gamow's theory of alpha decay.

The 'liquid-drop' model of the atomic nucleus

> On the basis, however, of present ideas about the behaviour of heavy nuclei [as proposed by Bohr], an entirely different and essentially classical picture of these new disintegration processes suggests itself. On account of their close packing and strong energy exchange, the particles in a heavy nucleus would be expected to move in a collective way which has some resemblance to the movement of a liquid-drop.

'Close packing and strong energy exchange' refers to the subnuclear forces as described earlier. 'If the movement is made sufficiently violent by adding energy, such a drop may divide itself into two smaller drops.'

The larger the nucleus, the greater the instability

> In the discussion of the energies involved in the deformation of nuclei, the concept of surface tension has been used and its value has been estimated from simple considerations regarding nuclear forces. It must be remembered, however, that the surface tension of a charged droplet is diminished by its charge, and a rough estimate shows that the surface tension of nuclei, decreasing with increasing nuclear charge, may become zero for atomic numbers of the order of 100.

Therefore, yes, it is theoretically possible for a large nucleus to undergo significant splitting

> It seems therefore possible that the uranium nucleus has only small stability of form, and may, after neutron capture, divide itself into two nuclei of roughly equal size (the precise ratio of sizes depending on finer structural features and

perhaps partly on chance). These two nuclei will repel each other and should gain a total kinetic energy of c. 200 MeV., as calculated from nuclear radius and charge. This amount of energy may actually be expected to be available from the difference in packing fraction between uranium and the elements in the middle of the periodic system.

The fission fragments and their subsequent decay

> After division, the high neutron/proton ratio of uranium will tend to readjust itself by beta decay to the lower value suitable for lighter elements. Probably each part will thus give rise to a chain of disintegrations. If one of the parts is an isotope of barium, the other will be krypton (Z=92-56).

The authors had therefore identified the second fission fragment as krypton, based on the necessity of the sum of the atomic numbers of krypton (Z=36) and barium (Z=56) adding up to that of uranium (Z=92).

Krypton, said the authors, 'might decay through rubidium, strontium and yttrium to zirconium', whereas 'barium might decay to strontium-yttrium-zirconium'.

Conclusion

> It is possible, and seems to us rather probable, that the periods [half-lives] which have been ascribed to elements beyond uranium are also [i.e. instead] due to light elements. From the chemical evidence, the two short periods (10 sec. and 40 sec.) so far ascribed to ^{239}U might be masurium isotopes (Z=43) decaying through ruthenium, rhodium, palladium and silver into cadmium.
>
> In all these cases it might not be necessary to assume nuclear isomerism; but the different radioactive periods belonging to the same chemical element may then be attributed to different isotopes of this element, since varying proportions of neutrons may be given to the two parts of the uranium nucleus.

In regard to the Berlin team's bombardment of thorium with neutrons, the authors suggested that fission had also occurred in this case.[12]

The second paper to be submitted on 16 January 1939 was by Frisch and entitled 'Physical Evidence for the Division of Heavy Nuclei under Neutron Bombardment'.

Frisch calculated that the energy liberated when the uranium element undergoes fission 'was estimated to be about 200 Mev, both from mass defect considerations and from the repulsion of the two nuclei resulting from the "fission" process'.

The 'mass defect' represents the mass of energy binding the nucleus. It is equivalent to the 'nuclear binding energy'.

> If this picture is correct, one would expect fast-moving nuclei of atomic number 40 to 50 and atomic weight 100 to 150, and up to 100 MeV energy, to emerge from a layer of uranium bombarded with neutrons. In spite of their high energy, these nuclei should have a range in air of a few millimeters only, on account of their high effective charge (estimated to be about 20), which implies very dense ionization. Each such particle should produce a total of about 3 million ion pairs.
>
> By means of a uranium-lined ionization chamber, connected to a linear amplifier, I have succeeded in demonstrating the occurrence of such bursts of ionization.

Frisch concluded that from his experiments,

> it can be estimated that the ionizing particles must have an atomic weight of at least about 70, assuming a reasonable connection between atomic weight and effective charge. This seems to be conclusive physical evidence for the breaking up of uranium nuclei into parts of comparable size, as indicated by the experiments of Hahn and Strassmann.

Furthermore, 'experiments with thorium instead of uranium gave quite similar results…'[13]

On 18 January 1939, Lise wrote to Hahn. She confessed that she had been 'somewhat secretive' about the two groundbreaking papers which she and Frisch had just sent to *Nature*. However, she promised to send Hahn a copy of the manuscript as soon as the papers were accepted. Meanwhile, a 'split' of uranium 'into two lighter nuclei' was 'energetically possible' she told Hahn, 'because of the deep valley in the mass defect curve between Z=40 and Z=60 and is also understandable on the basis of the liquid-drop model of the nucleus'.

The 'valley' is a measure of stability, obtained by plotting the number of protons and neutrons of a nucleus (horizontally) against the energy per nucleon of the nucleus (vertically).

'I am quite convinced', Lise continued, 'that the transurane series are those of light nuclei [i.e. they were not transuranes at all], except for the resonance process [whereby U-239 was created]'. Meanwhile, she suggested to Hahn that in his next paper, it would be 'nice' if he could indicate that it was because of earlier studies of uranium and thorium conducted by both himself, Strassmann and herself, that it had been possible to 'clarify the Curie-Savitch observations so quickly'.[14]

On 24 January 1939, Hahn wrote to Lise. He had now received the manuscripts of the two papers that Lise and Frisch had sent to *Nature*, and he was determined to fight a strong (but ineffectual) rearguard action. 'We do not believe in your view of the "transuranes"', he declared, an indication that he and Strassmann continued to believe in them.

> We have also thought of krypton, etc., as the second product of splitting. Until now we have not been able to confirm the presence of krypton or rubidium. But perhaps strontium and yttrium. The physicists here naturally have also thought about the difference between the atomic numbers 92-56, after the difference in atomic weights didn't work out.[15]

What Hahn omitted to say, as Ruth Lewin Sime pointed out, was that Hahn had only looked for strontium *after* receiving Lise's letter of 18 January stressing the paramountcy of atomic numbers. Hahn also failed to disclose that he and Strassmann had not begun to search for krypton (Z=36) until the evening of 24 January, the Meitner-Frisch manuscripts having arrived at the KWIC *that very morning*.[16] This refusal to acknowledge his sources (not for the first time) amounted to nothing less than blatant dishonesty on Hahn's part.

On 25 January 1939, Hahn informed Lise that, sure enough, he had identified both strontium, yttrium, and rubidium amongst the decay products.[17]

On 26 January 1939, Lise wrote to Hahn. 'Your results are really wonderful!'[18] It is likely that Lise meant this sincerely, whereas, had she meant it sarcastically, she might have been forgiven.

On 28 January 1939, an article entitled 'Proof of the Formation of Active Isotopes of Barium from Uranium and Thorium Irradiated with Neutrons: Proof of the Existence of More Active Fragments Produced by Uranium Fission', was submitted to *Die Naturwissenschaften* by Hahn and Strassmann. In it, they confirmed that what they had thought were isotopes of radium were 'evidently not radium but isotopes of barium'.[19] Again, Lise's name was not mentioned in the paper.

On 31 January 1939, Eva von Bahr-Bergius wrote to Swedish theoretical physicist Carl W. Oseen to say that Lise 'sounds rather unhappy. She says she feels like a charlatan, who receives money although she cannot accomplish much, and her life seems to her completely pointless'. The problem was that Lise had no assistant to help her. She had become 'so unaccustomed to simpler technical work such as glass blowing, soldering etc that she now cannot cope with such'.[20]

As for finance, this was not a problem, because she had funding from the Nobel Committee and she was also supported by Eva.[21] This amounted to 5,400 Swedish krona in 1938, rising to over 8,000 krona by 1946.[22]

In his reply, Oseen admitted that what Lise required was a fully equipped institute. As Sweden was unable to provide her with this, he suggested that she turn to Bohr, as it was by his 'mediation that she came here. You probably know that it was impossible to get a grant from the Wallenberg Fund. We have done the best we could', Oseen concluded.[23]

Wallenberg Fund: a reference to Sweden's Wallenberg Foundation, which supported the natural sciences.

On 5 February 1939, Lise wrote to Hahn. 'It would have been so nice for me if you had just written that we – independently of your wonderful findings – had come upon the necessity for the existence of the Kr-Rb-Sr [krypton-rubidium-strontium] series.' Lise had realised, yet again, that Hahn had given her no credit for making what she described as his 'wonderful findings' possible. She concluded,

> Now Siegbahn will gradually believe … that I never did anything and that you also did all the physics at Dahlem [the KWIC]. I am gradually losing all my courage. Forgive this unhappy letter. Sometimes I do not know what to do

> with my life. Probably there are many people who have emigrated who feel as I do, but still it is very hard.[24]

In this same letter, Lise also declared, 'I never wrote [before to say] how bad it really is'. But she omitted this sentence from the final draft.[25]

On 6 February 1939, Lise wrote to her brother, Walter Meitner.

> The Swedes are so superficial; I don't fit in here at all, and although I try not to show it, my inner insecurity is painful and prevents me from thinking calmly. Hahn has just published absolutely wonderful things based on our work together – uranium and thorium nuclei split into lighter nuclei such as barium and lanthanum, krypton, strontium etc. And much of these results make me happy for Hahn, both personally and scientifically.

However, 'Many people here must think I contributed absolutely nothing to it – and now I am so discouraged; although I believe I used to do good work, now I have lost my self-confidence.'[26] Lise, who had only ever acted with generosity and selflessness, merely asked for what was due to her – recognition.

Lise may or may not have suspected, at this stage, that Hahn's intention was to create the impression that she had played little or no part in his successes.

Hahn, in his next letter to Lise of 7 February 1939, confirmed that he had merely made use of her expertise, and furthermore was now in complete denial about the fact that he had done so. Said he, 'In all our work we absolutely never touched upon physics, instead we did only chemical separations over and over again. We know our limits and of course we also know that in this particular case it was useful to do only chemistry. In that regard the uranium work is for me a heaven-sent gift.'[27]

Had he been honest and open, like his colleague Strassmann, Hahn would have readily admitted that it had been at Lise's suggestion that the Berlin team had embarked on the uranium investigation in the first place; that she had guided it through every step of the way, pointing out what was feasible and what was not feasible, in terms of equating the findings with theoretical physics, and finally explaining Hahn's findings to him, when he did not understand them himself! But alas, for Hahn had reverted to his default position of frank dishonesty and dissimulation once again, as far as his relationship with Lise was concerned.

On 10 February 1939, Hahn and Strassmann's paper 'Proof of the Formation of Active Isotopes of Barium from Uranium and Thorium Irradiated with Neutrons: Proof of the Existence of More Active Fragments Produced by Uranium Fission', was published in *Die Naturwissenschaften*.

On 11 February 1939, Lise and Frisch's joint paper 'Disintegration of Uranium by Neutrons: A New Type of Nuclear Reaction' appeared in *Nature*. In their paper, the authors predicted that if one of the fragments 'is an isotope of barium [Z=56], then the other will be krypton [Z=36], which might decay through rubidium, strontium, and yttrium to zirconium'.[28]

On 18 February 1939, Frisch's paper 'Physical Evidence for the Division of Heavy Nuclei under Neutron Bombardment' appeared in *Nature*.

On 3 March 1939, Hahn wrote to Lise. He now had the effrontery to tell Lise that 'the priority for splitting uranium is gradually slipping away from Strassmann and me'. Also, Hahn objected to the phrase, 'A New Type of Nuclear Reaction' in the title of Lise and Frisch's paper and stated that 'Str [Strassmann] and I [had] already mentioned [fission of the uranium atom, which he called 'bursting'] in January … even a possible second fragment (masurium) is already in it'.

In the same letter, Hahn wrote, 'Strassmann and I know that we were as sure as possible of the splitting of uranium, without leaning on any other observation or hypothesis'. This was nonsense, and the correspondence between Hahn and Lise simply does not bear this out. The whole investigation had been a multidisciplinary one right from the start; the two chemists, Hahn and Strassmann, cooperating with the physicist Lise, and neither could have achieved their objectives without the other. In fact, had it not been for Lise, Hahn would still have been clinging to his beloved 'transuranes'!

'After we knew at the beginning of January that the transuranes were not masurium, etc.' continued the pompous and conceited Hahn, 'the search for the other fragments was self-understood'.

Finally, said Hahn, if those other than himself were to receive the credit for the discovery of nuclear fission, then 'there is nothing we can do'. However, 'I have not the slightest doubt that you and also Bohr are loyal'.[29] By 'loyal', Hahn was presumably expecting that Lise and Bohr would give him all the credit.

On 6 March 1939, Lise wrote to Hahn.

> Dear Otto, I think … that you or your gentleman have misunderstood some things. [Our] title, 'A New Type of Nuclear Reaction' referred *as a matter of course* to your and Strassmann's findings, and we only tried to show that one can explain this 'new nuclear reaction' *on the basis of the purely classical liquid-drop model*, and that it must be accompanied by energies of the order of magnitude 200 MeV. That is exactly what Bohr means when he says, word for word, 'that the authors (i.e. we) propose an *interpretation* of the remarkable findings of Hahn and Strassmann'. He discusses in conceptual detail only the theoretical aspect, and takes your findings as so certain, that he bases his discussion on them.[30]

On 7 March 1939, Lise wrote to Hahn. 'Dear Otto, You gave yourself the most beautiful possible birthday present – the wonderful discovery by Hahn and Strassmann. Tonight Otto Robert [Frisch] and I will drink a glass of wine to you. And perhaps in 10 years there will be a bottle of wine for us together – that will have to be a big one.' On 8 March 1939, Hahn celebrated his 60th birthday.

On 10 March 1939, Lise wrote to acquaint Hahn with a decisive experiment which she and Frisch had just completed. 'It really is the case that the two long transurane series [i.e. Processes 1 and 2] must be lighter elements. Actually, I am not surprised at our result, since after your discovery of the splitting of the uranium nucleus I no longer believed in the transuranes, as I wrote to you many times.'

Here was Lise, magnanimous as ever, giving Hahn credit for 'splitting the atom', when (a) he was not quite sure that he had done so, and (b) he did not understand the physics involved, even when it was explained to him.

'But you and Strassmann could not have made your beautiful discovery if we had not done the earlier uranium work,' Lise continued, pointing out quite justifiably that Hahn, yet again, had failed to acknowledge the ladder on which he had climbed.

Lise now explained that she and Frisch had established, beyond all doubt, that the 'transuranes' were, in fact, 'lighter nuclei. Exactly which ones they are you will have to find out; we are not going to try.'[31] In fact, Lise and Frisch had already predicted that the initial decay products would be barium and krypton.

On 13 March 1939, Hahn wrote to Lise.

> Dear Lise, This time, it is we who heartily congratulate you upon your exciting result with the recoil particles and the transuranes. We cannot find any holes in your interpretation and from your findings we must indeed declare that the transuranes are dead. For us – Strassmann and me – this result was, however, completely incomprehensible until now because we absolutely could not say what the transuranes might be. In any case you and [Frisch] were the first to achieve a completely clear result for the physicists based on experiment and not on vague suppositions.[32]

At last, Hahn had acknowledged Lise's role in unravelling the truth about the sorry 'transurane' saga.

Another World War was in the offing, after which Hahn, now free of all restraints, would have the opportunity to acknowledge Lise and Frisch's vital role in the discovery of nuclear fission. The question is, would he afford *them* the same loyalty that he now demanded of them?

On 24 March 1939, Lise wrote to Bohr (who was still in the USA) in glowing terms about the wonderful hospitality that he had afforded her at his Institute in Copenhagen.

> Not only did everyone from [George de] Hevesy to the youngest Mitarbeiter [male junior co-worker] strive to help me in the friendliest way with necessary materials and working space. The entire scientific attitude, the natural way of discussing problems with me in which I could ask and be asked anything, is wonderfully beneficial. Of course, I owe my thanks for this beautiful atmosphere above all to you.

This was in stark contrast to that which pertained in Stockholm.[33]

In March 1939, in a letter to *Naturewissenschaften*, Ida Noddack criticised Hahn for not citing her article of September 1935 (published in the journal *Zeitschrift für Angewandte Chemie*), in which she had suggested that it was possible for an atomic nucleus to break apart into 'several larger fragments'.

On 20 March 1939, Hahn wrote to Lise complaining that Ida 'accuses me of not citing her, after she predicted already in 1934 that uranium splits into lighter nuclei'.[34] To this, Lise responded by saying that Ida 'really has made a great fool of herself'.[35] How wrong both Hahn and Lise were, and how remiss of them both not to admit that Ida had been *absolutely right*!

In May 1939, Lise's personal effects at last arrived in Stockholm. But she found her furniture, china, and glassware shattered to pieces and her books desecrated.[36] The Nazi authorities had done their work well!

In summer 1939, Frisch travelled to Birmingham, UK. However, with the outbreak of war, he was unable to return to Copenhagen.

On 15 July 1939, Lise wrote to Hahn to correct his mistaken impression that she had regarded his work as an unimportant. 'It is a great step forward with such clear and elegant chemistry to identify transuranic elements,' she said. 'But you have misunderstood. In Bohr's work there was nothing about the possibility of splitting the atoms of heavy elements.' In regard to Hahn's 'comparison of the fission process to the droplet model of Bohr (already three years old) and not to our work,' said Lise, 'it seemed to me that you had misunderstood especially in connection with the following sentence when we had discussed the maintaining of the core charge.'

Core charge: the force of attraction between valence electrons (those in the outermost shell of the atom) and the core of the atom.

> In the work of Bohr there is understandably nothing to explain the possibility of splitting heavy nuclei [i.e. of splitting the atom]. The interpretation, that with heavy nuclei cohesive surface tension through the repulsive Coulomb forces of the high core charge, is almost reduced to zero hereby capturing the neutron and creating fission – this has been the content of our work. Your description could give the impression that you had not grasped this and that you have the opinion that this was already done by the work of Bohr.

Lise also reprimanded Hahn for failing, in an article of his entitled 'Existence of Transuranes' (June 1939), to acknowledge either the work of British physicist Norman Feather or the work of US physicist Philip Abelson.[37] Here is Hahn, again pretending that he had climbed the proverbial ladder all by himself!

Lise reiterated that she 'did not quite understand why you attributed the theoretical explanation of the fission process to Bohr's (3-year-old) liquid-drop model and not to [the] work [of myself and Frisch],' she said. This, and a recent disagreement that Hahn had had with Feather, led Lise to ask him the question, 'Doesn't that show that you're a little angry and aren't seeing things so clearly anymore?'[38] For Lise, in her appraisal of Hahn, the light was evidently beginning to dawn!

Lise proceeded to explain yet another concept in physics which Hahn had failed to comprehend, that when fission occurs – for example of U-239, U-236, or Th-233 – there were many 'fission possibilities'. For example, despite their having 'different atomic weights and different nuclear charges' these two elements could 'yield a series of identical isotopes … as well as isotopes which are not identical'. In other words, the atom may split in different ways, resulting in different fission products. The atomic weights of these isotopes would be 'in the range … from 80 to 150'. But, of course, the sum of the atomic numbers of the daughter nuclei must always equal the atomic number of the parent nucleus.

> What concerns the resonance process, is Bohr's opinion that it can lead to an explosion, whilst with rising temperature of the 'thermal' neutrons can reach dangerously high levels with the possibility that the neutrons go down quickly and when the resonance energy is gained the resonance process overwhelms everything else.
>
> Finally, I should like to say a word about our work on transuranium elements. I have the impression from your work that our proof of the non-existence of transuranium elements is no longer crucial because you misunderstood the meaning of the calculated decay curve.[39]

By this, Lise presumably meant that Hahn had mistakenly believed that his decay curves indicated the presence of transuranes. Whereas they in fact indicated the presence of fission products. Here, once again, Lise is pointing out to Hahn his failure to understand physics.

Note: The first transuranic element, Neptunium, was not synthesised until 1940. In fact, the Berlin team had actually produced a transuranic element (in 'Process 3'), in which they made U-239 (twenty-three minute half-life) which would decay to element 93, but they did not look for it or identify it.[40]

German physicist Walther Gerlach (1889–1979) quoted Hahn as having said in 1945 that 'Strassmann and I did not know what we were doing, and Professor Meitner did the main work'. But in a letter written a decade later in 1955, Hahn retracted this statement, saying, 'with all friendship to my lady colleague, this proposition was not correct'.[41]

However, in respect of fission, Gerlach quoted Einstein as having said of Hahn and Strassman, 'They did not understand the discovery correctly.'[42] This prompted the following response from Hahn. 'I have often read in the many messages of Prof. Einstein that we had no idea about what we were doing and that the main result of the work should be attached [i.e. attributed] to Professor Meitner.'[43]

In July 1939, Lise visited Cambridge at Bragg's invitation. He and Cockcroft now offered her a post at the Cavendish Laboratory and Girton College offered her a three-year contract.[44] However, having 'practically accepted', she decided to postpone her move until summer 1940.[45] However, on 3 September 1939 came war, and the arrangement fell through. Lise would come bitterly to regret her decision in the years to come.

Chapter 20

Another War

On 1 September 1939, Hitler invaded Poland. On 3 September 1939, Britain and France declared war on Germany.

At the outbreak of war, Auguste and Justinian's son Otto Frisch happened to be visiting Australian physicist Marcus ('Mark') Oliphant, Professor of Physics at the University of Birmingham, UK, who offered him a teaching post at the university. There, Frisch worked with German-British-Jewish theoretical physicist Rudolf Peierls under Oliphant's direction. He studied nuclear fission, and in particular the possibility of creating a 'chain reaction', i.e. a self-sustaining nuclear fission process spread by neutrons, with the release of vast amounts of energy.

From autumn 1939, deportations of Austrian Jews began in earnest, under the orders of (Otto) Adolf Eichmann, high SS official and a major organiser of the Holocaust. Tens of thousands were deported to occupied Poland, and to parts of the occupied Soviet Union, most of whom were murdered.[1]

> Nazi plans to force Jews to emigrate succeeded. By the end of 1941, 130,000 Jews had left Vienna, 30,000 of whom went to the USA. They left behind all of their property, but were forced to pay the Reichs Flight Tax, a tax on all émigrés from the Third Reich: some received financial support from international aid organisations so that they could pay this tax. Following the Wannsee Conference in January 1942, the Nazis resolved to completely annihilate the Jewish population, and the majority of the Jews who had stayed in Vienna became victims of the Holocaust. Of the more than 65,000 Viennese Jews who were deported to concentration camps, only a few more than 2,000 survived.[2]

By 1944, the only Jews remaining in Austria were those who were married to non-Jews, or those who had gone into hiding.[3]

The Holocaust, said Annie Ellerman, was an

> attempt to exterminate a whole section of the population, no matter whether their characters were good or bad. Nor was it only the Jews who suffered. Many Germans who objected to the regime on moral or religious grounds were equally persecuted. Roughly, two-thirds of my cases were Jewish, but the other third were Christians of purely German descent.[4]

'Righteous Among Nations' was an honorific whereby the State of Israel honoured non-Jews who had risked their lives to save Jews from extermination by the Nazis. It should not be forgotten that 109 Austrians were awarded this honour, and 601 Germans.

At Cambridge, the University's School of Nuclear Physics had now diverted its attention to the war effort. Cockcroft dissuaded Lise from relocating to England as she had planned. So, yet again, Lise was left high and dry. On 12 November 1939, she expressed her feelings to Hahn. 'Scientifically I am completely isolated, for months I speak with no one about physics, sit alone in my room and try to keep myself busy. You cannot call it "work".'[5]

In late 1939, when the KWIP was taken over by the army and allotted the task of conducting studies into whether nuclear fission could be employed for military purposes, Debye, who refused to become a German citizen, felt that he could no longer remain director. He took a six-month sabbatical and accepted a guest professorship at Cornell University (Ithaca, New York, USA), starting in January 1940. He extended the professorship for another six years.

Early in 1940 in Birmingham, UK, Lise's nephew Otto Frisch and Peierls calculated that only about 1 kilogram (2.2 pounds) in weight of pure uranium isotope U-235 would be sufficient to make a powerful nuclear device – the so-called 'critical mass'. They also suggested means by which U-235 could be separated, and how such a 'bomb' could be detonated. This information they communicated secretly to the British authorities.[6]

In March 1940, Frisch and Peierls sent a secret 'Memorandum' to the British government on the feasibility of producing nuclear weapons, including an estimate of the quantity of uranium required (critical mass) for a chain reaction to occur, which would be only a few pounds: a method of uranium separation, and a method of detonation.[7]

In April 1940, Norway and Sweden were invaded and occupied by the Germans. On 10 May 1940, the Netherlands suffered the same fate.

In 1936, the Berlin team had identified the presence of the element that was a genuine precursor to a 'transurane' (with a half-life of twenty-three minutes) as U-239. This was by the resonance capture of slow neutrons by U-238. And, furthermore, it was clear that U-239 would decay to the next higher element, 93. What a prize, thought Lise, if she could complete her work by isolating this new element! In this ambition, however, she was frustrated. It was winter 1940 and Siegbahn's cyclotron, which was necessary for the operation, was still not functional.

In the event, the first two transuranic elements were first synthesised in May 1940 by Edwin McMillan and Philip Abelson at the Berkeley Radiation Laboratory, University of California, Berkeley. They identified neptunium as element 93, a beta emitter that necessarily decayed to form plutonium, element 94.

On 30 September 1940, Lise described to Franck 'the great difficulties in the laboratory and Siegbahn's lack of interest in her scientific work. She regrets the scientific isolation'.[8]

On 23 January 1941, Lise wrote to von Laue mentioning German chemist and Nobel Laureate Carl Bosch's remark to her that 'one has to have a hobby besides the profession when getting old'. Von Laue had extolled the virtue of learning Greek. Whereupon, Lise replied that she had 'learnt the language [i.e. Greek] thinking that the world would have another dimension for her if she knew it'.[9] Lise, who was already familiar with several languages, was well placed for hobbies: reading widely, enjoying music, and walking in scenic places being her favourite leisure occupations.

On 11 May 1941, Lise wrote to von Laue and his wife Magda to say how 'she longs for a meadow full with spring flowers in the Alps'.[10] On 26 May 1941, Lise told Marga Planck that she was 'longing for the mountains'.[11] On 2 November 1941, Lise wrote to von Laue and Magda about her holiday in Dalarna 'and the surroundings with forest and flowers'.[12] However, on 29 December 1941, Lise was reflecting upon 'all the unhappy changes in the world'.[13]

On 10 January 1942, Franck's wife Ingrid died in the USA. On 14 January, Lise wrote to von Laue to say how at Christmas she had 'received telegrams from Otto Robert [Frisch] and her brothers and sisters in America'. In other words, she at least knew that they were safe.[14]

When German theoretical physicists Werner K. Heisenberg and Carl F. von Weizsäcker visited Copenhagen in September 1941, Lise was suspicious. And even more so when Heisenberg attempted to engage Bohr in a private conversation.[15] This prompted Lise, on 20 April 1942, to write a coded message to von Laue warning him about the two German scientists.[16]

On 26 February 1942, to Swedish physicist and oceanographer Hans Pettersson, Lise explained 'the background of why Siegbahn dislikes the idea of her getting an assistant; he is not interested in nuclear physics. She cannot expect any help in this matter from Siegbahn'.[17]

Albert Schweitzer (1875–1965) was an Alsatian-German theologian, philosopher, organist, and mission doctor in equatorial Africa. On 2 June 1942, Lise wrote to von Laue to say that Schweitzer's opinion 'that religiousness is the deep respect of life also for the smallest animal' was 'a wording she now accepts'.[18]

As already mentioned, proof of nuclear fission was provided by Lise and Frisch, and by Frisch himself by experimentation, following their epoch-making conversation at Kungälv in late December 1938. But in all the excitement that had followed, said Frisch,

> we had missed the most important point: the chain reaction. It was [chemist and physicist] Christian Møller, a Danish colleague, who first suggested to me that the fission fragments (the two freshly formed nuclei) might contain enough surplus energy each to eject a neutron or two; each of these might cause another fission and generate more neutrons. By such a 'chain reaction' the neutrons would multiply in uranium like rabbits in a meadow! So, from Møller's remark the exciting vision arose that by assembling enough pure uranium (with appropriate care!) one might start a controlled chain reaction and liberate nuclear energy on a scale that really mattered. Many others independently had the same thought, as I soon found out. Of course, the spectre of a bomb – an uncontrolled chain reaction – was there as well; but for a while anyhow, it looked as though it need not frighten us.[19]

(In an experiment led by Enrico Fermi, the first sustained nuclear chain reaction was achieved on 2 December 1942 at the University of Chicago.)

Frisch described 'the fanatical ingenuity of the allied physicists and engineers', many of whom, ironically, were refugees who had been forced to flee Germany by the Nazis, who were 'driven by the fear that Hitler might develop the decisive weapon before they did'.[20]

In October 1942, Heisenberg was appointed director of the KWIP.

On 21 November 1942, Lise opined to von Laue that in respect of the search for 'absolute truth, one has to give up this aim' and instead, 'have to think complementarian [i.e. complementarily], comparable with Pascal's method of thinking in polarities and has to search for superposed principles'.[21]

Blaise Pascal (1623–1662) was a French philosopher, mathematician, scientist, and inventor.

> Polarities are chronic, ongoing tensions between two paradoxically correct viewpoints. These dilemmas are inherent in individuals, in groups, in organizations (such as schools), and in society. The strain that comes from the shifting energy in a polarity system is unavoidable, unstoppable, and unsolvable. The polarity system must be tapped as a resource by using 'both/and' thinking over a traditional 'either/or' problem-solving approach of choosing one viewpoint – a pole – as the solution to the competing viewpoint. Polarity Thinking is a construct that describes a set of principles and tools for recognizing, predicting, and leveraging polarities in work and in life.[22]

On 1 January 1943, Lise told Franck, 'I cannot understand myself, having had the opportunity to stay in England in July 1939, when I was in Cambridge to give some lectures and Cockcroft proposed to me to stay there … that I did not do it. What relief if I could now do some helpful work!'[23]

On 8 January 1943 Lise, nostalgic as ever in a letter to von Laue, recalled 'an outing with the [von] Laues to Saale [Germany] where they had seen various birds'.[24] In late spring 1943, von Laue told Lise that he had holidayed in Berchtesgaden in Germany's Bavarian Alps. This name had ghastly connotations, it being the infamous 'Eagle's Nest' residence of Adolf Hitler.[25]

On 15 April 1943, Lise brought up the 'old chestnut' again when she complained bitterly to Hahn that her name had been deliberately omitted from previous scientific papers relating to experiments in which all three of them had participated, so that they only bore Hahn and Strassmann's names as authors and not hers.[26]

Was Lise aware of the murders and atrocities that were being perpetrated by the Nazis on an industrial scale in Germany and in the occupied territories? The answer is yes, because she had remained in close contact with, for example, Paul Rosbaud (who had been instrumental in helping her to escape to Holland in July 1938 and who was, in fact, passing information to British Intelligence), and also with von Laue.

In July 1943, Speer ordered all KWI research departments to relocate to southern Germany because of the danger of Allied bombing.

In September 1943, fearing imminent arrest by the Nazis on account of his Jewish heritage from his mother's side, Bohr fled with his family to Sweden. When, on 6 October 1943, he relocated to Britain, his family remained in Stockholm, where his wife Magrethe would have had a happy reunion with Lise.

On 31 October 1943, Lise told von Laue that she had a new assistant who was 'really good and a great help to her. Many small improvements of the apparatus were made by him and she no longer has to wait until the workshop has time to do it. But the possibilities of using the cyclotron are still limited'.[27] On 17 November 1943, Lise told Rosbaud that 'her work in the laboratory is going better', and she described her new assistant as both 'skilled and humane'.[28] On 8 December 1943, Bohr relocated from Britain to Washington, DC.

In late 1943, having become naturalised as a British citizen, Frisch, together with a group of British scientists, relocated to Los Alamos to join the US Manhattan Project. James Franck also joined the project.

Manhattan Project: code name for a project set up in 1942 by the USA in order to develop an atomic bomb.

When Lise was also invited, she vehemently declared, 'I will have nothing to do with a bomb.'[29]

The KWIC was bombed and severely damaged by the Allies on 11 February 1944. Of all the Kaiser Wilhelm Institutes, Hahn's Chemistry Institute was the most severely damaged. Following this event, only the physicists, Kurt Diebner and Karl Wirtz remained, working from a bunker in the grounds of the ruined KWIP.

In summer 1944, Heisenberg relocated to Hechingen, where he was subsequently joined by von Weizsäcker and theoretical nuclear physicist, Karl-Heinz Höcker. Finally, Diebner moved his independent reactor experimental station to the town of Stadtilm in Thüringia.[30]

On 30 April 1944, Lise told von Laue that 'the cyclotron is in use to make Na [sodium] and P [phosphorus] for the biologists only. She has never seen such a bad relationship between the staff and the co-workers'.[31]

On 20 June 1944, Lise told Hahn that the news of his son Hanno's 'serious injury and the amputation of his left arm, gave her a shock and she mentions how bitter it will be for Otto [Hahn] to tell it [i.e. break the news] to Edith'. Hahn had 'told her this in his card which arrived today'.[32]

On 1 September 1944, Lise told Strassmann that the cyclotron had been out of use for two months.[33] On 4 September 1944, she wrote to von Laue to say, with her dry sense of humour, 'I miss working with Otto Hahn. We worked together from 1920 to 1935 on many different projects. He had his own understandings and no interest for my problems in physics. In that way we remained good friends.'[34]

In her letter to von Laue, Lise quoted from memory, and with a few pardonable mistakes, the first four of the following lines from Shakespeare's tragedy, *Hamlet*. The passage undoubtedly reflected her own stoicism, when it came to the kind of triumphs and disasters that she had encountered in her life. The correct version, in which the eponymous hero, Hamlet praises his faithful friend, Horatio reads as follows:

> A man that Fortune's buffets and rewards
> Hast ta'en with equal thanks. And blessed are those
> Whose blood and judgment are so well commingled,
> That they are not a pipe for Fortune's finger
> To sound what stop she please. Give me that man
> That is not passion's slave, and I will wear him
> In my heart's core, ay, in my heart of hearts.
>
> Shakespeare, *Hamlet*, Act 3, Scene 2

On 6 June 1944 – 'D-Day' – Allied forces invaded Normandy. On 21 June 1944, Lise wrote to Eva von Bahr-Bergius to say,

> I am certainly glad that the invasion has finally begun, but I fear what the Germans will do when their situation appears

> hopeless. I am very anxious to know if the [German] robot-bombs [the 'V' weapons] have something to do with uranium bombs. I don't actually think so, but I do know that the institute that was working on those things was transferred to southern Germany, even though it was not hit by [Allied] bombs at all.

(Speer had ordered all research departments to relocate to southern Germany in July 1943, and the KWIC was bombed on 11 February 1944.)

'That makes me wonder, and I am disturbed to think that it may be possible to make uranium bombs after all.'[35]

When, in late 1944, the Royal Swedish Academy of Sciences (the 'Academy') announced the awarding of the Nobel Prize in Chemistry to Otto Hahn, Lise implored Hans Pettersson, 'Please do not speak of this. It could be dangerous for Hahn.'[36] The Nazi regime had forbidden German citizens to accept Nobel Prizes and Lise was desperately anxious to protect her former colleague. Alas, her loyalty to Hahn would not be reciprocated, even when he had ample opportunity to do so after the war had ended.

On 14 January 1945, Lise told Otto Stern, 'You may imagine how much I have since regretted that I did not stay directly in England. It would have meant the possibility to do some helpful work.'[37] Vienna was liberated by Soviet forces on 4 April 1945.

On 6 and 9 August 1945, atomic bombs were dropped on the Japanese cities of Hiroshima and Nagasaki by the USA. On 2 September 1945, the war in the Far East ended with the surrender of Japan.

Through all those dark times of war, isolation, and the dislocation of life caused by the Nazis, Lise continued, when time permitted, to derive pleasure from leisure pursuits, often escaping into a world of fantasy reminiscent of childhood. On 25 March 1940, to von Laue, Lise recalled a book that she had read, Selma Lagerlöv's *Christmas Tales*, in which, she declared, 'that Lagerlöv's death looks like a symbol to the present events'.[38] Selma was a Swedish children's picture book author and illustrator and Nobel Laureate who had died on 16 March 1940, aged 81.

On 4 July 1942, Lise asked von Laue if he and his wife, Magda had read Elsa Beskow's 'Hänschen im Blaubeerwald' – 'Peter in the Blueberry Forest'. Mrs Beskow was 'a beloved fairy tale lady [i.e. writer] in Sweden'.[39] Even though she was far away from her relations and from her native land, Lise could still dream of fairyland!

On 9 January 1944, Lise told von Laue that 'she loves Brahms – his music as well as the man'.[40] To von Laue and his wife Magda on 6 September 1944, Lise declared that she was 'always full of gratitude when listening to music she loves'. In respect of Schubert's song 'An die Musik', 'they have an unusually good Schubert singer who is half Swedish half Vienner [Viennese]'.[41]

On 28 March 1945, Lise told von Laue that she had been listening to German composer J.S. Bach's sacred oratorio the *St Matthew Passion*. 'She had intended to go to the performance with Magrethe Bohr, but it was sold out.'[42]

On 21 August 1945, Lise stated that she was in communication with Hahn 'through the British Legation' but did not know his whereabouts.[43] On 25 August 1945, Bohr returned to Copenhagen from the USA.

On 1 September 1945, Lise thanked Hilde Rosbaud for her letter 'with the good news that Paul [her husband] is alive'.[44]

Chapter 21

Farm Hall

'Operation Epsilon' was the codename for a programme intended to glean information from German scientists about their previous work in nuclear physics, including the Nazis' atomic bomb project. During May and June 1945, ten such German scientists including Hahn, who were suspected of attempting to create a German atomic bomb, were apprehended by Allied troops. They were taken to the UK and detained at Farm Hall, a large mansion in Cambridgeshire. Here, unbeknown to them, their conversations were monitored by secret listening devices. Their names were as follows:

- Erich Bagge: junior physicist and former student of Heisenberg, who had helped Diebner establish German fission research and later worked on isotope separation.
- Kurt Diebner: physicist and organiser of the German Army's fission project, who later performed reactor experiments independently of the Heisenberg group.
- Walther Gerlach: senior physicist and administrator of German fission research beginning in 1944.
- Otto Hahn: eminent radiochemist and co-discoverer of nuclear fission, for which he received the Nobel Prize in chemistry while at Farm Hall.
- Paul Harteck: physical chemist and Hamburg professor; worked on isotope separation and reactor designs.
- Werner Heisenberg: eminent quantum physicist and Nobel Prize winner. A leading scientific figure of the German effort, he headed main reactor experiments in Leipzig and Berlin.
- Horst Korsching: junior physicist in the Kaiser Wilhelm Institute for Physics in Berlin; worked on isotope separation.
- Max von Laue: eminent physicist and Nobel Prize winner for his work on X-rays; outspoken anti-Nazi; did not engage in fission research.

- Carl Friedrich von Weizsäcker: theoretical physicist; influential younger colleague and friend of Heisenberg.
- Karl Wirtz: physicist and head of reactor construction in the Berlin Kaiser Wilhelm Institute for Physics.

On the British side, important figures were:

- Major T.H. Rittner: British officer in charge at Farm Hall and editor of most of the reports.
- Lieutenant Commander Eric Welsh: Rittner's superior, a British naval intelligence officer stationed in London.
- Captain P.L.C. Brodie: Rittner's assistant and editor of the later Farm Hall reports.
- Samuel A. Goudsmit: distinguished Dutch-US physicist and scientific head of the Alsos Mission (a US intelligence gathering operation aimed at finding out how close the Germans were to developing an atomic weapon).
- Major General Leslie R. Groves: military commander of the Manhattan Project and Washington administrator of the Alsos Mission.
- Michael Perrin: physicist and official of the British atomic bomb programme.[1]
- Also, Professor Patrick M.S. Blackett, British experimental physicist (who would be awarded the Nobel Prize for Physics in 1948).

Unbeknown to the internees, Farm Hall was bugged, and their conversations were recorded.

On 6 August 1945, said Jeremy Bernstein, US theoretical physicist and science essayist, Major T.H. Rittner, British Intelligence officer in charge of Farm Hall, stated that, 'Shortly before dinner', he informed Hahn

> that an announcement had been made by the BBC that an atomic bomb had been dropped. Hahn was completely shattered by the news and said he felt personally responsible for the deaths of hundreds of thousands of people, as it was his original discovery which had made the bomb possible. He told me that he had originally contemplated suicide

> when he realised the terrible potentialities of his discovery and felt that now these have been realized and he was to blame.[2]

In his diary entry for 7 August 1945, following the announcement the evening before of the dropping of the atomic bomb on Hiroshima, Bagge wrote that Hahn was

> very shaken … because he dreads the thought that his discovery might have military consequences. The talk is of 300,000 Japanese dead. Poor Prof. Hahn! He told us that when he first realized what frightful effects uranium fission might have, he had not slept for many nights and had thought of taking his own life.[3]

This reaction of Hahn's seems implausible. Surely, as a member of the 'Uranium Club', which was actively working to produce an atomic weapon, as will be seen, Hahn must have been aware of the consequences were such a weapon ever to be used. Was he being disingenuous, or was he deluded enough to deny his involvement in the German atomic weapons project? Denial was a personality trait of Hahn's, as has already been demonstrated. The atomic bombs were dropped on Germany's ally, Japan. One wonders if Hahn would have been equally distressed had they been dropped on London or New York!

As for Heisenberg, he was simply incredulous. 'I don't believe a word of the whole thing,' he declared. 'I am willing to believe that it is a high-pressure bomb and I don't believe it has anything to do with uranium.'[4] The reason for Heisenberg's incredulity will be discussed shortly.

On 8 August 1945, the German scientists constructed a version of their involvement in the German atomic weapons project in which they denied that they had worked to create an atomic bomb. In his diary entry of 10 August 1945, Bagge noted that 'the idea took hold with our older gentlemen here that it was very important to compose, and deliver to the Major [Rittner] a statement to the effect that in Germany work was not done on the atom bomb, but rather on a stabilised reactor'.[5]

In their 'Memorandum', signed and issued on that same day, 8 August 1945, by the Farm Hall detainees, it was stated that 'Professor Meitner had left Berlin a half year prior to the discovery [of nuclear fission] and did not participate in the discovery'.[6] Again, that same day, this became a second memorandum which included the following statement by Otto Hahn to Major Rittner, 8 August 1945 (MC):

> As long as Prof. Meitner was in Germany the fission of uranium was out of the question. It was considered impossible. Based on extensive chemical investigations of the chemical elements which resulted from irradiating uranium with neutrons, Hahn and Strassmann were forced to assume by the end of 1938 that in these processes uranium splits into two pieces, of which one piece, the chemical element barium, was determined with certainty.
>
> The production of barium from uranium was communicated to Prof. Meitner in Stockholm in a number of letters even before publication in Germany. With her nephew Dr O. R. Frisch, she explained the experimental findings of Hahn and Strassmann, the 'nuclear fission' which had previously been thought impossible.

In modern parlance, this litany of half-truths would be termed 'political spin'. In the relevant section of the Memorandum, which Hahn undoubtedly wrote himself, he stressed the importance of the chemistry, but not the physics. He failed to mention that he only discovered barium as a fission product when Lise insisted that he and Strassmann check their results. Nor does he mention that he had hedged his bets, not being sure whether he had achieved nuclear fission or not, until what he had achieved was explained to him by Lise and Frisch in their theoretical calculations.

Von Laue referred to this version of events as a 'Lesart' – in other words, a false narrative.[7] He subsequently elaborated on this in a letter to Rosbaud, in which he stated that at Farm Hall in early August 1945,

> During the table conversation, the version was developed that the German atomic physicists really had not wanted the atomic bomb, either because it was impossible to achieve it during the expected duration of the war, or because they simply did not want to have it at all. The leader in these discussions was [von] Weizsäcker. I did not hear the mention of any ethical point of view. Heisenberg was mostly silent.[8]

From the Farm Hall transcripts, it is clear that Blackett was developing a cordial relationship with Hahn. For example, on 8 September 1945, he told Hahn, 'I may say that your reputation is very well known over here because of your very fine record as an anti-Nazi. It is very much appreciated, so don't you worry.'[9] Perhaps a desire on both men's part to recapture the camaraderie that had existed between scientists of different nationalities prior to the war was a factor in this.

It was true that Hahn had refused to join the Nazi Party. However, as a member of the 'Uranium Club', he had committed his institute to the fission project. But since the splitting of the atom, atomic research had moved decisively into the realm of physics, a subject which Hahn, as Lise had so often pointed out, understood nothing of.

Hahn was therefore regarded as one of the few relatively untainted Germans, i.e. a 'Good German' who was not a Nazi, who could lead that country's chemistry endeavours now that the war was over.

On that same day, 8 September 1945, Blackett gave a clue as to why there was disagreement between himself and Commander Welsh, when he told Heisenberg,

> There is absolutely no conceivable reason, in my view, for this complete blackout on information about your being here, and the fact that you have been kept incommunicado from everybody is just silly now. Up to the bomb being dropped there was a blackout on everything [but] now I don't see the slightest reason from any point of view why Schumacher should not come to see you, but this is not, in fact, our responsibility.[10]

Ernst Friedrich ('Fritz') Schumacher was a German-British statistician and economist who had emigrated to England in 1936. His sister Edith was married to Heisenberg.

Interviewed by Blackett at Farm Hall on 9 September 1945, Hahn declared, 'My great trouble is really my institute. What is the future of people who really behaved well during the war? I hardly had a man who was in the [Nazi] Party.'[11] However, as early as 3 May 1933, Lise had written to Hahn in the USA to say that 'A rather large Nat[ional] Soc[ialist] cell has formed in the institute, it is all quite methodical'.[12]

Hahn stated that in regard to his scientific publications,

> I told the people that if I do not publish our harmless things, we make the American and English people think we are making bombs, etc. Therefore, we show them that we do quite harmless things, but I told them you can never tell what will happen tomorrow. Therefore, I saved the people in my laboratory. They did not go to war because I told them, it was awfully important; of course, we knew that it was of no importance at all. We really were cheating our government.

(By 'cheating our government', Hahn presumably meant by *pretending* to make bombs.)

Bernstein, however, was highly sceptical of this account. Said he,

> Hahn's description of all of this is, of course, self-serving and only partially true. When the original uranium group of which Hahn was a member was assembled for the particular purpose of investigating nuclear weapons, the subject of uranium was made a state secret. There is no reason to think that at that time Hahn and the others thought they were 'cheating' their government. It should also be recalled that at the popular lecture series given on the 26th of February 1942 before such authorities as Bernard Rust [Minister of Science, Education, and National Culture in Nazi Germany], the title of the first speaker's lecture – Eric Schumann's – was, 'Nuclear Physics as a Weapon'. Hahn was the second speaker – he spoke about uranium fission – and the third speaker was Heisenberg. That was the lecture at which Heisenberg spoke about the use of reactors to power submarines and about plutonium ['element 94'] as an explosive fuel. Does Hahn really believe that they were all there 'cheating' their government?[13]

Heisenberg's lecture will be discussed in more detail shortly. Meanwhile, from 9–10 November 1945, a scientific conference was held in London to celebrate the 50th anniversary of the discovery of X-rays by German mechanical engineer and physicist William C. Röntgen (1845–1923), which had occurred on 8 November 1895.

Said Bagge,

> The Swedish physicists Siegbahn and Svedberg [Theodor ('Thé') Svedberg, who was actually a chemist and Nobel Laureate] seem to have come to the Röntgen celebration in London on the 9th of November 1945 and saw the English scientists there. A few days later the Nobel Prize was awarded to Hahn. This does not seem to be a chance [i.e. a coincidence].[14]

The truth is likely to be that, whereas the British scientists played no part in the decision to award the Nobel Prize to Hahn, they would have made it abundantly clear to their Swedish colleagues that they thoroughly endorsed it.

In mid-November 1945, von Laue told Hahn, 'You have not got the Nobel Prize as a consolation for the fact that we ten German scientists are shut up here, but I think that is their reason for giving it to you now instead of waiting till next year, which was probably their original intention.'[15]

Bagge stated in his diary that, on 18 November 1945, Hahn's attention was drawn to a report in the *Daily Telegraph* newspaper stating that he was to receive the Nobel Prize for the year 1944. Said Bagge, 'The Swedish Academy had evidently decided on this step only recently, probably influenced by our situation. A few weeks ago, the Swedish Prof. Westgren informed Mr. Hahn that unfortunately one could not welcome him in Stockholm this year.'

This was a reference to Swedish Professor of Chemistry Arne Westgren.

> Because of the global feeling about the atomic bomb they had shunned away from this option. But perhaps the English physicists helped a little. There is no doubt that in the small war between the Commander [Welsh] and Blackett, the Commander was ahead for the time being. But now the counter-offensive of the [British] scientists was coming.

Said Bernstein, 'By the first week in December, the Nobel Prize award to Hahn was confirmed. Bagge reports that, on the 4th, the Commander [Welsh] and two American officers appeared at Farm Hall to get Hahn to write a letter of acceptance without disclosing the reasons why he could not make the trip to Stockholm.'[16] This indicates that the British and US authorities were adamant that Hahn must accept the Nobel Prize.

> In his autobiography entitled *My Life* (published in 1968, the year of Lise's death), Hahn referred to an interview at Farm Hall in which he stated as follows. 'There was Professor Heisenberg's team, which was making experiments with a view to utilizing nuclear energy, but not in order to make bombs. The purpose was to build something like what is now called a reactor.' Whereupon the interviewer posed a question. 'After the war, Professor Heisenberg published a number of papers in which he too said clearly that no work had been done in Germany in building an atomic bomb. Was that for technical or for humanitarian reasons?' 'Probably both,' replied Hahn. 'I should have refused to work on an atomic bomb at any price.'[17]

The truth of these assertions by both Hahn and Heisenberg will be discussed shortly. Goudsmit, who personally interrogated the '19 professional scientists and engineers' of the Kaiser Wilhelm Institute for Physics (KWIP), formed the opinion that Hahn and von Laue 'had not played significant roles in the wartime fission project'.[18] On 3 January 1946, the ten German scientists returned to Germany.

Meanwhile, what of Lise? On 27 June 1945, she wrote to Hahn at Farm Hall to give him a severe admonishment.

> I am writing in a great hurry, even though I have so much to say that weighs on my heart. Please keep this in mind and read this with the certainty of my unbreakable friendship. I have written many letters to you in my thoughts in the last few months, because it was clear to me that even people like you and [von] Laue have not comprehended the reality of the situation.

Germany's 'misfortune', said Lise, was

> that you have all lost your standards of justice and fairness. You yourself told me in March 1938 that [Heinrich]

Hörlein told you that horrible things would be done to the Jews. So, he knew of the crimes that were planned and later carried out, but despite that he was a Party member and you – also in spite of everything – considered him to be a very decent person …

You all worked for Nazi Germany and you did not even try passive resistance. Granted, to absolve your consciences you helped some oppressed person here and there, but millions of innocent people were murdered and there was no protest. I must write this to you, as so much depends upon your understanding of what you have permitted to take place. I and many others are of the opinion that one path for you would be to deliver an open statement that you are aware that through your passivity you share responsibility for what has happened, and that you have the need to work for whatever can be done to make amends.

But many think it is too late for that. The people say that you first betrayed your friends, then your men and your children in that you let them give their lives in a criminal war, and finally you betrayed Germany herself, because even when the war was completely hopeless, you never once spoke out against the meaningless destruction of Germany. That sounds pitiless, but nevertheless I believe that the reason I write to you is in true friendship.

In the last few days, one has heard of the unbelievably gruesome things which took place in the concentration camps; it overwhelms everything one previously feared. When I heard, on English radio, a very detailed report by the English and Americans about Belsen and Buchenwald, I began to cry out loud and lay awake all night. And if you had seen those people who were brought here [to Sweden] from the camps.

Perhaps you will remember that while I was still in Germany (and now I know that it was not only stupid but very wrong that I did not leave at once) I often said to you: as long as only we have the sleepless nights and not you, things will not get better in Germany. But you had no sleepless

> nights, you did not want to see, it was too uncomfortable. I beg you to believe me that everything I write here is an attempt to help you.[19]

Lise entrusted her letter to post to Morris (Moe) Berg, a US citizen. Berg, who was a US intelligence agent, handed it instead to the OSS.[20]

OSS: Office of Strategic Services, wartime intelligence agency of the USA.

Of all her German colleagues and former colleagues, Lise discovered that only Max Planck acknowledged that Germans as a whole were responsible for the terrible crimes committed by the Nazis. And, as a result, he was sure that the German people would be punished. 'We have done the most horrible things. Terrible things must happen to us,' he told Lise.[21]

Lise would have been well aware of the brave manner in which Planck had confronted Hitler in person on 16 May 1933 about the dismissal of a colleague, Fritz Haber, a Jew, from his position as director of the KWIPCE. In Planck's own words:

> Following Hitler's seizure of power, I had the responsibility as president of the Kaiser Wilhelm Society of paying my respects to the *Führer*. I believed I should take this opportunity to put in a favorable word for my Jewish colleague Fritz Haber, without whose invention of the process for producing ammonia from nitrogen in air, the previous war [the First World War] would have been lost from the start. Hitler answered me with these words: 'I have nothing against Jews as such. But Jews are all Communists, and it is the latter who are my enemies; it is against them that my fight is directed.' I commented that there are different types of Jews, both worthy and worthless ones to humanity, with old families of the highest German culture among the former, and when I suggested that a distinction would have to be made between them after all, he replied: 'That's not right. A Jew is a Jew; all Jews stick together like burrs. Where there is one Jew, all kinds of other Jews gather right away. It would have been the duty of the Jews themselves

> to draw a dividing line between the various types. They did not do this, and that is why I must act against all Jews equally'. He ignored my comment that forcing worthy Jews to emigrate would be equivalent to mutilating ourselves outright, because we directly need their scientific work and their efforts would otherwise go primarily to the benefit of foreign countries.[22]

The Axis forces would soon discover this to their cost!

In her diary' on 7 August 1945, Lise wrote, 'The first uranium bomb has been used over Hiroshima, said to be the equivalent of 20,000 tons of ordinary explosives.'[23]

Chapter 22

Paul Rosbaud: Was Lise a Spy?

Paul W. M. Rosbaud was born on 18 November 1896 in Graz, Austria. He was the illegitimate son of Franz Heinnisser, choirmaster at Graz Cathedral, and Anna Rosbaud, a piano teacher.

During the First World War, Rosbaud served with the Austrian army. At the time of the armistice (signed on 3 November 1918), he surrendered to the British and was briefly imprisoned. He later wrote, 'My first two days as a prisoner under British guard were the origins of my long-time anglophilia. For the British soldiers, war was over and forgotten. They did not treat us as enemies but as unfortunate losers of the war. They did not fraternize, but they were polite and correct.'[1]

Rosbaud studied in Germany, including at the Kaiser William Institute in Berlin, and became a metallurgist.

In 1933, Rosbaud made contact with Major Francis E. ('Frank') Foley, passport control officer at the British Embassy in Berlin. Foley was also a member of the British secret intelligence agency MI6, and MI6's station chief in Berlin. Rosebaud himself now became a British agent and gave himself the codename 'Der Greif' – 'The Griffin'.[2] It was Foley who introduced Rosbaud to Lise.

In 1936, Rosbaud became editor of Germany's leading scientific periodical *Die Naturwissenchaften*, published by *Springer Verlag*, one of Germany's largest publishing houses. This brought him into contact with leading German scientists and involved him in travels throughout Europe, including the UK. He therefore had knowledge of all the latest scientific developments of the day.

In April 1938, Rosbaud, with Foley's help, arranged for his wife Hildegard (née Frank), who was Jewish, and their 10-year-old daughter, Angelika, to relocate to the safety of London. He, however, chose to remain in Germany, intent on doing his best to undermine the Nazi regime.

On 4 November 1939, two months after the outbreak of war on 3 September, the so-called 'Oslo Report', written by German mathematician and physicist Hans F. Meyer, was sent anonymously to the British Embassy in Oslo, Norway, from where the information was passed on to MI6 in London. The report contained information about the German development of radar, and of rocket development at Peenemünde, the launch site in north-eastern Germany. Unfortunately, his report was not taken seriously by British Intelligence, otherwise the bombing of London by V-1 and V-2 rockets might have been avoided.

During the Second World War, Foley continued to help Jews escape from the Reich, and as a scientific reporter permitted to travel throughout Germany, Rosbaud was also personally involved in assisting not only Jews, but also political prisoners. For example, he purchased the freedom of detainees by bribing the Gestapo, and he bribed SS guards to release concentration camp inmates. He himself visited the Mauthausen concentration camp in 1942, and the Theresienstadt concentration camp in 1943, where he witnessed the horrors at first hand.[3]

Rosbaud provided British Intelligence with invaluable information about German developments in jet-propelled aircraft, radar, 'flying bombs', and attempts to create an atomic bomb.[4] It was 'through Rosbaud', said US nuclear physicist and author Arnold Kramish, that 'the British knew everything they wanted to know about the German atomic program – from its inception and throughout the war – except during a year and a half hiatus in his reporting from the end of 1939'.[5]

Rosbaud had contact with the Norwegian Resistance networks. He also had contact with the French Resistance, through a French prisoner of war who worked in his office and was a physicist. In this way, his reports were smuggled to the UK. An important source of intelligence were Norwegian students studying at technical schools in Germany. One such person was Sverre Bergh, who reported on the development of V2 rockets at Peenemünde. This information was contained in a report prepared in 1943 for British Intelligence officer, Eric Welsh.[6]

Meanwhile, on 27 February 1940, Arnold Berliner paid Lise the compliment of another letter. Said he:

> One is pulled so far off balance spiritually, that the body also cannot endure it for long. The loneliness and loss of employment burdens my existence most severely. I read as much as my eyes permit, often, in fact, more. However, the joy I once had from it, when reading was a counterweight

> to professional work, that is gone. And then, a life without music! … A purely scientific experience, a performance of Figaro under Mahler, a lecture by Herr von Harnack … thank God we experienced these!

This was a reference to German Lutheran theologian, Carl Gustav Adolf von Harnack (1851–1930):

> But what we are living through now breeds … only the fear of fear itself. I have only now truly learned to understand that saying. My connection to physics is close to zero; luckily, friend Max [von Laue] keeps me informed of this and that. He is touchingly loyal and good; he visits every week for an hour or two.[7]

Von Laue was assiduous in keeping Lise informed about the welfare of Berliner, but the news was not good. On 2 March 1940, he told her that Berliner had become a virtual recluse in his Berlin apartment, declining to go outdoors 'so as not to have to wear the Jewish star, without which no non-Aryan was allowed to be seen on the street'.[8]

'Aryan': in Nazi ideology, relating to, or denoting a person of Caucasian race, not of Jewish descent.[9]

On 21 November 1940, Berliner wrote to Lise to say of his friend the Austrian-Jewish composer and conductor Gustav Mahler, 'I learned what a great musician is. Now I experience a great physicist. You have already had this good fortune with the other great Max [i.e. Max Planck].'[10]

On 22 March 1942, Berliner committed suicide by taking poison. He had been ordered to vacate his Berlin apartment by the end of that month when he would have been deported to an extermination camp. Von Laue, Rosbaud, and also Hahn, attended Berliner's funeral.

On 23 November 1942, Rosbaud's wife Hildegard wrote to Lise with the 'very sad news' that her father Karl Frank was a prisoner in Theresienstadt concentration camp. In fact, Frank had died a week earlier.[11]

Another Norwegian student/spy was Ragnar Winsnes, who was studying in Dresden, Germany. Winsnes met Rosbaud on only one occasion: in Berlin, on D-Day, 6 June 1944, the day of the Allied landings in Normandy. On that occasion, said Kramish, whose information was based on a meeting with Winsnes in person,[12] Rosbaud 'gave Winsnes the name, author, and year of publication of a book published by *Springer Verlag*', the pages of which 'contained a long message in some sort of code'. The codes were invented by Rosbaud, and Winsnes was to take only Rosbaud's coded messages with him to Stockholm, Sweden, where that particular book could be purchased. Both book and codes were then passed, directly or indirectly, to Cyril Cheshire.[13]

On 21 July 1944, the day after the failed July Plot to assassinate Hitler, Rosbaud left Berlin, but only temporarily.

The war in Europe ended on 8 May 1945. In December 1945, an exhausted Rosbaud was assisted by Frank Foley to leave Berlin for London, where he was reunited with his family.[14] Here in the UK, Rosbaud was subsequently photographed by Lise's sister-in-law (Walter's wife), the notable photographer Lotte Meitner-Graf.

Was Lise herself a spy? This question cannot be answered with certainty. However, said Kramish, she was not only 'a channel for Rosbaud to his family and friends in England', but, in addition, 'Technical books from Rosbaud came to Welsh through Meitner, and that is another indication that she was in contact with Cheshire.'

This was Cyril Cheshire, SIS Station Chief, Stockholm. (SIS: UK Secret Intelligence Service, also known as MI6.)

'Some of those books contained secret messages. It was her way of contributing to Hitler's defeat without working on the atomic bomb – which, in the final analysis, had nothing to do with his defeat. Hers was a meaningful contribution to the Allied victory over Germany.'[15]

On a postcard to Lise, dated 27 June 1944, said Kramish, Rosbaud had written, 'Recently, very little has been published concerning physics and mathematics. I shall give you eight special books that perhaps are of interest to your work program.' It was probable, said Kramish, that one or more of these books 'contained special messages'.[16]

Above left: Ludwig Boltzmann, aged 58.

Above right: Emma Planck with violin, 1906. (Archiv der Max-Planck-Gesellschaft, Berlin-Dahlem)

Right: Grete Planck, 1906. (Archiv der Max-Planck-Gesellschaft, Berlin-Dahlem)

Lise Meitner with Otto Hahn at the Friedrich Wilhelm University, Berlin, circa 1909. (Archiv der Max-Planck-Gesellschaft, Berlin-Dahlem)

The Kaiser Wilhelm Institute for Chemistry, circa 1912. (Archiv der Max-Planck-Gesellschaft, Berlin-Dahlem)

Lise and Eva von Bahr-Bergius at the Kaiser Wilhelm Institute for Chemistry, Berlin-Dahlem, 1914. (Churchill College Archives)

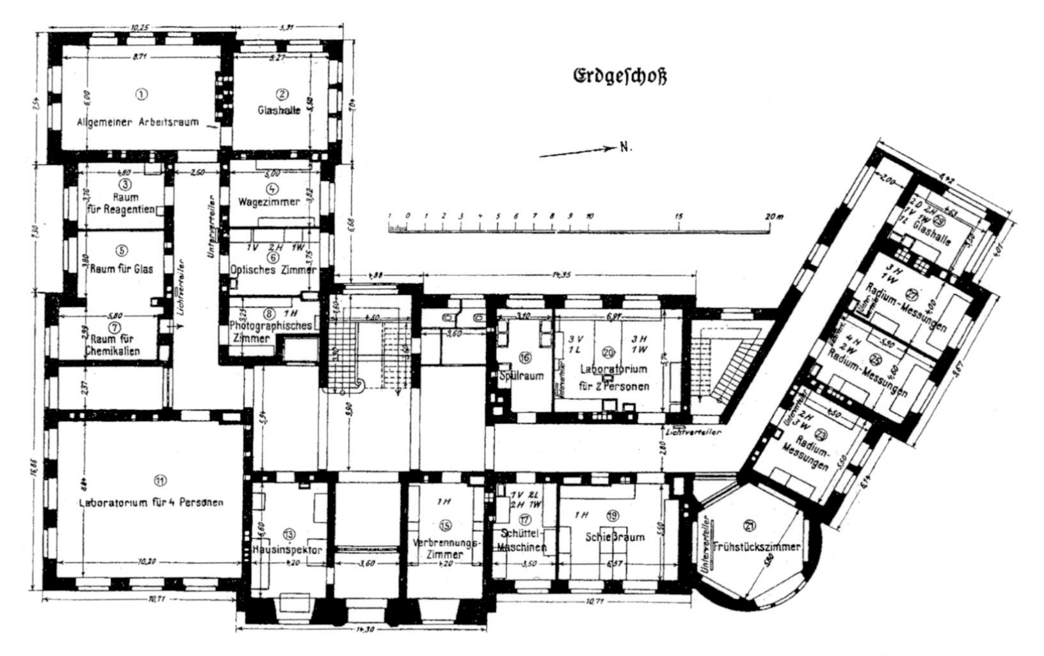

The Kaiser Wilhelm Institute for Chemistry, ground floor plan circa 1912. 29 – irradiation room; 20 – Hahn's private laboratory where Franz Strassmann led the chemical analysis and separation; 23, 25, 27, 29 – the Hahn-Meitner Department. In room 29, animated discussions took place on the subject of uranium and thorium. (Archiv der Max-Planck-Gesellschaft, Berlin-Dahlem)

Above left: Niels Bohr. (A.B. Lagrelius & Westphal, Stockholm)

Above right: Walter Meitner as a young officer in the Austrian army during the First World War. (Philip and Anne Meitner)

The 'Bonzenfreie Kolloquium' ('Colloquium Without Bigwigs'), Berlin-Dahlem April 1920, organised for Danish physicist Niels Bohr by Lise Meitner. Front row, left to right: Otto Stern, James Franck, Niels Bohr, Lise Meitner, Hans Geiger, Peter Pringsheim. Middle row, left to right: Wilhelm Lenz, Rudolph Ladenburg, Otto Hahn. Back row, left to right: Paul Knipping, Ernst Wagner, Otto von Baeyer, George de Hevesy, Wilhelm Westphal, Gustav Hertz. (Archiv der Max-Planck-Gesellschaft, Berlin-Dahlem)

Gathering at the Kaiser Wilhelm Institute for Physical Chemistry, 1929. From left (sitting) Hertha Sponer, Albert Einstein, Ingrid Franck, James Franck, Lise Meitner, Fritz Haber, Otto Hahn. Behind: Walter Grotrian, Wilhelm Westphal, Otto von Baeyer, Peter Pringsheim, Gustav Hertz. (Archiv der Max-Planck-Gesellschaft, Berlin-Dahlem)

Lise Meitner in her laboratory, 1931. (Archiv der Max-Planck-Gesellschaft, Berlin-Dahlem)

Above left: Max von Laue, Lise Meitner, and Dirk Coster in Berlin. (Courtesy of Anthea J. Coster)

Above right: Enrico Fermi. (US Department of Energy)

Left: Ida Noddack.

Above left: Otto Hahn. (Archiv der Max-Planck-Gesellschaft, Berlin-Dahlem)

Above right: Fritz Strassmann in Tailfingen, circa 1944–1945. (Archiv der Max-Planck-Gesellschaft, Berlin-Dahlem)

Right: Max Planck, circa 1936–1937. (Archiv der Max-Planck-Gesellschaft, Berlin-Dahlem)

Peter Debye at the Kaiser Wilhelm Institute for Physics, circa 1936. (Archiv der Max-Planck-Gesellschaft, Berlin-Dahlem)

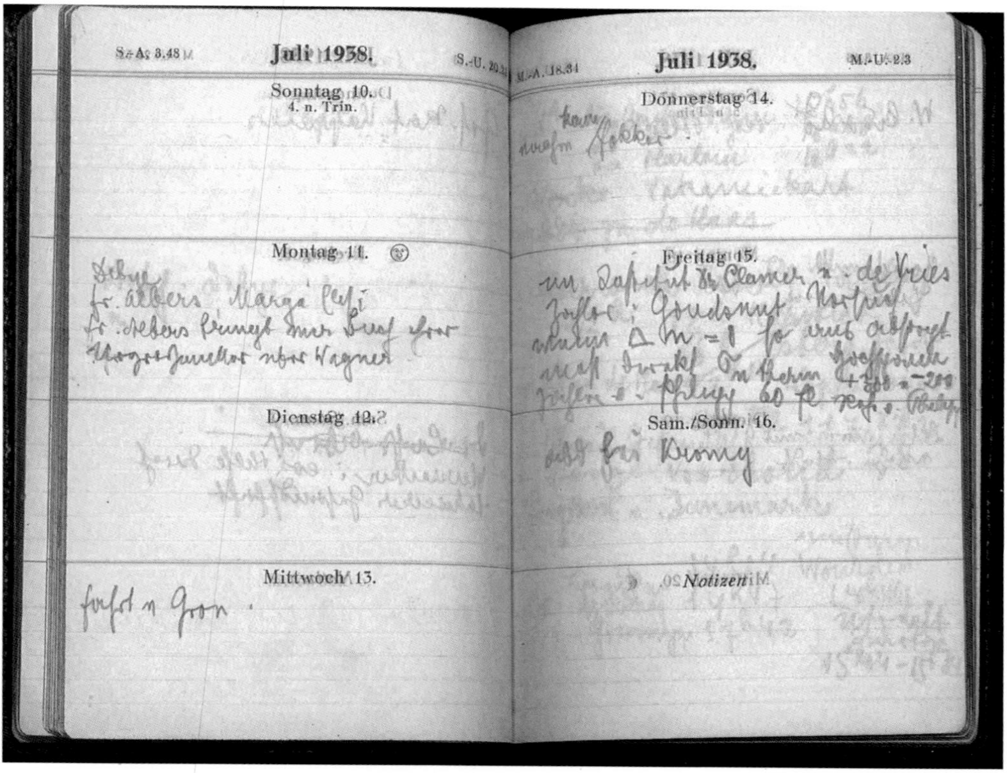

Juli 1938.

Sonntag 10.
4. n. Trin.

Montag 11.

Dienstag 12.

Mittwoch 13.

Juli 1938.

Donnerstag 14.

Freitag 15.

Sam./Sonn. 16.

Notizen

Lise Meitner's diary. (Photo by kind permission of Anne and Philip Meitner)

Lise Meitner's notebook. (Photo by kind permission of Anne and Philip Meitner)

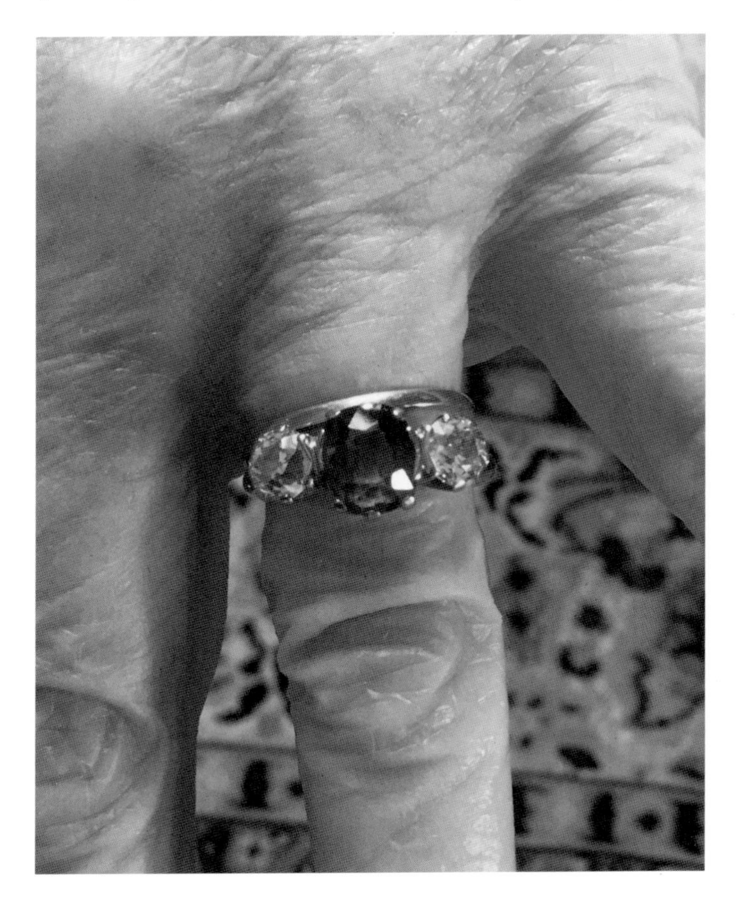

The diamond ring, given to Lise by Otto Hahn prior to her escape from Nazi Germany on 13 July 1938. Worn by Anne Meitner, wife of Philip. (Philip and Anne Meitner)

The diamond ring.

Above left: Dirk Coster, portrait by Netherlands painter Marcel Duran, University of Groningen, Netherlands. (Courtesy of Anthea J. Coster)

Above right: Adriaan Fokker, aged 55.

Above left: Rudolf E. Peierls.

Above right: Erich Bagge at Farm Hall, 1945. (Archiv der Max-Planck-Gesellschaft, Berlin-Dahlem)

Right: The bombed Kaiser Wilhelm Institute for Chemistry, 1944. (Archiv der Max-Planck-Gesellschaft, Berlin-Dahlem)

Paul Rosbaud, circa 1926–1927 at the Kaiser Wilhelm Institute for Silicate Research. (Archiv der Max-Planck-Gesellschaft, Berlin-Dahlem)

Walter Meitner and his father-in-law Wilhelm Graf playing chess together. (Philip and Anne Meitner)

Above left: Thé Svedberg.

Above right: Werner Heisenberg at Farm Hall, 1945. (Archiv der Max-Planck-Gesellschaft, Berlin-Dahlem)

Right: Manne Siegbahn. (Dutch National Archives, The Hague, Netherlands)

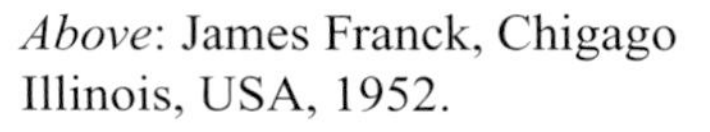

Above: James Franck, Chigago Illinois, USA, 1952.

Left: Gerta von Ubisch. (University of Heidelberg, Germany)

Page from a French passport, issued 1931. (By kind permission of Tom Topol)

Page from an Austrian passport, issued in 1936 by the Austrian Consul in Nuremberg, Germany. (By kind permission of Tom Topol)

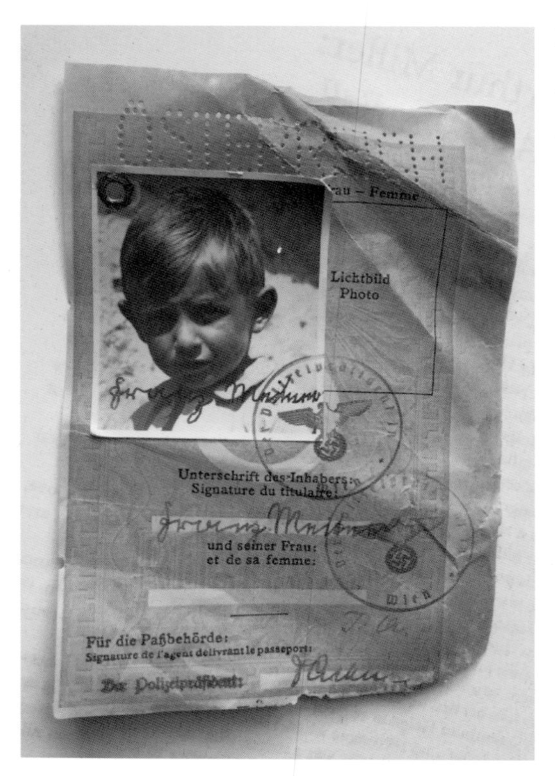

Frau – Femme
Lichtbild
Photo
Unterschrift des Inhabers:
Signature du titulaire:
und seiner Frau:
et de sa femme:
Für die Paßbehörde:
Signature de l'agent délivrant le passeport:
Der Polizeipräsident:

Philip Meitner's Austrian passport, 1938, stamped by the Head of Police, Vienna. (Courtesy of Philip and Anne Meitner)

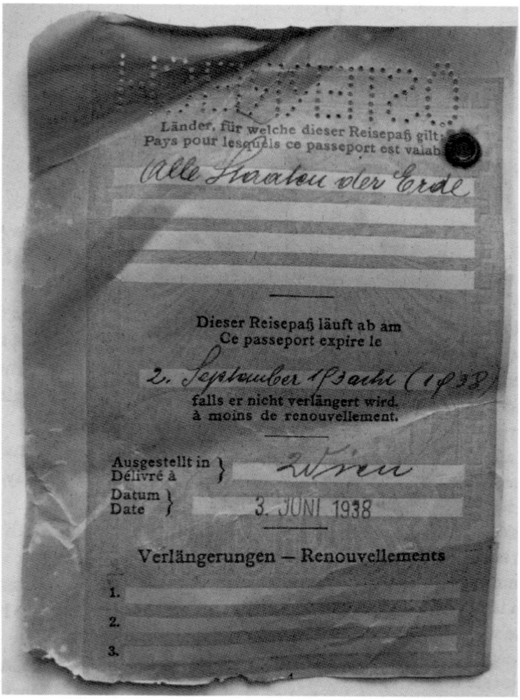

Länder, für welche dieser Reisepaß gilt:
Pays pour lesquels ce passeport est valable:
Alle Staaten der Erde

Dieser Reisepaß läuft ab am
Ce passeport expire le
2. September 1938
falls er nicht verlängert wird.
à moins de renouvellement.

Ausgestellt in / Délivré à: Wien
Datum / Date: 3. JUNI 1938

Verlängerungen – Renouvellements
1.
2.
3.

Philip Meitner's Austrian passport, reverse.

E.D. Letter Code AXWO Borough, U.D. or R.D. Wandsworth Registration District and Sub-district 24 - 5

	ADDRESS.	SCHEDULE. No.	SCHEDULE. Sub. No.	SURNAMES AND OTHER NAMES.	O, V, S, P. or I.	M. or F.	BIRTH- Day.	BIRTH- Year.	S, M, W. or D.	PERSONAL OCCUPATION.
	1	2	3	4	5	6	7	8	9	10
V.	81 West Hill	1	–							
See f. 16	83 do	2	1	Fry Sydney		M	8 Nov	00	S	Architectural model maker.
	do		2	Ogden. Francis K.		M.	21 July	92	S	Solicitor
	do		3	[illegible]		F	6 Jan	84	S	Domestic servant.
R.	do	3	–							
V.	do	4	–							
	85 West Hill.	5	1	Graf. Bertha		F	30 July	73	W	Private means
	do	6	1	Meitner Walter		M	15 Mar	91	M	Doctor of Chemistry.
	1.4.50 NH230 AXH		2	MEITNER-GRAF ~~Meitner~~ Lotte ~~Charlotte~~		F	17 Nov	99	M	Unpaid. Dom. du[ties]
	do	7	1	Bayly Leonard A.		M	30 Sept	03	M	Bank cashier.

National Register, England and Wales, 1939, showing Walter and Lotte Meitner and Bertha Graf residing at 86 West Hill, Putney, London.

Above left: Philip Meitner, a torch bearer for the July 1948 London Olympic Games. (Philip and Anne Meitner)

Above right: The Olympic torch. (Philip and Anne Meitner)

Grave of Walter Meitner, Church of St James, Bramley, Hampshire. (Courtesy of Reverend John Lenton)

Da ich für die vielen Beweise freundschaftlichen Gedenkens anlässlich meines 80. Geburtstages nicht persönlich danken kann, bitte ich meinen herzlichsten Dank in dieser Form entgegen zu nehmen.

Dear Philip and dear Anne,
Many thanks for your birthday-wire and all my best wishes for your moving in the new house!
Much love
Ever yours
Lise (Wuzerl)

Card from Lise to Philip and Anne Meitner thanking them for the telegram that they sent to her on the occasion of her 80th birthday. (Courtesy of Philip and Anne Meitner)

Lise Meitner with James and Ingrid Franck's daughter Lisa Lisco, circa 1962–1963. (Archiv der Max-Planck-Gesellschaft, Berlin-Dahlem)

Lise Meitner in 1966 at the Cambridge home of Max Perutz, being presented with the Enrico Fermi Award (made also to Hahn and Strassmann) by US chemist Glenn T. Seaborg, as Lotte Meitner-Graf looks on. (Philip and Anne Meitner)

Lise Meitner with Philip and Anne Meitner at their Hampshire Farm. (Philip and Anne Meitner)

Otto Robert Frisch at the piano in Cambridge. (Philip and Anne Meitner)

Lise Meitner at home in Cambridge. (Philip and Anne Meitner)

Left to right: Elisabeth and Gertrud Schiemann with Lise Meitner. (Archiv der Max-Planck-Gesellschaft, Berlin-Dahlem)

Left to right: one of the Planck twins, Emma or Grete Planck, Lise Meitner, and Elisabeth Schiemann. (Archiv der Max-Planck-Gesellschaft, Berlin-Dahlem)

Elisabeth Schiemann. (Archiv der Max-Planck-Gesellschaft, Berlin-Dahlem)

Grave of Lise Meitner, Church of St James, Bramley, Hampshire. (Courtesy of Reverend John Lenton)

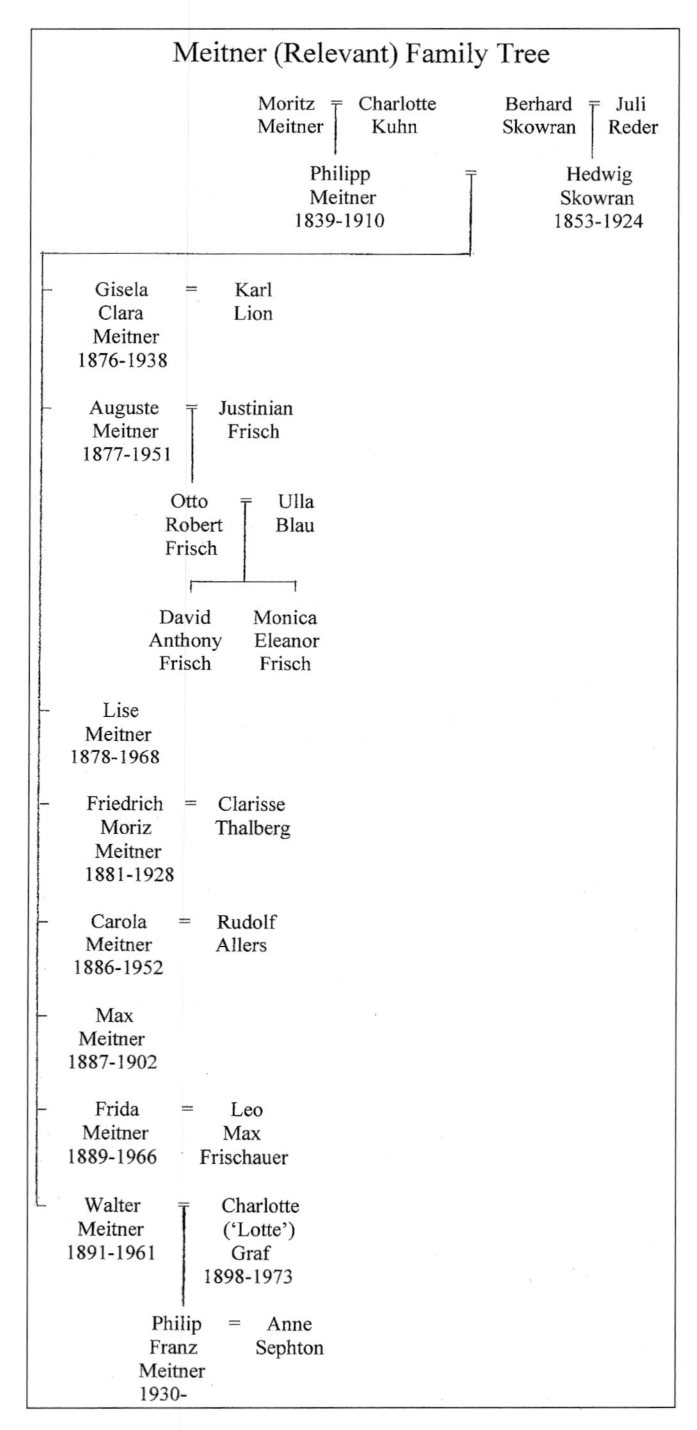

Meitner Family Tree.

Chapter 23

Fate of the Meitner Family

In September 1939, a National Register of citizens was created in the UK and this, together with *Ancestry*, has yielded valuable information as to what became of Lise's siblings and their families.

Gisela Clara Meitner, born 1876

She attended medical school and became a doctor. Gisela married Karl Lion, who was also a medical doctor. In autumn 1938, she left Vienna for England. According to the September 1939 UK Register, she and her husband were living in Cherry Orchard, Staines, Middlesex.

Auguste ('Gusti') Meitner, born 1877

She became a concert pianist. She married Justinian ('Jutz') Frisch, a lawyer, and they had a son, Otto. Otto Frisch became a physicist and he would one day play a vital role in a discovery in physics that would make him and Lise famous.

When the Nazis annexed Austria and began persecuting the Jews, Jutz lost his job. On 9 November 1938, he was arrested and imprisoned: first in Vienna, and then in the Dachau concentration camp, as already mentioned. However, Lise managed to obtain a Swedish passport for both him and his wife, Auguste, and they relocated to Stockholm in spring 1939.

Friedrich Moriz Meitner, born 1881

In 1913 he married Clarissa Thalberg. Friedrich was an engineer. His death occurred in August 1928. It was reported as 'Bergunfall' (mountain accident).

The September 1939 UK Register shows Clarissa and her son Johann to be living at Adelaide Road, London.

In 1940, Clarissa entered the USA via Montreal. Johann had preceded her and was living in Indiana. On 14 March 1941, she became a naturalised US citizen. Clarissa became a writer of children's books, adventure stories, and historical novels. She also translated works by G.K. Chesterton, H.G. Wells, and others.

Carola Meitner, born 1886

She married Rudolf ('Rudi') Allers, a professor of psychology. On 18 January 1938, the couple sailed from Genoa, Italy, to the USA and Washington, DC, where Allers accepted an invitation to work at the Catholic University.

Max Meitner, born 1887

Max had enrolled as a law student in Vienna in September 1907. In January 1908, he committed suicide by shooting himself.

Frida Meitner, born 1889

Frida married Leo Frischauer in 1917. He was a writer. The couple emigrated to the UK in 1938 before moving to New York, USA, arriving on 13 September 1939.

Walter Meitner, born 1891

He became a scientist specialising in chemistry. He married Charlotte ('Lotte') Graf, a professional photographer. The couple and their son Philip escaped to the UK in summer 1938 in dramatic circumstances, as will shortly be seen.

Chapter 24

The War Ends

The war in Europe ended on 8 May 1945 with the signing of the Armistice. In the Far East, the war ended on 2 September 1945, following the unconditional surrender of Japan.

It must have grieved Lise beyond words to hear how many friends, colleagues, and others had been lost. Her great passion was music, and Wikipedia's 'List of [notable] victims of Nazism' includes the following musicians: seven Czechs, four Germans, two Italians, one South African-British, one Dutch, and one Croatian. Also three Austrians: the composer Ernst Bachrich, the violinist/conductor Alma Rosé, and the composer, pianist, and conductor Marcel Tyberg.

In late August 1945, Lise learned from Rosbaud's wife Hildegard that he had survived the war. And on 25 October 1945, Rosbaud himself wrote to Lise from Berlin to say:

> I have experienced the greatest triumph of my life: I exist, and those who wished to exterminate us all have vanished forever … The greatest happiness for me, of course, is to be in contact with my wife and daughter again … I can hardly express how thankful I am for every line you wrote to me these last years. For me, every letter was a message from another and better world, and you helped me to hold on and never to lose courage.[1]

'A Gallup poll, taken in 1945 a fortnight after the dropping of the Hiroshima bomb, found overwhelming public support for use of the bomb against Japan, with 85% of Americans approving and just 10% disapproving.'[2]

When Lise's name and not Hahn's appeared widely in the press, under such headlines as 'A Jewess found the Clue' i.e. to nuclear fission (7 August 1945), Hahn was greatly put out.[3]

On 8 October 1945, Lise was elected a foreign member of Sweden's Royal Academy of Sciences, having been nominated, perhaps surprisingly, by Siegbahn. This was a great honour: the only other female member of the Academy having been Marie Curie, who had died in 1934.

On 22 October 1945, Lise stated that among the books she had read was *What is Life: With Mind and Matter and Autobiographical Sketches*, by Austrian-Irish physicist Erwin Schrödinger. This was 'not only very instructive but also full of Austrian charm'.[4]

As already mentioned, it was on 16 November 1945, while he was being held in captivity in England at Farm Hall, Cambridgeshire, that Hahn learned that he had been awarded the Nobel Prize.

Birgit Broomé Aminoff, a Swedish crystallographer, was wife of Gregori Aminoff, Professor of Mineralogy at the Swedish Museum of Natural History and who sat on the board of the Nobel Foundation. On that same day, 16 November 1945, Birgit wrote to Lise to say that in her opinion, the latter 'had reached a status equivalent to that of many Nobel Prize recipients'. In other words, Birgit felt that Lise should also have been recognised by the Nobel Committee.[5]

Lise responded in typically generous fashion.

> Surely Hahn fully deserved the Nobel Prize in chemistry. There is really no doubt about it. But I believe that Frisch and I contributed something not insignificant to the clarification of the process of uranium fission – how it originates and that it produces so much energy, and that was something very remote from Hahn [i.e. that Hahn had no expertise as far as the explanation in terms of theoretical physics was concerned]. For this reason, I found it a bit unjust that in the newspapers I was called the *Mitarbeiterin* [female junior co-worker] of Hahn in the same sense that Strassmann was. Your letter, therefore, was a double present; a warm understanding word can mean so much. A thousand thanks for it.[6]

Lise could not help but notice that, in the Swedish press, she was continually referred to as Hahn's *Medarbetare* (or in German, *Mitarbeiterin*) and yet she had been a distinguished physics professor at the KWIC, equal in rank to chemistry Professor Otto Hahn. This prompted her to write as follows on 5 December 1945, to Eva von Bahr-Bergius about an article that she had seen in the Swedish newspaper, *Dagens Nyheter*:

'The article … was almost insulting. Really, I was never just a Mitarbeiter of Hahn: I am, after all, a physicist, and haven't I done quite a few quite decent physical things?' Lise continued darkly, 'I know something about the particulars of the deciding Nobel session and hope to be able to tell you about it sometime in person.'[7]

In fact, prior to the awarding of the Nobel Prize to Hahn, the Nobel Chemistry Committee (NCC) had voted to review its decision – an unprecedented occurrence. However, the decision remained unchanged.[8]

Swedish physicist Oskar Klein was elected to Sweden's Royal Academy of Sciences on 28 February 1945. Klein was convinced that Manne Siegbahn, a member of the Nobel Physics Committee (NPC) and himself a Nobel Laureate, whom he described as a 'dangerous obstacle', had been influential in depriving Lise of the physics prize.[9]

On 23 December 1945, said Lise, referring to the execution of Planck's son Erwin on 23 January 1945 for his involvement in the attempt on Hitler's life – the July Plot of 20 January 1944 – 'I am afraid they have terribly tormented [i.e. tortured] him'.[10] She stated that she had had 'no contact with Otto Hahn since 25th March', and she believed both him and von Laue to be in Belgium. In fact, the two men were being detained at Farm Hall.[11] In January 1946, Hahn returned to Germany, where he became president of the KWIC, which was now located in Göttingen in the zone occupied by the British.

On 14 January 1946, said Lise, the Swedish Atomic Committee (founded November 1945) had 'offered her a key position for establishing nuclear physics in Sweden'.[12]

On 16 January 1946, to Franck, Lise spoke of 'the wrong information by Hahn about the truth of the German atomic bomb'.[13] In other words, Hahn was lying, and the Germans *had* been attempting to produce an atomic weapon. Lise also stated that she had 'not been very well in recent weeks' and had 'needed to rest, but the doctor believes that it was overwork and I have the best intention to take a few weeks leave in February'.[14]

On 18 January 1946, Lise stated to Norwegian theoretical physicist Egil Hylleraas that, despite reports in the press, 'Hahn was always an opponent of the Nazis'.[15]

Lise was now to visit the USA, where she taught for a time at the Catholic University of America in Washington, DC. Here, she was reunited with her sisters Carola ('Lola') and Frida, and also with her nephew, Otto Frisch. She arrived in New York on 25 January 1946. In February 1946, Lise was welcomed to a meeting of the American Physics Society in New York. On 9 February, at a banquet in Washington DC given by the Women's National Press Club, she sat next to US President Harry S. Truman and was given the accolade 'Woman of the Year'. Lise also met the President's wife Bess and also Mrs Anna E. Roosevelt Halsted, daughter of the late President Franklin D. Roosevelt. [16]

Lise visited the universities of Princeton, Columbia, and Harvard, and met with Einstein, James Chadwick, and US army officer Leslie R. Groves, director of the Manhattan Project. However, much to her dismay, the world's press portrayed her as the Jewess who had fled to the USA, bringing with her the secrets of the atomic bomb. On 8 July 1946, she returned to England aboard the liner *Queen Mary*.

On 29 June 1946, Franck married Hertha Sponer, Professor of Physics at Duke University, Durham, North Carolina, USA.

In August 1946, Lise was interviewed in Sweden by Swedish-born *New York Times* reporter George Axelsson who wrote an article entitled 'Is the Atom Terror Exaggerated?' which was published in the UK's *Saturday Evening Post*. It gave a valuable insight into Lise's modus vivendi:

> When in the midst of an absorbing experiment, Professor Meitner forgets the clock. She sends out for a sandwich and some apples and may then keep on until the late hours. She is a frugal eater with decided vegetarian leanings. She loves coffee, and her hobbies are flowers and long walks – if she has time, she does twenty miles on foot every day. 'It keeps me young and alert', she explains.[17]

Following the dropping of the atomic bombs on Hiroshima and Nagasaki on 6 and 9 August 1945, Lise declared (in August 1946),

> I do not see why everybody is making such a fuss over me. I did not design any atomic bomb. I don't even know what one looks like, nor how it works technically. I must stress that I myself, have not in any way worked on the smashing of the atom with the idea of producing death-dealing weapons.

> You must not blame us scientists for the use to which war technicians have put our discoveries.

Said she, we must look on nuclear fission 'as a revolutionizing scientific discovery; but perhaps, even so, only the first step on the road to something greater and still more valuable – mastering the art of using atomic energy for the benefit of mankind'.[18]

On 23 August 1946, Lise declared that 'in spite of the 30 years spent in Germany she has never become a German'.[19]

On 15 September 1946, Lise stated that she had met the Plancks in London. The death of Planck's son Erwin, 'who was killed by the Nazis in the beginning of 1945 was too much for him. But when he had had a good rest and I was alone with him, he was wonderful as ever'.[20]

Meanwhile, Otto Hahn was in denial about German wartime atrocities. To Lise, on 17 September 1946, he wrote, 'I would almost doubt that the behaviour of the [Allied] occupying forces is so much nobler than that of the Germans in the occupying countries.'[21]

In September 1946, at British insistence, the Kaiser Wilhelm Society's name was changed to the Max Planck Society and the institutes were renamed accordingly. Surely, contributing factors in this decision were that one of its institutes, the KWI for Anthropology, Human Genetics, and Eugenics had conducted fiendish medical experimentation on human beings, including children, in collaboration with such notorious people as Dr Josef Mengele. And, of course, both the KWIC and the KWIP were associated with the Nazi atomic bomb project, as will be seen.

Meanwhile, Lise and Hahn continued to receive nominations for the Nobel Prize. In that year of 1946, for physics, Lise received four nominations and Hahn, one nomination. For chemistry, Lise received one nomination and Hahn one nomination.

As regards the forthcoming Nobel ceremonies, Lise wrote to her sister Lola Allers on 27 October 1946 as follows. 'Like it or not, I must attend the Nobel banquet, which I've never done before. But if I don't go this time, when the Hahns are being honored, I fear it might be misunderstood.'[22]

In Sweden, Lise declared to von Laue on 12 November 1946, 'One speaks a foreign language. I don't just mean the external language. I mean the conceptual aspects. [In other words, the culture was different.] One is homeless. I do not want you to experience this and not to understand it.'[23] Here, Lise is anticipating von Laue's visit to Stockholm for the forthcoming Nobel Prize ceremony.

On 15 November 1946, Lise wrote to Hahn in regard to that year's Nobel Prize for Physics having been awarded to US physicist, Percy W. Bridgman. 'The possibility that I might become your fellow prize-winner has finally been swept away. If you are interested, I could tell you something about that.'[24] Lise received no reply. Had Hahn responded positively, how fascinating it would have been to have heard Lise's thoughts on the subject!

On 19 November 1946, Lise said that 'of the modern composers she prefers [Danish composer, conductor, and violinist] Carl Nielsen'.[25] In regard to her visit to the USA, she 'had given 36 lectures at a college in Washington'.[26]

On 22 November 1946, Lise confided to Bohr's wife, Margrethe in respect of the Nobel ceremony. 'Of course, I am looking forward to it, but it will not be easy.'[27]

Chapter 25

How Hahn and Not Lise Became Sole Contender For a Nobel Prize

The pre-eminence of German chemistry

At the time of Lise's departure from Germany in July 1938, the country was pre-eminent in chemistry. But atomic theory, in respect of nuclear physics was, in comparison, in an embryonic stage. This is reflected in the fact that, between 1901 and 1944, Germans were awarded no less than seventeen Nobel Prizes in this discipline (and twelve in physics). This compared with Sweden's three prizes in chemistry (and two in physics).

The Nobel Chemistry Committee (NCC) therefore carried more 'clout' than the Nobel Physics Committee (NPC), and the latter would probably have waited for the former to take the initiative in respect of awarding Nobel Prizes.[1]

A matter of prestige

The Chemistry Committee was composed of five distinguished Swedish chemists who were, therefore, anxious to claim the discovery of fission for the science of chemistry alone, along with the prestige that this would inevitably carry.

Did the discovery of nuclear fission principally involve chemists or physicists?

Hahn promoted the idea that physics played only a minor role in the discovery. Whereas, in fact, both disciplines were involved up to the hilt.

'Chemical bonds' between Germany and Sweden

Traditionally there was a close relationship between Germany and Sweden, particularly in the sciences.

Acceptance

Whereas Hahn was accepted without question by the Swedish scientific community, Lise felt isolated and a stranger in Siegbahn's institute in Stockholm.

Political bonds between Germany and Sweden

Hermann Göring, born in Bavaria, Germany on 12 January 1893, had been a highly decorated fighter pilot during the First World War. From 1919 to 1921 he lived in Sweden, where he worked as a pilot for the Swedish airline, Svensk Lufttravik. When, in February 1920, Göring was asked to fly Count Eric von Rosen, explorer and ethnographer, from Stockholm to his home, Rockelstad Castle, this event changed his life.

Von Rosen was married to Mary, daughter of Baron Carl A. Fock, a colonel in the Swedish army whose family had emigrated to Sweden from Westphalia (north-western Germany; prior to 1918 it was part of the Kingdom of Prussia). Göring was destined to become Commander-in-Chief of the Luftwaffe and Hitler's designated successor.

It so happened that Mary's younger sister Baroness Carin von Kantzow, a divorcee, was visiting that weekend, and for Göring it was love at first sight! The marriage of Göring, the dashing aviator and war hero, to noblewoman Carin on 3 February 1922 not only captured the hearts of the Swedes, it was also a significant moment in the relationship between Germany and Sweden.

In 1921, the couple set up home in Germany. Sadly, however, Carin contracted tuberculosis, and when she died on 17 October 1931 at the age of 42, Göring was devastated. Hitler himself attended the funeral. Following Carin's death, Göring paid frequent visits to his Swedish relatives by marriage.

Hermann Göring, Sweden's saviour

Operation Weserübung was the codename for the proposed German invasion of Norway, Sweden, and Denmark. Göring, however, had assured his father-in-law Eric von Rosen that, in the event of war, Sweden's neutrality would be respected. He therefore remonstrated with Hitler, who agreed for Sweden to be exempted from the plans on condition that Germany's supplies of iron ore were continued, and that German troops be allowed transit across Swedish soil. On 9 April 1940, the German invasion of Norway and Denmark duly commenced.

Trading links between Germany and Sweden during the Second World War

During the Second World War, Germany was heavily dependent on Sweden for supplies of its high-grade iron ore (containing 55% to 67% iron) from its northern mines. Between 1939 and 1942 an estimated 10 million tons were exported, first from the Swedish ports of Luleå and Oxelösund, and later from the Norwegian port of Narvik.

All this considered, and in view of the cordial relations between the two countries, there was no reason for Germany to invade Sweden.

Hahn the propagandist and supplier of false information

Hahn repeatedly tried to write Lise out of the history books. For example, in 1950 he stated that physicists had considered fission 'impossible'. Whereas the truth was that Lise and Frisch had proved that it *was* theoretically possible.[2] And in 1964 he went so far as to say that fission had been 'forbidden' by physicists.[3] This was a despicable distortion of the truth on Hahn's part.

In the light of his behaviour, the adjectives that describe Hahn best would appear to be: one-dimensional, pragmatic, disingenuous, and increasingly deluded. In fact, Hahn had so depended on Lise that he literally begged her on several occasions to explain his results to him and suggest a way forward. By contrast, Lise, who was devoted to her science, had always shown Hahn the utmost loyalty: a loyalty which many might say was entirely misplaced and undeserved by him. But as always with Lise, the maintenance of friendships, wherever possible, was the overriding factor.

Hahn the showman

Following the publication of his scientific papers and those of Lise and Frisch in early 1939, Hahn was quick off the mark. Having obtained permission from the Nazi authorities, he rushed post-haste to Oslo (Norway), Gothenburg and Stockholm (Sweden), and Copenhagen (Denmark), where he gave lectures on fission. Doubtless in these lectures, the great 'I am' attributed the discovery to himself, mentioned the name of his colleague Strassmann only en passant, and those of Lise and Frisch only as a footnote (thus avoiding conflict with the Nazi authorities).

Lise: the weakness of her current position

In Stockholm, where Lise was attempting to re-establish herself, she had no professorship nor, as yet, a department of her own. It is therefore unlikely that either the US, British, or Swedish authorities could envisage a post-war role for her. As such, from a political viewpoint, Hahn held all the cards, as far as obtaining the support of these countries was concerned. Lise, on the other hand, was not 'high-profile', nor would she have desired to be.

During the war years, Lise was relatively isolated in neutral Sweden, having been obliged to leave Germany. Furthermore, the Berlin team omitted her from its scientific papers, to which she had contributed, albeit from a distance. Personally speaking, Lise was modest, unobtrusive, self-effacing, and perhaps over-zealous in her praise and promotion of Hahn, to her own relative detriment. Hahn, on the other hand, was a showman, confident, and out to blow his own proverbial trumpet.

Lise's desire to protect Hahn

During her time in Stockholm and up to the end of the Second World War, Lise kept quiet about her role in liaising with and advising the

Berlin team in order to protect Hahn, who would lose his job, and perhaps his life, were the Nazis to discover that he had collaborated with an ethnic Jew.

The personal touch

When it came to nominees for Nobel Prizes, the Swedes liked to know who they were dealing with, i.e. they liked to meet the candidates in person. Hahn would have been aware of this, and his March 1939 lecture tour may be seen as him making a pitch for the Nobel Prize.

Also, Hahn was known to the Swedish scientific community, having appeared in Sweden in person in 1943 on his appointment as a foreign member of the Royal Swedish Academy of Sciences.

The composition of the NCC in the NPC

In 1944 and 1945, all members of the NCC were Swedish chemists and all members of the NPC were Swedish physicists, with the sole exception of Hans von Euler-Chelpin of the Chemistry Committee, who was a biochemist.[4]

Impact of the war

It was wartime, and Sweden was relatively isolated. Normal interaction with foreign scientists was greatly curtailed, and there was no foreign input as far as the deliberations of either the NCC or the NPC were concerned.

Behind closed doors

Each committee operated like a private club, in a country with a population of only about 6.5 million. Its members knew each other personally; they had probably attended the same Swedish universities of either Stockholm or Uppsala, and their families probably socialised together.

Deliberations were kept secret and not recorded, which means that, for an outsider, reaching a conclusion as to the basis for any particular Nobel Prize being awarded and the rationale for it is largely a matter for conjecture.

Lack of experience

The science of nuclear fission was in its infancy, and it is highly unlikely that either the physicists or the chemists on the two committees (like Hahn himself) had a proper understanding of the theory behind it.

An additional factor was that, because Hahn had deliberately omitted Lise's name from the Berlin team's scientific papers that were published in her absence, the committee members would have assumed that her contribution to the Berlin team's research had ended when she left Germany in July 1938.

Pro-German bias on the committee

The awarding of the Nobel Prize to Hahn may have been seen by the committee members, and the members of the Assembly which sanctioned the final decision, as a 'thank you' to Germany for sparing them invasion, whilst at the same time in no way condoning the Nazis or their behaviour. (Both Hahn and Strassmann had refused to join the Nazi Party.)

Swedish patience

All in all, Swedes probably adopted a 'wait and see' attitude towards the Nazis. Certainly, the invasion of their Scandinavian neighbours by Germany would have infuriated and disgusted them. But they knew that the war would not go on forever. Had Hahn been a rabid Nazi, it is highly unlikely that he would have been considered for a Nobel Prize.

The gender factor

The two all-male committees may have had reservations about awarding the Nobel Prize to Lise, both because she was a woman and because she was resident in Sweden. Had this been the case, were she ever to be granted Swedish citizenship (which she was, in 1949) the committee members might even have found her sitting next to them in their future deliberations! In the male-dominated world of science, Lise was seen only as a distraction.

Lise's enforced absence from Berlin

Lise was absent from Berlin at the time when the crucial papers on nuclear fission were published, by the Berlin team on the one hand, and by herself and Frisch on the other. Therefore, the Nobel Committee members and Assembly members may not have realised that she was still deeply involved in Hahn and Strassmann's research, albeit from a distance of about 700 miles. This is understandable. But did it never occur to Siegbahn to walk down the corridor of his institute and consult Lise on the matter? Evidently not.

Academic output

A factor in Lise's favour was that during the war years, despite the initial lack of facilities in Sweden and the failure of Siegbahn to cooperate, she succeeded in publishing seven scientific papers.[5]

Anti-Semitism

This was probably not a factor. After all, the Swedish National Socialist Workers' (Nazi) Party did exist, but its membership was small, and it had negligible influence.

It should not be forgotten that Sweden gave refuge to about 900 Jews from occupied Norway and about 7,000 Jews from occupied Denmark during the war years. Also, thanks to the efforts of Swedish nobleman and diplomat Count Folk Bernadotte, the last surviving 14,000 women in Germany's Ravensbrück concentration camp, of whom about 2,000 were Jews, were rescued and transferred to Sweden on a temporary basis.

The Swedes had no objection to Jews working in science, or any other occupation.

Nazism

Would the award to Hahn of the Nobel Prize be seen as the Swedes condoning Nazism? No, this was not their intention. In fact, there was a strong anti-Nazi sentiment among Swedes who, as already mentioned, deplored the Nazi invasion of their neighbours.

Hahn's persona

Hahn was amiable and charming when it suited him (viz his demeanour at Farm Hall, which had so impressed Blackett) and he would have made a good impression in Sweden on this account. After all, the Swedish scientists had met Hahn personally, as already mentioned. The Swedes were also surely aware that what they regarded as his discovery would play a crucial part in the development of nuclear power for peaceful purposes, which they could look forward to benefitting from.

Hahn as a future leader of German science?

This was undoubtedly how the Swedes perceived him.

Was Hahn motivated by greed?

Hahn was surely aware that, had he been awarded the prize jointly with Lise, in that case the prize would have been divided in two and his share would be halved. Furthermore, the awarding of a Nobel Prize, with the prestige accruing to it, could result in vast sums of money being donated to projects in which the recipient was involved. So, his motto may have been 'winner takes all'.

Was the dropping of the two atomic bombs by the USA on Japan on 6 and 9 August 1945 likely to affect the issue?

The atomic bombing of Japan was in total conflict with the Nobel organisation's ideals of peace and brotherhood for mankind. Furthermore, because Hahn was regarded as the discoverer of nuclear fission, this event had come at an inopportune time in respect of his candidature for the Nobel Prize.

There is no doubt that Hahn had contributed to the discovery of fission, knowledge of which enabled the USA to manufacture atomic bombs. However, according to him, he had played no direct part in the attempted manufacture of the German atomic bomb by the Nazis, and he appeared to be genuinely horrified by the events of Hiroshima and Nagasaki. But was Hahn once again being disingenuous? This will be discussed shortly.

Chapter 26

Nobel Nominations and Deliberations: Reason and Unreason

Alfred Bernhard Nobel (1833–1896) was a Swedish businessman, engineer, inventor, and philanthropist. In his will he set aside the bulk of his estate to establish a set of international awards known as the Nobel Prizes.

For each category of Nobel Prize, i.e. Chemistry, Physics, and so on, nominations were required to be submitted prior to 1 February of the relevant year. A committee (appointed by the Academy) consisting of five members made its recommendations in the form of a special report, which was summarised as a general report, which became a recommendation.

Members of the Academy were divided into sections called 'classes', depending on their field of expertise viz. the Physics Class, the Chemistry Class, etc. This recommendation of the Committee was submitted to the relevant section of the Academy (which numbered about 100 members at this time). Whereupon, the final recommendation was made to the full Assembly, which, having made its final decision, made an official announcement at the beginning of October.

The procedure was for the relevant Nobel committee to send a confidential invitation to persons whom it considered competent and qualified to nominate a particular person for a particular prize. This could apply worldwide, but in practice nominators were largely drawn from Sweden and elsewhere in Scandinavia.

In his will, Nobel stipulated that 'the prizes for physics and chemistry shall be awarded by the Swedish Academy of Sciences' ('The Academy'). The physics prize should go to 'the person who shall have made the most important discovery or invention within the field of physics', and the chemistry prize should go to 'the person who shall have made the most important chemical discovery or improvement'.

Nominations

1939

In this year, following Lise and Frisch's paper detailing the explanation of fission, and Frisch's subsequent paper proving that fission had actually occurred, the Nobel Prize nominations were as follows:

Chemistry: Lise and Hahn jointly, by Svedberg.

1940 to 1942 inclusive

It being wartime, no Nobel Prizes were awarded. However, nominations continued to be made.

1941

Chemistry: Lise and Hahn one joint nomination (with US biochemist Wendell Stanley), and Hahn one nomination from Westgren. (Every year, from 1941 to 1946 inclusive, Westgren would nominate Hahn for the Chemistry Prize.)

Physics: Lise and Hahn jointly, by James Franck. Hahn and Strassmann jointly, by Samuel A. Goudsmit, plus one nomination for Hahn.

1942

Chemistry: Lise and Hahn one joint nomination, plus one for Hahn.

1943

Chemistry: Hahn one nomination.

Physics: Lise and Hahn jointly, by James Franck, and one nomination for Hahn (but significantly *not* for Lise) from Siegbahn.

1944

Chemistry: Hahn one nomination from Westgren. Otherwise, Hahn would have received no nominations in chemistry for 1944, and as he had none in physics either, he would therefore not have been eligible to receive the prize.

As for Lise, she received no nominations in this year, and she was therefore not eligible to receive the prize.

In that year of 1944, the Chemistry Committee proposed Hahn for the Chemistry Prize. This was despite the fact that others had received more nominations than his one nomination. For example, Sir Robert

Robinson (6); Gustav Komppa (6); Linus Pauling (3); Gilbert Lewis (3); Jacques Tréfonël (3); George de Hevesy (2); and Vincent du Vigneaud (2).

At first glance, this may seem extraordinary. However, it was often the case that the prize for a candidate was held over until the following year. Also, however many nominations the candidate received in order to be eligible, he or she had to fulfil the requirements of the Nobel Foundation. In the event, the Academy endorsed de Hevesy for the (reserved) 1943 Chemistry Prize but postponed its decision on the 1944 Chemistry Prize.

The war in Europe ended on 8 May 1945.

1945

Chemistry: Hahn one nomination.

Physics: Lise (jointly with Frisch) one nomination (from Oskar Klein). Hahn two nominations.

Deliberations

It fell to Chemistry Committee member Thé Svedberg to report on the committee's deliberations. He stated as follows.

> It seems that sharing the Prize between Hahn and Meitner for the discovery of uranium fission, or in common for their work with uranium fission products should not be questioned. Therefore, the sharing of the Prize could also possibly be proposed to a great extent for the totality of their common work in the field of radioactivity.[1]

This seems both reasonable and equitable on the part of Svedberg, if somewhat illogical in that Lise was a physicist and not a chemist!

1940

The Chemistry Committee recommended that Hahn should receive that year's Nobel Prize. However, both the chemistry section of the Academy and the Academy itself rejected the award for Hahn.

1941

The Physics Committee, showing a complete lack of understanding of the matter, stated that Hahn and Lise's work appeared to 'belong to chemistry', and the decision was therefore handed over to the Chemistry Committee.[2]

Chemistry Committee member Svedberg reported that Lise had not performed work 'of great importance in the past two years', and her publications and those of Frisch in 1939 'had not significantly influenced developments in the field'. On the basis of Svedberg's recommendation, the committee decided that the Nobel Prize in chemistry should be awarded to Hahn alone.[3]

Is it conceivable that members of the Physics Committee, of the Chemistry Committee, and of the Assembly, did not actually have sight of the Lise Meitner-Otto Frisch papers of January 1939, which confirmed that nuclear fission had occurred; contained the first theoretical explanation of how it had occurred; and made it perfectly clear (from the fact that reference was made to Hahn and Strassmann in both papers) that this had been a multidisciplinary achievement i.e. involving Hahn and Strassmann also? No, said Professor Karl Grandin, Director, Centre for the History of Science, Royal Swedish Academy of Sciences, Stockholm, Sweden, 'they all had it and discussed it'.[4]

1942

Swedish chemist Wilhelm Palmaer nominated Hahn and Lise jointly for the chemistry prize. (But Palmaer died in June that same year.)

Westgren attributed the theoretical explanation of fission primarily to Bohr. He did concede, however, that had Lise remained in Germany after 1938, instead of being forced to leave in 'unhappy circumstances', a joint award would have been 'justified'.[5]

1943

Westgren was elected to the Chemistry Committee, of which he became chairman. He was also appointed permanent secretary of the Academy. In that year, he successfully proposed Hahn for foreign membership of the Academy. In view of the fact that Hahn was currently a contender for a Nobel Prize, this action by Westgren may perhaps be considered to be 'out of order'.

1944
The Nobel Committee for Chemistry decided that the Nobel Prize should be awarded to Hahn. The full Assembly, however, decided that the decision should be deferred. This appeared to be a journey without end, with everybody going round in circles.

1945
Oskar Klein argued that Lise and Frisch were co-discoverers of fission together with Hahn.

In late February 1945, Klein, a keen advocate of Lise's candidacy, was elected a member of the Academy. The outcome of Klein's appointment was that Physics Committee member Erik Hulthén was asked to evaluate the contribution made by Lise and Frisch. This he did, in a 'Special Report' dated 9 June 1945:

> It should be apparent that Meitner and Frisch's contribution to the clarification of the nuclear fission problem's physical side is indeed very significant, but they share the honour with a large number of other researchers in the field. Now, it is always a difficult matter to make a definite judgment in priority issues when the contributions have been made in such a rapid succession as in this case. It might, therefore, be that the real historical development has been different from what can be observed from the facts cited here. However, since no other documents are available to me, I cannot (this year) justify, to endorse the proposal regarding a prize award for Meitner and Frisch's efforts.[6]

Hulthén's remark, that no other documents were available to him, is true to the extent that once Lise had left Germany her name no longer appeared on the Berlin team's scientific papers that were published in her absence. However, the salient point is that Lise and Frisch's two fission papers of January 1939 *were* available to him.

But for Hulthén to state that Lise and Frisch shared the honour of the discovery with many other researchers was patent nonsense, for as Frisch stated, until that moment in time, 'Nobody had ever found a nuclear disintegration creating far removed elements.'[7] Bohr himself was astonished to have confirmation from Lise and Frisch that the atom had been split, so how could the discovery possibly be attributed to anyone else? Furthermore, this was the discovery on which all subsequent scientific research into nuclear fission was based.

On 11 September 1945, Bohr wrote to Klein as follows.

> There is a general consensus in the [scientific] community of Lise Meitner and Robert Frisch's contribution to the development. This might well be decisive help for the Nobel Committee's deliberations. It would not only be a well-deserved encouragement, but possibly also of significance for the whole case's international side, if Meitner and Frisch could be considered for a prize awarded at the same time as [one for] Hahn.[8]

In late September 1945 the Chemistry Committee, having decided that yet again the decision should be deferred, duly reported to the Academy.

Is it possible that the NCC and Assembly (perhaps mindful of Fermi's previous premature announcement of his discovery of 'transuranes') had doubts about whether or not Hahn had achieved fission, and also about the explanation provided for it by Lise and Frisch? If so, this is understandable since it was a revolutionary discovery.

However, in autumn 1945, a paper entitled 'Atomic Energy for Military Purposes', written about the Manhattan Project by US physicist Henry de Wolf Smyth was published by the *Maple Press*, York, Pennsylvania. This document, however, gave no real idea of the crucial role that Lise had played in the discovery of fission. The relevant part read as follows:

> Just before Bohr left Denmark, two of his colleagues, O. R. Frisch and L. Meitner (both refugees from Germany), had told him their guess that the absorption of a neutron by a uranium nucleus sometimes caused that nucleus to split into approximately equal parts with the release of enormous quantities of energy, a process that soon began to be called nuclear 'fission'. The occasion for this hypothesis was the important discovery of O. Hahn and F. Strassmann in Germany (published in *Naturwissenschaften* in early January 1939) which proved that an isotope of barium was produced by neutron bombardment of uranium.

Nevertheless, with the explosion of the atomic bombs, the Nobel authorities could have been left in no doubt as to the fact that fission had been achieved!

On 15 November 1945, only two months after the dropping of the two atomic bombs on Japan, the Academy announced that the 1944 Nobel Prize for Chemistry would be awarded to Hahn. Furthermore, the deferred 1944 and 1945 Nobel Prizes for both physics and chemistry would be presented at the December 1946 ceremonies.

On 17 November 1945, Klein wrote to Bohr to inform him that 'At the poll, just over half of the votes were cast for Hahn and slightly less than half for postponement. As far as I could understand, this surprising result was due to a (perhaps not entirely unjustified) fear of some opportunistic, political reasons – the desire to keep up with America.'[9]

The decision of the Academy was made despite the protestations of Westgren, Svedberg, and Klein, who demanded that matters should be delayed prior to further information being available from the USA. This, of course, was extremely unlikely, as all scientific papers relating to nuclear fission were classified as top secret by the military authorities and security services.

Göran Liljestrand, a professor at the Karolinska Institute for medical education and a member of the Academy, rejected their argument and 'spoke strongly in favour of Hahn'. (Some might regard this too as being 'out of order', Liljestrand being a pharmacologist!)[10]

Composition of the Chemistry Committee, 1944 and 1945

The committee remained unchanged. Its five members included:

- Arne Westgren (chairman): Swedish chemist and metallurgist
- Bror Holmberg: Swedish chemist
- Hans von Euler-Chelpin: German-born Swedish biochemist
- Arne Fredga: Swedish chemist
- Thé Svedberg: Swedish chemist

Composition of the Physics Committee, 1944 and 1945

1944: Its five members included Henning Pleijel (chairman), Erik Hulthén, Carl W. Oseen, Axel Lindh, and Manne Siegbahn. All were Swedish physicists.

In 1945: The same, except that Swedish physicist Ivar Waller had replaced Carl W. Oseen.

Apart from what has already been mentioned, what else was going on behind the scenes?

The Chemistry Committee

Arne Westgren had served as joint secretary of the Physics Committee and the Chemistry Committee from 1926 to 1942. In 1942, he became a member of the Chemistry Committee, and in 1944 he was appointed its chairman. He was therefore in a highly influential position. Every year, from 1941 to 1946 inclusive, Westgren had nominated Hahn for chemistry, a total of six times. In fact, had it not been for Westgren, Hahn would have received no nominations in chemistry for 1944, and he would therefore not have been eligible for the prize in that year. Why Westgren was desperately keen for Hahn to succeed, and why he never once nominated Lise, is not clear.

Hans von Euler-Chelpin, a German, had obtained Swedish citizenship in 1902. In the First World War he had served in the German Air Force. In the Second World War he had worked in a diplomatic mission representing Germany. His sympathies were probably, therefore, with his fellow countryman Hahn.

The Physics Committee

It is curious that Siegbahn (a Nobel Laureate himself) never nominated Lise, his colleague at the Nobel Institute, for a Nobel Prize. This will be discussed shortly.

The 'old boy network'

When a vacancy occurred, members of the Academy elected a replacement by secret ballot. Members of each Committee were elected by the Academy (bar one, who was elected by the President of the corresponding section of the Nobel Institute).[11]

Doubtless many trade-offs and intrigues took place behind the scenes, by colleagues who knew each other well and had even previously worked together. For example, in 1919–1920, Westgren and Siegbahn had worked together at Lund University on X-ray diffraction for metallurgical purposes.[12]

Göran Liljestrand, who had spoken so forcefully in favour of Hahn, had worked with Ulf S. von Euler, son of Chemistry Committee member, Hans von Euler-Chelpin.

The above factors may have each played a greater or lesser part in explaining why Hahn was awarded the Nobel Prize, and not Lise. However, because of the traditional secrecy attached to the Nobel Prize decision-making process, the whole truth remains to be discovered.

Chapter 27

Hahn's Moment of Glory: Dissenting Voices

On 2 December 1946, Hahn set out for Sweden where, on his arrival, he was met by Lise. In the delayed Nobel Prize ceremony, which took place in Stockholm on 10 December 1946, Swedish biochemist Professor Arne W.K. Tiselius addressed the Nobel Laureates-to-be in turn. To Hahn, he said:

> On 10 December 1945, precisely one year ago, you were unfortunately prevented from attending the Nobel Prizegiving ceremony in order to receive your prize here in person. But on that occasion the chairman of the Nobel Prize Committee for Chemistry gave a detailed account of the results of your researches. Today, therefore, I must confine myself to expressing our great pleasure that you are able to be here now to receive your Prize and our congratulations in person.
>
> The splitting of the nuclei of heavy atoms has had such consequences that all of us, indeed the whole world, look forward to its future development with great expectations, but also with great anxiety. I am convinced, Professor Hahn, that just as your great discovery was the result of your profound researches into the nature of atomic nuclei, researches that were carried out without any consideration of any possible practical use that might arise, so too the future vigorous development of research in this field as a consequence of your work, is bound to give you particularly great satisfaction. I am also convinced that you, Professor Hahn, share with us the hope that ultimately it will turn out to be a blessing for all mankind.

> Professor Hahn, I herewith convey to you most sincere congratulations on behalf of the Academy and ask you now to receive, from the hand of his Majesty the King, the Nobel Prize for Chemistry for the year 1944.

This was King Gustav V of Sweden.

In his speech at the Nobel banquet, which Hahn proudly reproduced in full in his autobiography, he wallowed in self-pity, both for himself and for the German people. Germany, he said,

> has probably become the most unfortunate country in the world. Truly, it cannot be said that all Germans, least of all, German scientists, in the last thirteen years, went over to Hitler with banners flying. As for German youth, perhaps the attitude taken by many of them ought not to be judged too harshly as is sometimes done. They had no chance to make up their own minds; there was no independent press, no foreign broadcasting; and they could not go and see foreign countries for themselves.[1]

This was a curious statement for Hahn to make because up until the late 1930s, the 'Hitler Youth' holidayed abroad in vast numbers in many European countries, including the UK.

'There are probably not many people outside Germany who know the extent of the oppression under which we laboured during the last ten or twelve years,' continued Hahn.[2]

Such denial and self-indulgence on the part of Hahn beggars belief. To get matters in perspective, a colleague of the author was present at the liberation of the Bergen-Belsen concentration camp on 15 April 1945. *That* was an example of oppression!

Three days later, on 13 December 1946, Hahn delivered his Nobel lecture. He began by describing atomic theory since the time when Henri Becquerel became the first person to discover evidence of radioactivity, in uranium in 1896. He described Fermi's experiment in bombarding uranium with neutrons. 'Lise Meitner and I decided to repeat Fermi's experiments,' he declared, failing to mention that this had been entirely Lise's idea. He stated that both he, Lise, and Strassmann had all believed that they had created three 'so-called transuraniums [or 'transuranes'] – elements higher than uranium'.

It is true that the Berlin team, including Lise, did originally believe in the three transuranes, although Lise had reservations and was able to provide a satisfactory theoretical explanation for only one of them. As for the alleged findings for the other two transuranes, this did not accord with current atomic theory.

Having concluded 'that radium isotopes had been produced', said Hahn, he subsequently concluded that it was not radium but barium that had been produced. But, again, he failed to mention that he had found this out only because Lise had insisted that he and Strassman checked their results. This result, he said, was 'in opposition to all the phenomena observed up to the present in nuclear physics' i.e. the idea that the uranium nucleus could have split ('bursting', as he put it) to produce a fragment as large as a barium isotope. The question was, what was the identity of the other fragment, assuming that there were only two?

'As a second partner [barium] in the new process we assumed an element with an atomic weight of about 100, as in that case the combined atomic weights would be that of uranium, for example 138+101 (e.g. element 43) gives 239!'

Here, Hahn demonstrated, yet again, his failure to understand a fundamental law of chemistry, laid down in 1913 by British physicist, Henry G.J. Moseley, who stated that an element is defined not by its atomic weight but by its atomic number (or 'Z' number, which is equal to the number of protons in its atomic nucleus).

As applied to this situation, the atomic number of barium (56) plus the atomic number of the 'second partner' i.e. the other fission product must total the atomic number of uranium, which is 92. Therefore, the second fission product must have the atomic number 36, which is krypton. This Hahn should have realised immediately.

Hahn did, however, acknowledge that 'Lise Meitner and O. [Otto] R. Frisch' had

> explained with the aid of Bohr's model of the original nucleus … the possibility of a breakdown of heavy atomic nuclei [i.e. a heavy atomic nucleus] into two lighter ones. The great repulsive energy of the fragments produced by the

> splitting was first demonstrated experimentally by Frisch and afterwards by F. Joliot. Meitner and Frisch soon proved that the active breakdown products, previously considered to be transuraniums were, in fact, not transuraniums but fragments produced by the splitting.

Finally, in his Nobel lecture, Hahn did explain that the atomic number of barium (56) must be subtracted from the atomic number of uranium (92), in order to identify the second fission product – krypton (36). But he did not go so far as to admit that it was Lise who had come to this conclusion, and not himself![3]

In his autobiography (published in 1968), Hahn stated that he 'handed over a largish sum to Professor Strassman'.[4] In fact, it was less than 10% of the prize money, and Strassmann's wife Maria referred to it disdainfully as 'a tip'.[5] Hahn donated nothing to Lise.[6]

Conclusion

Between 1924 and 1965, Lise received a total of forty-eight nominations, twenty-nine for physics and nineteen for chemistry.

Between 1914 and 1947, Hahn received a total of thirty-nine nominations, twenty-three for chemistry and sixteen for physics.

In 1994, Austrian-born British molecular biologist Max Perutz described Hahn as

> one of the world's leading radiochemists. After the war Meitner stressed, in an interview on German television, that Hahn had been the only person in the world with chemical methods sufficiently refined to separate the infinitesimally small quantities of new radioactive elements produced by the irradiation of uranium with neutrons from the bulk of the uranium itself, as well as from the accompanying, naturally present radium and its radioactive decay products.

True as this may be, it does not alter the fact that the intellectual impetus for the Berlin team was provided by Lise.

The discovery of fission, said Perutz, 'was a remarkable feat, for which Hahn deserved the Nobel Prize, but I thought that the Nobel Committee for Chemistry had been narrow-minded in not awarding it jointly to him and his physicist colleague, Meitner.'[7]

In their decision to deny Lise the Nobel Prize (and Strassmann and Frisch, for that matter), the Nobel Committees and Assembly were guilty of ignorance, confusion, and politicking. The great error was to ignore the fact (a) that Lise had been involved, every step of the way (a perusal of Lise and Frisch's fission papers, which members saw and read, ought to have told them that), (b) that Lise and Frisch alone had provided verification that fission had occurred, and also the scientific explanation for it (this, Hahn, with his limited knowledge of physics, would have been incapable of doing), and (c) that the discovery of fission was a multidisciplinary achievement that required the cooperation of both chemists and physicists.

In defence of the NCC, members were operating in the dark as far as Lise was concerned, in as much as Hahn, as leader of the Berlin team had, in effect, falsified the records by omitting her name from his and Strassmann's scientific papers. He had pulled the proverbial wool over their eyes.

Therefore, Hahn was culpable for not admitting Lise's role. The Nobel Institute was culpable for not doing the decent thing and putting matters right, even when the full facts of the case became clear. But perhaps they would have regarded this as a loss of face.

The discovery of nuclear fission dwarfed all others of the time, as the Nobel authorities would doubtless have been aware, with its potential of nuclear power for both peaceful and military purposes. The logical and equitable decision should, therefore, have been to award the chemistry prize to Hahn and Strassmann, and the physics prize to Meitner and Frisch. (Frisch was already a distinguished scientist in his own right for his work at Hamburg under Otto Stern.)

It fell to Strassmann to sum up the situation perfectly. Said he,

> What difference does it make that Lise Meitner did not *directly* participate in the 'discovery'? Her initiative was the beginning of the joint work with Hahn – *4 years later she belonged to our team* – and she was bound to us intellectually from Sweden through the correspondence 'Hahn-Meitner'.

> She was the intellectual leader of our team, and therefore she belonged to us – even if she was not actually present for the 'discovery of fission'.[8]

Strassmann himself was a gentleman and a man of honour, and if Hahn had deserved the Nobel Prize, then so also had he.

Almost a decade later, to James Franck, Lise declared that the fact that she

> did not get the Nobel Prize, which at the time would have been a material help to me or for me was not disappointing and I have not thought about it for many years and I would not have wanted it without O. R. [Otto Robert Frisch] because that would have been a great injustice. You can be sure that it is not an unhealed wound.

This of course, implies that once, yes, she had felt wounded by this injustice.[9]

Lise's life was in no way defined by the fact that she was not awarded the Nobel Prize: the decision being a poor reflection on that organisation, rather than on herself. Fortunately, more enlightened organisations were in no doubt as to her abilities and achievements, and only too willing to recognise them.

Chapter 28

The Alleged Nazi Bomb

The discovery of nuclear fission did not go unnoticed by the German military authorities. On 22 April 1939, after hearing a colloquium paper by German experimental physicist Wilhelm Hanle on the use of uranium fission in an *Uranmaschine* (uranium machine, i.e. nuclear reactor), German theoretical physicist Georg Joos, along with Hanle, notified Wilhelm Dames at the Reichs Ministry of Education of the potential military applications of nuclear energy. This would be given to Abraham Esau, head of the physics section of the Reichs Research Council at the Reichs Ministry of Education.[1]

The outcome was that a group of three leading German physicists created the first 'Uranium Club' (Uranverein). However, in August 1939 they were called up for military service.

Paul Harteck was Director of the Physical Chemistry Department at the University of Hamburg and an advisor to the Army Ordnance Office (HWA). On 24 April 1939, along with his teaching assistant Wilhelm Groth, Harteck made contact with the Reichs Ministry of War (RKM) to alert them to the potential military applications of nuclear chain reactions. This initiative led, later in the year, to the creation of the second Uranium Club, one of whose members was Hahn.[2]

In the same year, nuclear physicist and chemist Josef Mattauch 'took on the direction of the newly-established department for mass spectroscopy and atomic physics' at the KWIC.

Aware of the enormous threat that these developments posed to the Allies, Hungarian-German-US physicist and inventor Leo Szilard, in August 1939, persuaded Einstein to acquaint US President Franklin D. Roosevelt of this.

With the outbreak of World War II on 1 September 1939, the Army Office of Weaponry conducted studies starting in October 1939 to determine to what extent nuclear fission, as discovered by Otto Hahn and Fritz Strassmann in the Kaiser Wilhelm Institute for Chemistry the previous year, could be applied militarily.

In December 1939, Heisenberg became head of a small nuclear fission research group in Leipzig, where the 'Leipzig L-IV' test reactor was built.

'The majority of the Kaiser Wilhelm Institute for Physics', with the exception of von Laue's and chemist and inventor Wilhelm Schüler's departments,

> were placed under the immediate authority of the Army Office of Weaponry in 1940. The overall leadership was in the hands of Kurt Diebner and [nuclear physicist] Heinz Pose, while Otto Hahn and Werner Heisenberg were charged with the scientific directorship. The Institute's research funds had to be used 'for the problem of attaining energy from uranium fission',[3] in other words for the construction of an 'Uranbrenner' (uranium burner) as a reactor was then called; while the Army Office of Weaponry attempted to coordinate the work on military problems with scientific groups in other cities.[4]

On 3 May 1940, German troops in Norway seized control of the Vemork Norsk Hydro plant in the town of Rjukan, in the Telemark region of Norway. This was the world's only heavy water production facility.

Heavy water: water in which the hydrogen in the molecules is partly or wholly replaced by the isotope deuterium, used especially as a moderator in nuclear reaction.[5]

In late 1941, Heisenberg gave a lecture to top Nazi officials and the German military. This was subsequently published as an approximately 130 page report headed 'For a Bomb'. In it, Heisenberg discussed using enriched U-235 as the fissile material, with graphite as a moderator.[6]

As already mentioned, on 26 February 1942 at the House of German Research in Berlin-Dahlem, Heisenberg gave a lecture entitled 'The Theoretical Foundations for obtaining Energy from Fission of Uranium'. Present were Minister of Education Bernhard Rust, Albert Vögler, representatives of the Nazi Party, and of the German state.[7] Vögler was a German politician, an industrialist and an important executive in the munitions industry. There were also presentations by Hahn, and by Austrian physical chemist, Paul Harteck, and several others.[8]

Heisenberg's first sentence said it all. 'The work on the uranium problem' was 'done in the framework of the Army Weapons Bureau task force'.

'Obtaining energy from uranium fission is undoubtedly possible if enrichment in the 235 92U isotope is successful,' said Heisenberg. Whereas, 'Production of *pure* 235U would lead to an explosive of unimaginable force.'

Furthermore, if a nuclear reactor were to be built, this could be used on the one hand 'for energy production' and on the other 'to obtain a hugely powerful explosive'.

Heisenberg admitted that 'without generous support of the research work – with materials, radioactive sources, funds, as obtained from the Army Weapons Bureau, it would not have been possible to progress'.

So here was Heisenberg holding out to his Nazi overlords the prospect of atomic weapon production and offering them his full cooperation and expertise.[9]

In April 1942, Heisenberg achieved the first neutron multiplication in the Leipzig test reactor. But on 23 June 1942, in an accident, the Leipzig L-IV test reactor exploded.

Meanwhile, when von Laue informed Lise on 5 June 1942 that Heisenberg was to relocate from Leipzig to take charge of the KWIP in Berlin, Lise was suspicious. And on 20 September 1942 she wrote to German-Jewish physicist Max Born to say that she considered this to be 'quite an interesting fact'.[10] In other words, she suspected that Heisenberg was now supremo of the Nazi fission project.

In June 1942, Germany's Minister for Munitions Albert Speer stated as follows:

> I asked Heisenberg how nuclear physics could be applied to the manufacture of atom bombs. His answer was by no means encouraging. He declared, to be sure, that the scientific solution had already been found and that theoretically, nothing stood in the way of building such a bomb. But the technical prerequisites for production would take years to develop: two years at the earliest, even provided that the program was given maximum support.[11]
>
> Hitler had sometimes spoken to me about the possibility of an atom bomb, but the idea quite obviously strained

> his intellectual capacity. He was also unable to grasp the revolutionary nature of nuclear physics. In the twenty-two-hundred written points of reference for my conferences with Hitler, nuclear fission comes up only once, and then it is mentioned with extreme brevity. Hitler did sometimes comment on its prospects, but what I told him of my conference with the physicists confirmed his view that there was not much profit in the matter. Actually, Professor Heisenberg had not given any final answer to my question of whether a successful nuclear fission could be kept under control with absolute certainty or might continue as a chain reaction. I am sure that Hitler would have not hesitated for a moment, to employ atom bombs against England.[12]

Hitler abhorred Jewish scientists, and the significant involvement of Lise and Frisch in the discovery and elucidation of nuclear fission may also have been a factor in his failure to endorse the nuclear project.

> No method was known that would have allowed production of an atomic explosive without enormous and therefore, impossible technical equipment … [Therefore] the work was to go forward as before on a comparatively small scale. Thus, the only attainable goal was the development of a uranium pile [nuclear reactor].[13]
>
> On the suggestion of the nuclear physicists, we settled the project to develop an atom bomb by the autumn of 1942, after I had again queried [questioned] them about deadlines and been told that we could not count on anything before three or four years. The war would certainly have been decided long before then. Instead, I authorised the development of an energy-producing uranium motor for propelling machinery [e.g. submarines].[14]

The nuclear weapon research project 'was then taken out of the field of responsibility of Army Office and transferred, at Speer's request, in a reduced form to the Reichs Research Office (Abraham Esau) and other institutions'.[15] However, although the project had been downgraded, funding continued from the military and it was then split into the areas of uranium and heavy water production, uranium isotope separation, and the *Uranmaschine*.

Isotope separation: the separation of U-235 from U-238 in natural uranium ore. Whereupon, the U-235, which readily undergoes fission, is retained and the U-238, in which the probability of fission occurring is very low, is discarded.

It was, in effect, broken up between institutes where the different directors dominated the research and set their own research agendas. The dominant personnel, facilities, and areas of research were:

- Walther Bothe: Director of the Institute for Physics at the Kaiser Wilhelm Institute for Medical Research, in Heidelberg. (Measurement of nuclear constants.)
- Nuclear constant: a number expressing a relation or property which remains the same in all circumstances, or for the same substance under the same conditions.[16]
- Klaus Clusius: Director of the Institute for Physical Chemistry at the Ludwig Maximilian University of Munich. (Isotope separation and heavy water production.)
- Kurt Diebner: Director of the Army Ordnance Office (HWA) Testing Station in Gottow (Brandenburg region of Germany) and of the Reichs Research Council Experimental Station in Stadtilm, Thüringia; he was also an advisor to the HWA on nuclear physics. (Measurement of nuclear constants.)
- Otto Hahn: Director of the Kaiser Wilhelm Institute for Chemistry in Berlin-Dahlem. (Transuranic elements, fission products, isotope separation, and measurement of nuclear constants.)
- Paul Harteck: Director of the Physical Chemistry Department of the University of Hamburg. (Heavy water production and isotope production.)
- Werner Heisenberg: Director of the Department of Theoretical Physics at the University of Leipzig until summer 1942; thereafter Acting Director of the Kaiser Wilhelm Institute for Physics in Berlin-Dahlem. (*Uranmaschine*, isotope separation, and measurement of nuclear constants.)
- Hans Kopfermann: Director of the Second Experimental Physics Institute at the Georg-August University of Göttingen. (Isotope separation.)

- Nikolaus Riehl: Scientific Director of the Auergesellschaft.[17]
- Auergesellschaft: an industrial firm with its headquarters in Berlin. In 1939, its Oranienburg plant began production of high-purity uranium oxide on an industrial scale.

In all, a total of sixty scientists (physicists, chemists, and physical chemists) were involved. This, however, was dwarfed both in manpower and financial resources by the Manhattan Project.

> The Kaiser Wilhelm Society then took over control of its institute again, and in October 1942 appointed Heisenberg as Director of the Kaiser Wilhelm Institute; Max von Laue remained vice director. Heisenberg continued to work on the construction of the uranium burner, for which large-scale experiments were conducted in Dahlem, accompanied by theoretic calculations about production, distribution, and absorption of neutrons in the reactor. The most important material for the construction of a reactor, pure uranium, and heavy water and pure carbon as moderators, had, due to the war, become ever more difficult to obtain.

Moderators: designed to reduce the speed of fast neutrons.

> Nevertheless, in the winter of 1943–1944 Heisenberg and his assistants, along with the Heidelberg physicists from the Kaiser Wilhelm Institute for Medical Research, succeeded in constructing a 'model reactor' with 1.5 tons of heavy water and about the same amount of uranium in the newly constructed bunker laboratory at the foot of the 'Turm der Blitze' (Lightning Tower).

The bunker was euphemistically named 'The Virus House', presumably to deter the curious. 'The model reactor produced "three times the number of neutrons shot at it".'[18]

On 28 February 1943, the Vemork Norsk Hydro heavy water production plant was destroyed by the Norwegian Resistance in 'Operation Gunnerside'.

In that year, at the KWIC's department for mass spectroscopy and atomic physics,

> a large wooden barracks was built on the property. With funds from the Reichs Ministry of Aviation and the Industry Bank, it was also possible, in 1943, to build a solid structure ('Minerva') for two high-voltage plants: one for 1.2 million volts for neutron production, and one for 3–5 million volts for producing energy-enhanced particle beams (e.g. protons and deuterons).[19]

As already mentioned, in July 1943, due to the danger of Allied bombing, Speer ordered all KWI atomic research departments to relocate to the Württemberg region of south-western Germany.

Hahn and the KWIC relocated to Tailfingen. Gerlach pursued his reactor research in Haigerloch. Meanwhile, the KWIP relocated in part to Hechingen and in part to the Baden-Würtemberg hills west of Munich. All these three towns, Tailfingen, Haigerloch, and Hechingen, were located in the same region of south-western Germany.

> The experiments were continued in a former textile factory in Hechingen and in the granite basement of Haigerloch, where a final attempt resulted in 7 times the number of neutrons being released, but 'the amount of material available was insufficient for the reactor to go "critical"'.[20]

Finally, further experiments were brought to a halt by the arrival of US troops in April and May 1945.

When Heisenberg learned of the dropping of the atomic bomb on the city of Hiroshima on 6 August 1945, he was incredulous. Why? Brilliant scientist though he was, Heisenberg had made a fundamental miscalculation in respect of the quantity of uranium – critical mass – required for an atomic weapon of 13 tons: equivalent in size to a bouncy-ball 4 feet in height. This would have been far too heavy for an aircraft to carry. But there was another problem. At the current rate of production, it would have taken the Germans about 150 years to produce this quantity of uranium! This is what convinced Speer, in his conversation with Heisenberg in June 1942, to abandon any notion that the atomic bomb had a role to play during the course of the Second World War. Frisch and Peierls, however, had made the correct calculation of the size of the critical mass, i.e. about 1 kilogram (2.2 pounds), or about equivalent in size to a golf ball, and they had reported as much to the British Government. As for the Manhattan Project, such a quantity of uranium (1kg) could be produced every few days.[21]

From what has been said, it is clear beyond doubt that all the members of the Uranium Club, Hahn included, were deeply involved in the Nazi atomic bomb-making project. So why did they not simply put their hands up and admit that, yes, they had been attempting to produce an atomic weapon? Were they afraid that they might share the same fate as their countrymen at the Nuremberg War Crimes Tribunal (20 November 1945–1 October 1946) and have a noose put around their necks? At the trial, the indictments were for conspiracy against peace, initiating and waging wars of aggression, participating in war crimes, and crimes against humanity. Such a confession would not have chimed with their narrative – 'Lesart' – that they had not in fact wanted a bomb. Furthermore, it would have meant a loss of face, in that they had failed to manufacture such a device.

To Franck on 16 January 1946, as already mentioned, Lise spoke of 'the wrong information by Hahn about the truth of the German atomic bomb'. As far as Hahn is concerned, perhaps this was the most damning indictment of all!

Chapter 29

Niels Bohr: The Truth at Last!

On 6 February 2002, four decades after the death of Niels Bohr, the Bohr family 'decided to release all documents deposited at the Niels Bohr Archive, either written or dictated by Niels Bohr, pertaining specifically to the meeting between Bohr and Heisenberg [and von Weizsäcker] in September 1941'.

In an undated letter to Heisenberg circa 1957 (but not sent), in respect of a newly published book *Brighter than a Thousand Suns* by Austrian writer Robert Jungk, Bohr declared, 'I am greatly amazed to see how much your memory has deceived you in your letter to the author of the book'. In respect of their meeting in Copenhagen in September 1941, said Bohr, 'I remember every word of our conversations, which took place on a background of extreme sorrow and tension for us here in Denmark.' Both he, Heisenberg, and von Weizsäcker had expressed their

> definite conviction that Germany would win and that it was therefore quite foolish for us to maintain the hope of a different outcome of the war and to be reticent as regards all German offers of cooperation. I also remember quite clearly our conversation in my room at the Institute, where in vague terms you spoke in a manner that could only give me the firm impression that, under your leadership, everything was being done in Germany to develop atomic weapons and that you said that there was no need to talk about details since you were completely familiar with them, and had spent the past two years working more or less exclusively on such preparations.

In a draft of a letter to Heisenberg (again unsent), Bohr said that, 'you informed me that it was your conviction that the war, if it lasted sufficiently long, would be decided with atomic weapons, and [I did] not sense even the slightest hint that you and your friends were making efforts in another direction.'

In undated 'Notes to Heisenberg', Bohr referred to a visit to Copenhagen in 1943 by German physicist Hans Jensen, who 'described the efforts to increase the production of heavy water in Norway and mentioned in this connection that, for him and other German physicists, it was only a matter of an industrial application of atomic energy'.

In a letter to Heisenberg drafted circa 1962 (but not sent), Bohr remembered 'quite clearly the impression it made on me' when Heisenberg had declared once again that the war,

> if it lasted long enough, would be decided with atomic weapons. I did not respond to this at all, but as you perhaps regarded this as an expression of doubt, you related how in the preceding years you had devoted yourself almost exclusively to the question and were quite certain that it could be done, but you gave no hint about efforts on the part of German scientists to prevent such a development.

Finally, in a draft letter to Heisenberg (again not sent), Bohr described the difficulties raised by their September 1941 meeting. Said he, 'It brought us, who lived only on the hope of defeat for German Nazism, in a difficult situation to meet and talk to someone who expressed as strongly as you and Weizsäcker your certain conviction of a German victory and confidence in what it would bring.' In respect of their conversation, said Bohr, 'I carefully fixed in my mind every word that was uttered.'

In respect of atomic weapons, said Bohr,

> I had to understand that in recent years you [Heisenberg and his colleagues] had occupied yourself almost exclusively with this question and did not doubt that it could be done. It is, therefore, quite incomprehensible to me that you should think that you hinted to me that the German physicists would do all they could to prevent such an application of atomic science. During the conversation, which was only very brief, I was naturally very cautious, but nevertheless thought a lot about its content. My alarm was not lessened by hearing from the others at the Institute that Weizsäcker

> had stated how fortunate it would be for the position of science in Germany after the victory that you could help so significantly towards this end.[1]

However, if Heisenberg and von Weizsäcker believed that they could involve Bohr in the Nazi atomic bomb project, they were sadly mistaken.

These letters by Bohr dispel the myth that German scientists had been opposed to the Nazi bomb project and had played no part in it. They also indicate that Lise had been right to be suspicious of the visit of the two German scientists to Bohr in Copenhagen in September 1941. Finally, they confirm von Laue's description of the German scientist's 'Memorandum' in which they claimed not to have wanted the bomb as a 'Lesart' – false narrative. After all, other German scientists were working enthusiastically on V-rockets, munitions, radar, nerve agents, and other warlike projects, so why should anyone believe that the atomic scientists were any different?

Hahn, as a member of the Uranium Club, was privy to all its dealings, and worked as one of a team on the Nazi atomic bomb project. Yet during the war, said Hahn, he had been occupied solely with 'harmless things'. 'I should have refused to work on an atomic bomb at any price', and he 'did not want to have it'. Bohr's correspondence therefore gives the lie to all these statements by Hahn, who was a deeply embedded atomic bomb researcher.

It is sobering to think that had Heisenberg not grossly overestimated the critical mass of uranium required to achieve a self-sustaining chain reaction, his conversation with Speer might have taken an entirely different turn. The Nazis may have pumped money and resources into the project, allowing Heisenberg and his colleagues to develop the atomic bomb, which, according to Speer, Hitler would not have hesitated to use.

The whole extraordinary story of the atomic bomb and who got there first rested on a series of extraordinary coincidences. Lise being driven out of Germany by the Nazis; her momentous meeting with Frisch in Sweden; Heisenberg's miscalculation of critical mass, which led Speer to downgrade the Nazi bomb project; Frisch becoming stranded in England at the outbreak of war, where he and Peierls (who ironically was a former student of Heisenberg) correctly calculated the critical mass; and the flight of German scientists to the USA, including many Jews who led the Manhattan Project.

Chapter 30

Manne Siegbahn: A Thorn in Lise's Side

Karl Manne Georg Siegbahn (known as Manne) was born on 3 December 1886 at Örebro, Sweden. In 1911 he was awarded a doctorate in Physics from the University of Lund, and in 1912 he began his research work on X-ray spectroscopy. In 1920, he was appointed Professor of Physics at the University of Lund.

As already mentioned, Lise had met Siegbahn in spring 1921 when, at his invitation, she spent several weeks in Sweden as visiting professor at the University of Lund.

In 1923, Siegbahn was appointed Professor of Physics at the University of Uppsala. In 1924, he was awarded the Nobel Prize in Physics 'for his discoveries and research in the field of X-ray spectroscopy'. This provided a means of measuring photons and particles of light that have wavelengths in the X-ray portion of the electromagnetic spectrum. 'When an atom is unstable or is bombarded with high-energy particles, its electrons transition from one energy level to another.' Whereupon, 'the element absorbs and releases high energy X-ray photons in a way that is characteristic of atoms that make up that particular chemical element'.[1]

In respect of the awarding of Nobel Prizes, Robert M. Friedman, author of *The Politics of Excellence* (2001) described just how ruthless Siegbahn and other committee members were when it came to guarding their own interests by the sidelining of funds. Said he, they

> tried to generate more money for research. They desired to withhold the prize as often as possible. By first reserving a prize and then not awarding it the following year, the committee – with the Academy's assent – could assist in building up either the main fund, interest from which provides money for the prizes, or the committee's special fund, interest from which could be used for research grants. Adding money to these funds became a committee obsession.

> Siegbahn, who was now firmly in place in Uppsala, already had begun searching for more money for new instruments. Recognizing the ease with which grants from the committee's special fund could be obtained, he also concurred with the aim of trying not to find worthy candidates.
>
> When all members could agree on the agenda, the committee could dispatch and dismiss the nominees, assuring the Academy that no candidate could be found whose achievements fulfilled the high standards stipulated by Nobel's testament. Aiding the process, Oseen's hypercritical stance and keen rhetoric skills could find fault with virtually any candidate.[2]

In the 10 November 1936 issue of Sweden's 'respected Gothenburg newspaper', *Goteborgs Handels- och Sjofartstidning*, physicist and oceanographer Hans Pettersson (son of former Chemistry Committee member Otto Pettersson) published an article demanding that the Academy and its committees explain themselves. The newspaper stated, said Friedman, that 'Nobel's money was intended first and foremost for the prizes. Was it right for the Academy to declare in a period of spectacular scientific accomplishment that no candidate merited a prize, and then to divert the prize money to benefit local research?'[3]

Not for nothing had chemist Oskar Widman, himself a Swede, declared in 1926 that to sit on a Nobel Committee was 'like sitting on a quagmire – one doesn't have firm footing under one's feet'.[4]

In 1937, Siegbahn was appointed Research Professor of Experimental Physics at the Nobel Institute of the Royal Swedish Academy of Sciences, Stockholm, of which he became Director in the same year.

As for Lise, on 12 February 1939 she told Hahn that Eva Bahr-Bergius had confirmed to her what she herself had always suspected, that Siegbahn 'actually did not want to have me' at his institute'.[5]

When Siegbahn's cyclotron did finally come into operation in early 1942, Lise told Hahn, 'Things are irradiated only for Manne'.[6]

When the decision was made to award the Nobel Prize to Hahn but not to Lise, Hans Pettersson wrote to her on 16 November 1945:

> [we] are indignant about the one-sidedness of the distribution of the Nobel Prize. We are certainly glad that

> Hahn got the chemistry prize, but by all rights the physics prize should have gone to you. I personally, am quite sure that this would have been the case had not Sweden's most practised *krokbensläggare* [one who pulls others down – an undoubted reference to Siegbahn] been against it, for dark reasons of prestige.[7]

Swedish scientist Svante A. Arrhenius (1859–1927), referring to Siegbahn's notorious high-handedness, had once referred to the 'small popes' of Swedish science, 'especially Siegbahn'. Swedish engineer and physicist Professor Gudmund Borelius and Oskar Klein took the same view.[8]

On 17 November 1945, Klein wrote to Bohr. 'I got a strong impression that there is widespread sympathy for another prize to be given to Lise Meitner and Frisch, or maybe to LM alone. However, I do not know Siegbahn's position'. The awarding of a prize to all three of them 'at the same time would have been much more suited for creating harmony both for everyone involved, and in all the circles now disputing who made the greatest effort'.[9]

Had he chosen to do so, Siegbahn, as an influential member of the NPC, could have presented a powerful case for Lise (and Frisch) to be awarded the Nobel Prize for Physics. And this would have demonstrated to the world that the discovery of nuclear fission had involved the disciplines of both physics and chemistry. After all, like other committee members and Assembly members, he had seen and read Lise and Frisch's fission papers: so it must have been perfectly clear to him that Lise had been closely involved with the Berlin team's researches right up until the present time. And had he chosen simply to stroll down the corridor to her office, he could have ascertained from her just how crucial her role had been. Alas, he evidently did not feel inclined to do so.

The question therefore arises: why did Siegbahn nominate Hahn for a Nobel Prize, but not Lise? Perhaps for these reasons. Had the Nobel Prize been awarded to Lise, this may well have had the following implications. She would have attracted enormous funding for research into the generation of nuclear power for peaceful purposes, had she chosen to pursue that course of study, which is likely, given her contribution to fission. She would also have found enormous favour with the Swedish government, this now being a top priority. Her work would have eclipsed that of Siegbahn, 'the small pope', who was principally concerned with the practical aspects of spectroscopy. She would have knocked Siegbahn off his metaphorical perch as ruler of all he surveyed in his Nobel Institute. For all these reasons, Lise would have gained added prestige – not that this would have concerned her unduly – and won the hearts of the Swedish people to boot!

Chapter 31

Lise's Integrity and Hatred of Dishonesty

On 16 January 1946, Lise had told Franck that she did not believe Hahn's description of the behaviour of German astrophysicist Walter Grotrian (1890–1954), a former colleague of hers. But there, 'Hahn is much too thoughtful to be a judge of character'. Heavy sarcasm, on Lise's part! As for Grotrian, 'He is not very clever or deeply thoughtful and his writing to you [Franck] in an attempt to distort the past, is regrettable. It shows a lack of honesty, but I did not trust him. Perhaps it is only a lack of courage in my convictions.'

In fact, Lise had personally remonstrated with Grotrian, in regard to a wartime visit he had made to an astronomical observatory in Tromsø in occupied Norway. 'It remains incomprehensible to me that a fair-minded scientist – and that is what I have always known you to be and valued you for – would consider it an appropriate mission to organize scientific work in an unlawfully occupied country for the benefit of those in power'.[1] In other words, Lise questioned Grotrian's integrity.

In respect of German physicist Wilhelm Westphal (1882–1978), Lise told Franck, 'he was one of the worst people, about whom it is painful for me to think'. At the end of the Second World War 'immediately after the Russians entered Berlin, he wrote an article in the newspaper in which he promoted himself as the protector of Planck and the representative of democracy'. By contrast,

> At the beginning of the Hitler regime, he not only became a Nazi, which one might ascribe to a lack of courage; but he was a convinced Nazi with a big picture of Hitler hanging in his house. And you certainly know that after the 1914 war, he was [such] an ardent democrat and he would have denounced a nationalist colleague and thrown him out of the country.

> If a person adapts his attitude to his respective circumstances and he then tells me he has a good conscience … then I have nothing to add. He has no conscience. It is very regrettable that he got around the naïve Americans, but I hope he was not able to get around you too. Most of the leading Nazis were creatures of Wilhelm Westphal, without any guidelines, without conscience, and without the least feeling for truthfulness.
>
> These people were and are, Germany's misfortune. Perhaps one can do Westphal's children a service, if you consider honestly what a flimsy character he is. Incidentally, Hahn dismissed Westphal with a couple of short words. He is certainly not worth more.
>
> More serious to consider are the appointment of both Hahn and von Laue which divided many decent Germans.

In autumn 1946, the British had decided that the Kaiser Wilhelm Society was to be dissolved and 'started again in Göttingen',[2] which lay within the British zone of occupation. On 11 September 1946, it was renamed the Max Planck Society for the Advancement of Science, with Hahn as its president. Meanwhile, von Laue was appointed acting director of the Max Planck Institute for Physics (formerly the Kaiser Wilhelm Institute for Physics) at Göttingen and titular (nominal) professor at Göttingen University. These were the appointments to which Lise referred.

Lise continued,

> Hahn came here [to Stockholm, to receive the Nobel Prize in person] for two reasons. First that the Germans, particularly from the viewpoint of the Americans, had caused bitter wrongs. He wrote a few words to me before his arrival saying that the Americans were now doing the same to Germany as the Germans had done in Poland and Russia.
>
> Even though I assured him that he could not seriously mean, and cannot have forgotten that 2 million people died in Poland and practically all cultural facilities had been systematically destroyed, he repeated the same words out loud at a meeting with Stern and me, about which Stern was very unhappy. He [Hahn] simply behaved unreasonably; he

suppressed the past with all his might, even though he hated and despised the Nazis.

His second main motive is to bring Germany back to international recognition but because he is neither strong nor thoughtful, he simply denies what is happening, or he trivialises it.

In his first interview for Sweden [i.e. for the Swedes] he said nothing about the past, or [expressed] a wish that Germany should revert to being a legitimate state and be developed as an equal partner in Europe. After a few words about the crisis in Germany he said he was happy that Germany was not blamed for building the atomic bomb and thus be burdened with the senseless killing of so many thousands of people. I tried to make clear to him that he should explain why he would be contented, when Germany had done such terrible things; but he did not go back to that.

Stern said to me, that going around in Germany was the stab-in-the-back story [meaning, presumably, that the German scientists had deliberately 'stabbed the Nazi regime in the back' by holding back the development of the atomic bomb] and now the word is being spread that Germans did not make the atom bomb for reasons of decency.

Naturally, I said to Hahn that he could help Germany by refuting incorrect claims that the Allies knew surprisingly little about the preconditions for an explosive chain reaction, and it was a great disadvantage for Germany when decent people like him resorted to the wrong reasons for justification.

At the time, it seemed to make sense to him, but in all his utterances there is the same tone. Forget the past and emphasise the injustice which Germany is suffering. That I had a part in his busy past – in his interviews – there is nothing. When he speaks of his lifelong work and our long-term partnership, only my name is mentioned [i.e. but not Lise's achievements]. I have had a number of indignant enquiries about Hahn's claims; among others, from Eva von Bahr.

It was very clear to me, that Hahn was hardly aware of his unfriendliness and after his return [from the Nobel

Prizegiving ceremony] he thanked me very naïvely for my 'great friendliness'. Naturally, the reunion with him was somewhat painful, but I was ready for it, no personal debates and to that I held firmly. As well as Hahn, [his wife] Edith looked surprisingly young and unchanged. In Göttingen they now have fewer difficulties according to some reports and they get a big parcel from here every month.

As regards Max von Laue, said Lise, he

> is better able to think than Hahn, but his naïve attitude is not very different from that of Hahn. Perhaps our generation is too old to see things clearly and no longer has the strength to mount a meaningful struggle against the prevailing mental confusion which goes back a hundred years [i.e. anti-Semitism], and in which Nazism found only a horrible expression. It seems to me that there is only an uncertain future for Germany, and for the future of the world. I am supposed to be busy at present because I am preparing some workrooms and have got new fellow-workers. but the doctor has advised me to reduce my workload, and he is probably right.
>
> Give Hertha [Franck's wife] my love I will write to her soon. I have been so happy to know that you all had a happy Christmas together. I hope that you recover from your head cold. Lisa [Franck's daughter by his first wife Ingrid Josefson] and family greet you, your letters are always the best greeting – I have not forgotten you. Look after yourself and keep well. With sincere friendship.[3]

Chapter 32

Lise's Humanity

In a letter to von Laue of 12 November 1946, Lise expressed her concern for the people of Germany, which in the circumstances some might find surprising. 'Liaison with the British occupying power is a good start for a better future for the people,' she declared.

Those who lived outside that country

> make a mistake if they think that we are unaware of the great distress in Germany. But sadly, there is even greater distress in other countries, e.g. Poland and Austria, and so one must give aid as I have seen in [i.e. given by] America and here [in Stockholm] where there are many independent bodies [i.e. charitable organizations]. One wishes, from the heart, to give more help if it were possible. In the last eight weeks, I have sent seven parcels to Germany – among them one to you and one to Hilde [von Laue's daughter by his wife Magdalene, née Degen]. Who knows when they will arrive? Sadly, on Hilde's present, I have just put Tailfingen and no street address, but I have written her a card so that they can make enquiries at the post office. Hahn's coming here has pleased many people and I believe that you would be happy here.
>
> I wish so much that Germany will return to peace, order, and efficiency and I welcome every step that I may contribute. But the whole world faces so many extraordinarily difficult problems that the questions of form and prestige are meaningless, without fully understanding.
>
> I have tried to understand what the ideology and the disgrace of the Nazis has created in the future of Germany.

> I believe one of the relevant causes was that education was neglected and the nurturing of character was forgotten.

Lise referred to German mathematician and Nazi Ludwig Bieberbach (1886–1982) as 'a man who ran a specialised unit, who was considered a scholar, who wanted to cultivate the young but who was unable to have any moral conviction'.

Bieberbach, she said, was someone 'who ran his section very well and worked scientifically but thought nothing about things outside his domain. Such people we had by the thousand and they were, in my opinion, Germany's misfortune'.

By contrast, said Lise, 'In England, university teachers are really a spiritual and moral elite. Science and art are, I believe, no place for mass production [i.e. indoctrination] and it is particularly questionable for science. In art, mass production will have only a minor effect on aesthetic taste, but the uneducated scientist will damage the character of his students'.

'Forgive me, that I say so much, but this matter is close to my heart. I am fortified by a book which you gave me – *Paideia*.'

Paideia, by German classicist Werner Jaeger (1881–1961), describes how the ancient Greeks conceived a notion of the ideal human personality.

> And for me, I was fortunate to be Planck's assistant. Hahn will confirm how often, long before Hitler came, that we had a great human responsibility for our younger fellow-workers; day by day, and in their overall development in everything that we said and did. How are young people in Germany supposed to think normally again and to learn from responsible teachers?[1]

Said Krafft in January 1988,

> Members of the staff of the Institute never went to Hahn with their personal problems, but to Lise Meitner, and if he ever heard about these matters it was, for the most, Lise Meitner who had told him! She was the true life and

soul of the Institute and her motherly care for the welfare of the members of her former staff is expressed in many of her lessons to Otto Hahn … Lise Meitner was the one who could induce Otto Hahn to grant the penniless Fritz Strassmann a support of DM [Reichsmarks] 50 per month from mid-1934, taken from a private fund he [Hahn] had at his disposal for special contingencies. As Strassmann never talked much about his personal affairs, his 'boss' probably did not even realize his need.[2]

Chapter 33

The Peace

As already mentioned, the war in Europe ended on 8 May 1945, and in the Far East on 2 September 1945.

To Eva von Bahr-Bergius on 24 December 1946, Lise wrote of her disillusionment with Hahn. At the Nobel Prize event, and the interviews that he had given in its wake she said, 'I found it quite painful' that he 'did not say one word about me, to say nothing of our thirty years of work together. I am part of the suppressed past'. And, in a rare criticism of Hahn, she concluded, 'I have struggled all these years not to become bitter or distrustful, one must take people as they are. But joy in living suffers with this attempt.'[1]

To her sister Lola Allers, on 29 December 1946, Lise described Hahn as being

> completely permeated with the idea that Germans are being treated unjustly, especially by the Americans which, from a certain point of view is understandable. Less understandable to me, he absolutely suppresses the Nazi crimes, and is therefore led to very wrong convictions. Probably one cannot be such a charming person and also very deep.[2]

In that year, Lise received five nominations for physics (including from Niels Bohr, Max von Laue, and James Franck) and one for chemistry. However, Hulthén reiterated the negative comments that he had made to the Nobel Physics Committee about Lise and Frisch the previous year. The committee and the physics class [of the Academy] 'accepted his [flawed] reasoning', despite Klein's protestations.[3]

Lise now left Siegbahn's Institute and commenced at the Royal Institute of Technology, the Royal Swedish Academy of Sciences' Research Institute for Experimental Physics. Its director was Swedish engineer and physicist Professor Gudmund Borelius. Here, she was provided with her own laboratory, a professor's salary from the Swedish Atomic Committee, and two assistants and one technician. 'The laboratory would receive the equivalent of several hundreds of millions SEK in research grants and Meitner worked, among other things, with beta spectrometers that she bought.'[4] Manna from heaven, in sharp contrast to Manne from Sweden!

Furthermore, there was 'good cooperation with Sigvard Eklund, a colleague of Siegbahn', who occupied the adjacent room,[5] and whom Lise described as 'a very good younger physicist' and a 'fair and pleasant person'.[6] Lise's brief was to create a nuclear physics section: the goal being to produce limitless atomic energy, which for Sweden had now become a top priority.

Meanwhile, in that same year, Frisch returned to England and joined the staff of the Atomic Energy Research Establishment at Harwell, Oxfordshire, of which he subsequently became head of the Nuclear Physics Division.

To James Franck, on 6 January 1947, Lise wrote of von Laue that he was 'better qualified for thoughtful reflection than Hahn', but nonetheless, 'his fundamental attitude is not very different from Hahn's'.[7] This was said in the context of Germans being incapable of considering the suffering of others and acknowledging the harm that they had done.

To Franck, on 16 January 1947, Lise said of Hahn, 'he does not have a very strong character, nor is he a very thoughtful person. He deceives himself about the facts or belittles their importance.' It seemed that for Lise, at long last, the light was beginning to dawn, as far as her view of Hahn was concerned!

Lise described herself as being part of

> the suppressed past. Hahn never, in any of his interviews about his life's work, mentioned our long years of work together; nor did he even mention my name. It is clear to me that Hahn was hardly aware of his lack of friendship, and he wrote to me after his return thanking me completely naïvely for my 'great friendship'.[8]

This is the classic description of someone who is in denial and, in respect of Hahn, Lise was at last coming to the realisation that their friendship was an entirely one-sided affair.

On 31 January 1947, Lise told von Laue that 'she was overworked' and had been 'in bed for nearly three weeks'.[9]

On 28 February 1947, Gerta von Ubisch wrote to Lise from Norway. Since graduating from the Friedrich Wilhelm University she had become a botanist and plant geneticist. Gerta became the first woman to be awarded a doctorate at Heidelberg University, where she taught and became Assistant Professor of Botany. However, because she was of Jewish heritage, she was dismissed from her post in 1933. She subsequently went to live in Brazil. 'As a biologist a tropical country naturally appealed to me. I had always wanted to go to a country where the flora was unknown to me,' she told Lise. Gerta subsequently relocated to Norway, where she was now living with her brother. 'Now I would very much like to know from you how things are with Elisabeth Schiemann' (their mutual friend from university days), she said.[10]

On Hahn's birthday, 8 March 1947, Lise sent presents for both him and his wife Edith and for their son Hanno and his family.[11]

On 1 July 1947, Lise wrote to Gerta von Ubisch in Norway to bring her up to date with events since her arrival in Sweden. But first, she reflected upon 'her loneliness and shyness' when she had first come to Berlin in 1907.[12] As for Sweden,

> It all went smoothly and so I came to be here. At the end of August I wrote to the KWG to tell them that I was in Sweden, that I wished to remain here and asking for my terms of retirement. In reply, I received a few words of thanks for my past work but was told that I should not receive a pension. However, I did receive money from the Stockholm Academy of Science and the use of a room in Siegbahn's Institute.
>
> During the first four years I had no help or assistance and I had to learn again all the small things which I had not done for twenty-five years. I do not need to tell you what that meant! I was a lot better off than you because I had no serious money problems, but I was completely isolated, both as a person and as a scientist, and I felt that I did not belong anywhere.
>
> It is much better now, but how many more years of work can I reasonably expect? The sister, who was once with you

> in Lichterfelde, is my youngest sister and she lives with her husband in New York. Last year I travelled to America: it was a great blessing, after so many years, to be able to see my brothers and sisters who now live in England and America.[13]

On 13 July 1947, said Lise, English colleagues had told her that 'the German physicists are working well. But they are full of self-pity and they are unable to understand what had really happened', i.e. during the Third Reich.[14]

On 4 August 1947, in respect of an invitation that Lise had received from von Laue to visit Germany, she pointed out to him that since the Anschluss her Austrian passport was no longer recognised, and to enter any of the Allied forces' four zones of occupation, permission would be required (i.e. British in the north-west, French in the south-west; Soviet in the north-east, and US in the south-east). Also, she feared that she would experience 'the psychological problems of witnessing the social problems as Germany recovered from the damage of the war'. In other words, this would be too upsetting for her. Lise told von Laue that she sent 'clothes and other used items to Germany through a relief agency in Stockholm'.

In respect of an invitation to Germany, to the 'Physikertagung' – Physics Conference – she said, she had 'two scruples. One is of a technical kind. She had only a Nansen passport'.

The Nansen passport was issued by the Office of the High Commissioner for Refugees under the Protection of the League of Nations in London. Such passports were issued to stateless people and refugees who required travel documents but could not obtain them from a national authority.

'The second is a mental problem.' He, von Laue, 'certainly knows how important it would be for her to see the old friends and to speak with them. But her point of view is different from theirs. Her experience' with Otto and Edith Hahn in Stockholm and with Elisabeth Schiemann in London had 'made her frightened'.[15] In other words, Lise was afraid that by speaking out against their failure to acknowledge the suffering caused by Germans during the Nazi era, she would lose the Hahns and Elisabeth as friends.[16]

On 9 August 1947, Lise told Erwin Schrödinger that 'the great restrictions' in the Swedish budget had 'postponed her research professorship [which she had previously been offered] and the new building. She has settled in three small rooms; has established a department for nuclear physics; and is trying "to make the best of it".'[17]

Lise visited Paris in autumn 1947 for the ceremony to commemorate the death of Rutherford ten years previously, on 19 October 1937. 'On her way back, she passed through Germany and saw the destroyed [city of] Aachen. In Hamburg and Cologne, she saw people waiting for local trains and she was glad that they didn't look too bad and had good clothing.'[18]

In October 1947, Lise declared that she was 'worried about England's loss of power. She was disturbed when she was in England and saw how poor the country had become'.[19]

On 21 December 1947, Lise told Strassmann that 'her sister, Augusta and brother-in-law, Justinian Frisch had moved to Cambridge, UK, to be with their son, Otto Robert Frisch.'[20]

In 1947, Lise received six nominations in physics (three jointly with Frisch, and one jointly with Hahn from de Broglie) and six in chemistry (one of which was from Planck). Hahn received one nomination (jointly with Lise, as above). However, despite the fact that, in physics, none of the other nominees had more than three nominations, Lise was passed over for the Nobel Prize yet again. Instead, it was awarded to English physicist Sir Edward V. Appleton.

In that year, Max Planck nominated Lise once for physics and once for chemistry. Yet even this endorsement from arguably the world's leading physicist failed to sway the committee.

Also in that year, Frisch was appointed Jacksonian Professor of Natural Philosophy at Cambridge and elected to a Fellowship in Trinity College. (He retired in 1972.)

On 10 January 1948, Lise explained to Eva von Bahr-Bergius,

> I personally believe that I cannot live in Germany. From all I see in letters from my German friends, and other things I hear about Germany, the Germans still do not comprehend what has happened, and they have completely forgotten all the horrors that did not personally happen to them. I think I would not be able to breathe in such an atmosphere.[21]

Albert Einstein was more blunt. He had an 'irrefutable aversion' to German public life and would take no part in it, 'simply out of a need for cleanliness'.[22]

On 27 January 1948, Lise declared that she could not understand why Walter Grotrian 'voluntarily joined the German Air Force'. However, she did not 'feel competent to pass a moral judgement. But because she loved the old Germany, she has become very worried about the lack of resistance against the untruths and now she is worried about the Germans again'.[23] In other words, Lise felt that the Germans remained in denial.

On 1 February 1948, said Lise, she had been reading a book 'by Silens [see below] and his opinion about the Nazi era and the background to that time' including the Versailles Peace Agreement; inflation; destruction of the Christian faith; the influence of German composer, Richard Wagner; German philosopher, Johann Fichte; and German philosopher, Friedrich Nietzsche; and the 'Sozialdemokraten and their political power'.[24]

'Silens' was presumably a reference to Lars Gunnar Sillen (1916–1970), a Stockholm chemist and writer, including about science. 'Sozialdemokraten' was the Social Democratic Party, founded in 1863 and banned in 1933 by the new Nazi Government.

On 7 March 1948, Lise referred to the 'Preis der Stadt Wien' (City of Vienna Prize). 'She was very glad about this prize from her native city. She has strong links with Austria.'[25]

On 1 June 1948, to Max Born, Lise fondly remembered 'a musical evening at Planck's home with Planck at the piano and Einstein on the violin'.[26]

What of Fritz Strassmann? When Hahn was detained at Farm Hall, Strassmann became Director of the Chemistry Section of the KWIC at Tailfingen. In 1946, he was appointed Professor of Inorganic and Nuclear Chemistry at the University of Mainz.

The KWIC was to be relocated to Mainz in western Germany and renamed the Max Planck Institute for Chemistry. Strassmann, with the agreement of the now President of the Kaiser Wilhelm Society, Otto Hahn, invited Lise to return to her former position as head of physics, and also to be director of the new institute at Mainz.

On 6 June 1948, Lise explained to Hahn why she could not accept the position at Mainz.

> It would be a similar battle to the one I waged – with very little success – in the years '33–'38, and today it is very clear to me that I committed a great moral wrong by not leaving in '33, because staying had the result of supporting Hitlerism.

> These moral conflicts do not exist today of course, but … my personal situation would not be very different now than it was then. I would not have the trust of my Mitarbeiter and therefore would not be truly useful.'[28]

On 16 June 1948, Hahn replied as follows.

> You speak of the battle you waged. What battle was that? Would you, if you had been in our place, have acted differently from so many of us, namely, to make forced concessions and to be inwardly very unhappy about them? One cannot do anything to counteract a terror regime. How can one constantly reproach an entire people for their behaviour during such times? We all know that Hitler was responsible for the war and the unspeakable misery all over the world, but there must be some sort of world understanding also for the German people.[29]

To introduce a note of reality for a moment. During the Second World War, when the population of Germany was approximately 70 million, a total of about 13,600,000 soldiers served in the army; in the regular police, 651,000 (consisting of Orpo 400,000, Sipo 245,000, SD 6,500); SS paramilitary 250,000; concentration camp staff 22,000; making a total of 14,523,500. This is about 21% of the German population as a whole, or perhaps 25% of the adult population, all of whom were either directly or indirectly responsible for rounding up 'undesirables' for slave labour or extermination. This is to say nothing of the untold number of civilians who enthusiastically joined in the proceedings, for example by violence or by denouncing those neighbours who bravely tried to 'do the right thing'.

On 27 June 1948, Lise elaborated on why she had declined to become head of the physics department at the Max Planck Institute for Chemistry in Mainz, 'where Strassmann is head of the chemical department. She refused because she feared that she would never get the complete trust of her colleagues, owing to her Jewish descent and because she is an Austrian'.[30]

On 7 September 1948, Lise told von Laue that she proposed to visit her brothers and sisters in England and to take part in conferences on nuclear fission at Harwell, Birmingham, and Bristol.[31]

In that year, Hahn nominated both Lise and Otto Frisch for the Nobel Prize in physics. Why this sudden change of heart? Hahn was surely now aware that the proverbial cat was out of the bag, and the whole world had now learned of Lise and Frisch's crucial role in the confirmation and explanation of nuclear fission. The likelihood is, therefore, that he thought it expedient to recognise Lise and her nephew in this way, in order to maintain some degree of credibility for himself.

On 7 November 1948, which was Lise's 70th birthday, she received greetings from the President of Austria, Karl Renner, and from Wolfgang Denk, Rector of the University of Vienna.

On 4 December 1948, the Free University of Berlin was founded, and the former KWIC building became the Otto Hahn Building (which today accommodates the biochemical department).

On 15 February 1949, in response to a communication from Mrs Le Roy Sherman Edwards of the New York City Federation of Women's Clubs, Lise declared that it was 'a great encouragement for her to keep believing that science is an element of unity between the different countries and can contribute towards attaining a higher standard of mutual understanding, without which there can be no peace'.[32]

In that year, Lise, jointly with Hahn, was awarded the Max Planck Medal of the German Physical Society.

On 26 February 1950, Lise reminded von Laue that they had first met in 1907 'when she came to Planck's lecture and von Laue was his assistant'.[33]

On 8 June 1950, Lise expressed her thanks to Paul von Winterstein of the Austrian Legation in Stockholm 'for his valuable help in getting her Austrian citizenship back and the remission of the fee'.[34]

On 3 December 1950, said Lise, 'she had visited Austria for the first time for more than 12 years. "But to my surprise, in spite of many depressing observations, I had a strong feeling of happiness. Vienna is so intimately related to the deepest recesses of mind and feeling belonging to my youth".'[35]

When the occasion demanded it, Lise was not slow to express her opinion. For example, on 7 June 1952, when she was asked to lend her name to a girls' scout troupe in Berlin, she declined, saying that 'of course she has liked walking and climbing since youth, but asks whether that is sufficient'.[36]

On 11 October 1952, Lise was wondering which party to vote for in the forthcoming Swedish elections and reflecting on the fact that this was the first time in her life that she was able to vote in an election.[37]

To Schrödinger's wife Annemarie ('Anny' née Bertel), on 30 January 1953, Lise remembered 'the time 20 years ago when they were sitting in her flat in Dahlem listening to the radio and heard the results of the election which elected Hitler'.[38]

On 30 March 1953, at a lecture given to the Austrian UNESCO Commission in Vienna, Lise spoke from the heart. Said she, 'Science makes people reach selfishly for truth and objectivity; it teaches people to accept reality, with wonder and admiration, not to mention the deep joy and awe that the natural order of things brings to the true scientist'.[39]

On 22 June 1953, Lise wrote to Hahn on a matter which rankled with her deeply.

> Now I want to write something personal, which disturbs me and which I ask you to read with our more than 40-year friendship in mind, and with the desire to understand me. In the report of the MPG [Max Planck Society] there is a reference to a lecture I gave in Berlin (a purely physics lecture) and I am referred to as the 'long-time Mitarbeiterin of our president [i.e. Hahn]'. At the same time I read an article in the [scientific] periodical *Naturwissenschaftlichen Rundschau* by Heisenberg *about the relationship between physics and chemistry* in the last 75 years, where the only mention of me … is as follows: 'Hahn's long-time Mitarbeiterin, Frl. [Fräulein] Meitner'.
>
> In 1917 I was officially entrusted by the directors of the KWI for Chemistry to create the physics section, and I headed it for 21 years. Try for once, to imagine yourself in my place! What would you say if you were only characterized as the 'long-time Mitarbeiter' of mine? [which many might consider to be a fairer and more accurate appraisal]. After the last 15 years, which I wouldn't wish on any good friend, should my scientific past also be taken from me? Is that fair? And why is it happening?[40]

To this, Hahn made no reply.[41]

Another deception was perpetrated by the Deutsches Museum of Science and Technology in Munich, in order to further expunge Lise's name from the record books. When the museum celebrated its 50th anniversary in May 1953, on display was a wooden table on which was placed apparatus allegedly used for the discovery of fission in 1938. Above the table appeared a caption which read 'ARBEITSTISCH VON OTTO HAHN' ('WORKTABLE OF OTTO HAHN'). The workbench was located in a shrine-like alcove and contained in a glass cabinet, reminiscent of the display of sacred reliquaries in mediaeval times.

The workbench table had been saved for posterity by Arnold Flammersfeld, a former student of Lise's at the KWIC. There was no mention of Lise, and Strassmann's name only appeared as if en passant, 'on a marble tablet on the wall behind the table'. Some thirty years later, as if to add insult to injury, the museum put up another sign, far smaller, and stating that Lise had been Hahn's *Mitarbeiterin*.

However, as Ruth Lewin Sime points out, experiments were carried out in three different rooms and there is no indication as in which particular room the table was located. Also, 'in actual experiments, the instruments shown would not have been used on a single table, or even in the same room'.[42]

Hahn had been very much involved with the exhibition and in the 1960s he made 'a brief audiotape to accompany the display'. In it, true to form, he mentioned Strassmann, but omitted Lise. So here yet again, we have Hahn being economical with the truth in order to enhance his own reputation at the expense of others.

Since 1953 various efforts have been made by the museum, under pressure from scientists and historians both in Germany and worldwide, to put matters right.

However, this 'mistake', which can only be described as a deliberate deception, was not corrected until 1991, when the museum revised the display and expanded the text to include the names of Lise and Strassmann.

In his autobiography Hahn stated as follows. 'On the 12th of September 1953, the Otto Hahn Prize for Chemistry and Physics was founded in Munich by the Society of German Chemists and the Association of the Physics Societies of Germany.' When Lise was awarded the prize in 1955, together with German chemist Heinrich Wieland, both were presented with a gold medal and 25,000 Marks. 'There was a great celebration in honour of Lise, and she was moved to tears,' said Hahn. The irony of this would not have escaped her!

On 15 October 1953, Lise described to Hahn the celebrations which had occurred on the occasion of her 75th birthday, eight days previously. In her letter, her tone towards her former colleague was warm. 'It was a good day for me,' she said. Bohr sent her a gramophone, and Walter came to visit, bringing with him a birthday present from Frisch, namely some gramophone records. She had enjoyed 'a big party' and received 'messages from [presumably British governmental] ministers, senior scientists, 120 letters, flowers from London, New York, Vienna'. Her messages included ones from Theodor Heuss, President of West Germany; James Chadwick; and Australian physicist, Marcus Oliphant. Her birthday had also been commemorated in a special programme broadcast by 'RIAS', a radio station broadcasting from the American sector of Berlin.[43]

On 19 January 1954, Lise declared to Franck that when she had visited Cambridge, UK 'she was very impressed by Blackett, not only by his science but also by his personality'.[44]

In Youngstown, Ohio on 15 October 1954, Lise declared, regarding 'women in the field of science' and her own experience as a girl, that it happened 'more by chance than by design that I eventually became an atomic physicist'.[45]

Demonstrating how she kept in touch with her former colleagues, Lise described to Franck on 28 November 1954 how she had met Stern and Pauli in Zürich; the Hahns in Garmisch; and the Schrödingers in Alpbach, where the von Laues 'came for the day'.[46]

On 17 December 1954, Lise told Strassmann that 'her interest in physics has not lessened and she follows the developments'.[47]

In that year, 'the main commanders of the Swedish Armed Forces started to demand obtaining tactical nuclear weapons for Sweden. According to them, it was the only way to preserve the non-engagement of the state which otherwise would have to seek shelter under the atomic umbrella of one of the powers.'[48]

On 18 January 1955, Lise told von Laue that she was often depressed about the Max Planck Institute for Chemistry at Mainz 'because there is no cooperation between chemistry and physics like it was in the old institute'.[49]

On 24 February 1955, Lise described 'the mentality of the Viennese and how people wish to forget sad things. This, she had also observed in Germany'.[50]

On 30 April 1955, Lise declared that 'Mörl is right in thinking that Frisch and she gave the first explanation of uranium fission'.[51]

This was a reference to Anton von Mörl zu Pfalzen und Sichelburg, a lawyer and politician in the Austrian government which had preceded the Anschluss. At the time of the Anschluss, and because of his association with the old order, he was arrested and sent to Dachau, where he remained until September 1940. After the war he held political office in the local government for the Tyrol in Innsbruck. Along the way, he wrote books on scientific subjects.

On 6 September 1955, to von Laue, Lise referred to the numerous honours and acknowledgements which she had received. She was 'full of gratitude'. However, 'she always needs a little time to overcome her embarrassment'.[52]

In that year, said Lise somewhat dryly to her dear friend James Franck, 'It is interesting for me to receive the first Otto Hahn Prize.'[53]

On 7 October 1955, Lise was in Copenhagen for the celebration of Niels Bohr's 70th birthday.[54]

On 4 March 1956 Lise told Franck that she had met Hahn in Mainz at the opening of the new Max Planck Institute for Chemistry 'which is very newly equipped and modern, like most things in Germany'.[55]

On 8 March 1956, Lise stated that she and Hahn were to give lectures in Graz, where 'she proposes to speak on atoms and elementary particles'.[56]

In 1959, at the age of 80, Lise travelled to Germany to attend Hahn's 80th birthday celebrations on 8 March. She also travelled to the USA to Bryn Mawr College, Pennsylvania where she gave lectures; to Washington, DC; to Durham, North Carolina to visit the Francks; to Chicago; and to New York to visit her sisters and their families. Finally, she went to Vienna where she lectured on the subject of 'Memories of Fifty Years in Physics'.[57]

Meanwhile, Lise enjoyed attending musical concerts; repeatedly posed questions to her nephew, Otto Frisch about recent developments in physics; and kept up to date with the scientific journals.

On 18 June 1959, Lise declared 'that Planck and his family represented the finest flower of German civilisation and their friendship is one of the best things in her life'.[58]

On 21 November 1959, when asked, 'Was the uranium-splitting idea your own, or jointly that of yourself and your nephew, O.R. Frisch?' Lise 'confirmed that it was a joint discovery'.[59]

In that year, a new scientific institute was opened at Wansee on the outskirts of Berlin, in the presence of Willy Brandt, the city's mayor. It was given the name the Hahn-Meitner Institut für Kernforschung (Nuclear Research) and is now the Helmholtz-Zentrum Berlin für Materialien und Energie (Helmholtz Centre for Materials and Energy).

In 1960, Lise retired from her research work in Sweden and relocated to Cambridge to be nearer to her nephew Otto Frisch and his wife Ulla (née Blau, a graphic artist from Vienna) and their son, David Anthony ('Tony') and daughter, Monica Eleanor.

Chapter 34

Walter Meitner, Lise's Beloved Youngest Sibling, and His Family

For a biographer, the ideal situation is to meet the subject of the biography in person. However, this was obviously not possible in the case of myself and Lise Meitner. The next best thing would be to meet a relation, but as most of Lise's relatives had emigrated to the USA, this again was a forlorn hope. But there was one other possibility, one other glimmer of hope.

I knew from my reading that Lise had been buried in the churchyard of the Church of St James, Bramley, near Basingstoke in Hampshire, and it therefore occurred to me that there might be a relation of hers living in that county. Accordingly, I looked up telephone numbers for Hampshire on the Internet and, sure enough, there was a single 'Meitner', namely Philip.

With some trepidation, I picked up the telephone, dialled the number, and discovered that the person on the other end of the line was indeed the late Walter's son, Philip. Philip and his wife Anne kindly invited me to their home, and one winter's day in 2020 I set out on the 35 mile journey to Hampshire (the adjacent county to my own county of Dorset). How could I have known that this would be one of the most memorable days of my life?

Having left the motorway, I quickly found myself deep in the heart of the Hampshire countryside; motoring along narrow lanes which had once simply been tracks through the woods. And on the banks at the roadside and beneath the trees were snowdrops.

I kept my eye open to register the occasional passing place, which would come in useful if a vehicle was to approach from the opposite direction. Fortunately, the road was fairly clear. I noticed several familiar signposts; Badger Farm, Oliver's Battery (a reference to Oliver Cromwell), and Romsey Road, for example. These were already familiar to me because I had spent my early childhood in Stanmore, in nearby Winchester. My late mother Jean once told me how she and her brothers would push their bicycles all the way up to the top of Stanmore Lane, prior to setting off for these very locations, Farley Mount being a local beauty spot with wonderful views.

I rang the doorbell. Anne Meitner greeted me at the door and introduced me to Philip. During the course of the conversation we immediately established a rapport. Three of Anne's relatives had been general practitioners; one in Bournemouth, the adjacent town to my own home town of Poole. I myself had been in medical practice until a back injury cut short my career.

Anne told me how, as a child living in Bournemouth, she had seen the sky turn red as Poole burned, after German air raids. Likewise, I remember my parents telling me how they saw the sky turn red as Southampton (9 miles from their home city of Winchester) burned, following the enemy bombing 'Blitz' of 30 November and 1 December 1940.

Anne told me how one of her childhood friends from Poole named June Phillips had been killed by an enemy incendiary bomb, and I recalled being told how the Lagland Street Infants' School, which was within a stone's throw of my former surgery in Poole, had been bombed on 28 August 1940 and partially destroyed. The Meitners told me that they used to keep a boat on Poole Harbour. I can see the harbour from my lounge window!

I had learned from my research that Philip's father Walter had died on 29 June 1961 and been laid to rest in the churchyard of St James's church, Bramley, Hampshire. After coffee, kindly provided by Anne, I asked how it came about that Lise, who had died on 27 October 1968, also came to be buried at Bramley. At the time, said Anne, she and her husband Philip were farming at Sherfield-on-Loddon. However, Sherfield's churchyard was only available for that parish's own parishioners; so she approached the vicar of Bramley, a village about 2 miles distant, and it was agreed that Lise too, should be buried at Bramley. So, the two siblings, who had been so close in life, were finally at rest together.

Philip told me that the Meitners originated from Bohemia-Moravia (which became Czechoslovakia in 1918). His paternal 'Meitner' grandfather, Philipp, wished to study law, but there was no law school in Prague, the Czech capital. Whereupon he opted to study at the law school in Budapest, Hungary. To this end, he was required to become fluent in Hungarian; a feat which he achieved in the space of six months.

In 1873, Philipp married Hedwig Skowran, whose forebears had emigrated from Russia to avoid Jewish persecution. Shortly afterwards, the family relocated to Vienna, Austria, where Philipp established himself in legal practice: the emperor, Kaiser Josef II, having relaxed the laws in regard to Jewish immigration and employment.

Philipp and Hedwig's youngest child, Walter, was born on 15 March 1891. He was therefore twelve years Lise's junior. Walter became a research chemist. In Vienna he found himself living in the same block of flats as aspiring portrait photographer Lotte Graf, whom he married in 1924.

Walter and Lotte's only child, Philip Franz Meitner (born 22 February 1930), became a pupil at the Evangelical School, which was within walking distance of his home in the Leopoldstadt district of Vienna. In the early days, he was accompanied to and fro by his nanny, but later he made the journey on his own, carrying his school satchel on his back.[1]

I asked Philip how he had managed to escape the Nazis. 'A brave Frenchwoman who was a Roman Catholic and a friend of the family, who used to come to the house to teach my father the French language, took a number of children out of Vienna by adding them to her passport and pretending that they were hers,' he replied. 'I was only able to leave Austria because I was on her passport as her child'.

Philip had fond memories of the Frenchwoman holding him tenderly on her knee. She was successful, and the 7-year-old Philip left Germany and arrived in England on 16 June 1938. Philip subsequently learned that the Frenchwoman succeeded in saving two more children in this way. But she was eventually discovered and shot by the Germans.

I was invited to the Meitners' again on 17 March 2020 and on this occasion Philip gave further details of his escape from Vienna. On 16 June 1938, his parents took him to the city's railway station where he was met by the Frenchwoman. She was quite young, he said, probably in her late twenties. He did not know if she was married. During the journey, and realising that Philip was upset at leaving his family, the Frenchwoman sat Philip on her knee and cradled him in her arms.

Having arrived at Calais the pair disembarked from the train and boarded the boat to Dover. From there, they caught a train to London. The journey took place in one day, said Philip.

The Frenchwoman returned to Vienna, leaving Philip in the care of friends of the family: the Frankels, who would now care for him at their home in Wimbledon, as had previously been arranged.

Paul Herzberg Frankel was born in Vienna on 1 November 1903. His father Ludwig (born in Ukraine 1862) was a successful Viennese barrister.

It is likely that Ludwig and Philipp Meitner, Lise's father, had become acquainted as a result of both being members of the legal profession (although Ludwig was more than two decades Philipp's junior).

In September 1939, the aforementioned National Register of citizens of England and Wales was created. (No census was therefore taken in 1941: the census normally being taken in the first year of each new decade.) This register was put to use on 29 September, when identity cards were issued for every man, woman, and child. In the 1939 register, Paul Herzberg Frankel's address is given as 11 Lake Close, Wimbledon, where he lived with his wife Helen Hedwig (née Spizer, born Vienna 1908). His occupation was given as 'Sales Manager Mineral Oils'.

Paul Frankel, a petroleum economist, came to Britain in 1938 from Poland. He worked first with oil brokers and then with Manchester Oil Refineries, of which he became a director.

From now on, Philip would attend the nearby Beltane School, whose co-directors were Dr Ernst Bulova and his wife Ilse. They were both Austrians from Berlin, who had left Germany in 1933 as refugees from the Nazis. The aim of the school was to offer support to thirty refugee children. It was founded on Montessori principles. Maria Montessori (1870–1952) was an Italian physician and teacher who developed a child-centred educational approach to education and learning. The school, accordingly, sought to develop young children's natural interests and activities rather than employing the use of formal teaching methods.

It is not known whether the brave Frenchwoman possessed a French passport or an Austrian passport or both, but either way, adding Philip's name would have been a simple matter. I am grateful to passport collector and expert Tom Topol, who kindly provided me with specimen images of both passports: one issued in France in 1931, and the other at the Austrian Consulate in Nuremberg, Germany in 1936.[2] On the French passport the only particulars requested were 'Name, First Name, and Date of Birth'; on the Austrian passport, 'Name, Age, Sex'.

All the Frenchwoman had to do, therefore, was to enter Philip's details and presumably, instead of entering *his* surname, enter her own. However, a visa would also have been required; so how might this have been obtained?

Following the Anschluss, said Helen Fry, biographer of Thomas J. Kendrick, Passport Officer at the British Consulate in Vienna, 'A memo contained in FO [Foreign Office] 372/3283 [and dated 27 April 1938] from Cresswell at the Passport Office in London stated, "We have had several enquiries about the trick of adding the name of an Austrian child to a British passport".'[3]

This was a reference to British diplomat Jeremy M. Cresswell.

Furthermore, Helen stated that the files of the British Foreign Office contain two examples where a child has been added to a passport of a British businessman or woman in such circumstances.[4] Furthermore, it is highly likely that Philip's visa was issued by Kendrick, or by one of his staff, as will be seen.[5]

Finally, the Meitners showed me a surviving page from Philip's passport, which was evidently not used in his escape. On it, his name was written in longhand on both the passport photograph and on the passport itself. It was issued on 3 June 1938 by the Nazis (the Anschluss having occurred on 12 March), stamped by the Head of Police in Vienna, and it expired on 2 September 1938. Passport expert Tom Topol later told me that 'In Austria after the Anschluss, it was the police departments that issued passports. Philip Franz Meitner's passport is Austrian, and the two stamps on the passport are those of the Head of Police Vienna, as was routinely the case.'[6]

There was an air of mystery about the passport: for the signature was not Philip's handwriting, nor was it the handwriting of his mother Lotte, said Anne. Finally, it evidently played no part in Philip's escape.

In August 1938, two months after the escape of their son Philip, Walter and Lotte also escaped to England. How was this possible?

Said Helen Fry,

> When the noted Austrian black & white portrait photographer Lotte Meitner-Graf [Walter's wife] walked into the Passport Office … Kendrick's secretary Clara Holmes exclaimed in surprise, 'Whatever are you doing here?' Clara knew Lotte and was part of her circle of friends. 'I'm Jewish', she replied with sadness in her eyes. Meitner-Graf [the name Lotte Meitner adopted when she became a photographer] was a close friend and Clara had never realised her Jewishness. It had not been of any relevance until that moment. Clara enabled her to emigrate to England where Meitner-Graf built up a phenomenal career as a renowned photographer.[7]

Kendrick was born in Cape Town, South Africa in 1881. His father John was a US-born merchant and his mother Katherine Reddin was a South African. In 1910 he married Nora Wecke, daughter of a German manager of a diamond mine.

Kendrick, who was fluent in German, French, and Dutch, tried his hand at several occupations: mining engineer, stockbroker, and farmer. During the First World War he served in France in British Army Intelligence Corps and subsequently at GHQ in Cologne, Germany with the British Army of Occupation.[8]

On 1 January 1925, Kendrick, now aged 44, arrived in the Austrian capital Vienna, where he was appointed Passport Control Officer at the Passport Office, located at 6, Metternichgasse.[9] He was also 'Station Chief' for the Secret Intelligence Service MI6 (also known as SIS) at the city's British Consulate.

In April 1938, the British Home Office 'announced that Passport Control Officers could no longer issue temporary visitor's visas to refugees. All visas had to be for emigration proper, and accompanied by a guarantor who vouched that the refugee in question would not be a financial drain on the state'.[10] 'From 2 May 1938 the Consul-Generals would have to ensure that passports bore a British visa for the United Kingdom.'[11]

Said Helen Fry,

> Kendrick preferred to work within the boundaries of British immigration laws, but he became increasingly frustrated by the number of people who could not be helped through legitimate means. He began to issue visas on the flimsiest of evidence and for Jews who did not quite meet the criteria.[12] With pressure from London to limit immigration, Kendrick began to issue false passports.[13]

It is highly likely, therefore, that Philip and Lotte's visas were issued by one of Kendrick's staff, or by Kendrick himself.

On 17 August 1938, only two months after Philip's escape, Kendrick was arrested by the Gestapo for espionage. He was released on 20 August after intervention by the British Foreign Office.

In June 1967, Kendrick, who had the rank of army colonel, visited Lotte's studio at her invitation and had his photographic portrait taken by her – doubtless a little 'thank you' to him for making possible her escape from Nazi Germany.[14]

Walter and Lotte's departure from Vienna took place in the following way. 'One night,' said Philip, 'the British military attaché in Austria turned up at our house in Vienna and informed my father that the British government wanted him to come to England.' Walter was a research chemist, and he was told that a job awaited. An RAF aircraft was waiting at the airport to transport him and his wife Lotte, and he had only two hours to get his stuff together. There was no other way out because the Nazis had forbidden any Jew to leave the country. 'But I think it was Lise that the British government was really interested in,' Philip continued.

On his arrival in England in August 1938, at the age of 47, Walter was provided with a flat in Putney. He continued his scientific studies at Manchester University, returning home at weekends. It was probably through the influence of petroleum economist Paul Frankel, a friend of the family, that Walter subsequently took up a post with ICI (Imperial Chemical Industries), working with dyestuffs, which were his particular interest: he was fascinated with colours. More will be said about Frankel shortly.

Philip Meitner spent his life farming the rich Hampshire countryside. 'But why a farmer?' I enquired. He told me that his maternal grandfather William Graf, who was a lawyer, had owned a small farm on the outskirts of Vienna. Philip used to visit the farm as a little boy, and he loved it.

Philip began by renting a farm at Sherfield-on-Loddon. One day, he was invited to a party in London, and here he met Anne (née Sephton, from Lancashire) who was currently an undergraduate at University College. She subsequently became a Fleet Street journalist. They were married in 1956.

In 1953 a paper by Walter entitled 'Radioactive Isotopes in Roller Printing' was published in the 1953 edition of *Proceedings of the Textile Institute and the Society of Dyers & Colourists*. Meanwhile, in that year, Lotte opened her own photographic studio at 23 Old Bond Street, London under the name Lotte Meitner-Graf.

The Meitners told me that when Lise lived in Stockholm, and latterly when she lived in Cambridge, she often used to visit their Hampshire farm. 'I got the impression that Lise was not very happy in Stockholm,' said Philip.

What sort of person was Lise? 'She was charming, delightful, and self-effacing,' said Anne, 'but interested in everything when she came to the farm. She was particularly interested in the farm's refrigeration units.' Once a physicist, always a physicist, I thought! Lise was a scientist from first to last.

I had noticed from the many photographs that exist that Lise was always immaculately and stylishly dressed. 'She was highly disciplined in her life.' Was she fond of pets? 'No,' said Philip. He himself had a spaniel called Toby.

Was Lise political in any way? 'Definitely not,' said Anne. 'She did not promote feminism, nor did she promote Jewishness or Judaism. She did not bang the drum for either of those two causes.'

'Did Lise smoke in her later years?' I asked, recalling that I had seen a photograph of her holding a cigarette.

Philip smiled. 'Yes, Turkish. Turkish cigarettes were her favourite,' he replied.

The Meitners now showed me some photographs. There was a handsome gentleman attired in military uniform. This was Walter (born 1891), a young officer in the Austrian army at the beginning of the First World War. He served first on the Russian Front and subsequently in Italy. And there was Lise, at the Cambridge home of Max Perutz in 1966, receiving the Enrico Fermi Award (made also to Hahn and Strassmann), as Walter's wife Lotte looked on. Administered by the US government Department of Energy, this was to honour scientists of international stature for their lifetime achievement in the development, use, or production of energy.

The award was presented to Lise by US chemist Dr Glenn T. Seaborg, who had come over specially from the USA for the purpose. In another, Lise was sitting at a desk in her apartment in Cambridge, surrounded by books!

There was a youthful Philip, attired in athletic whites and carrying the Olympic torch, no less. Philip was a pupil at Leighton Park school, Reading, Berkshire, founded on Quaker principles. As already mentioned, the Quakers played an important part in the rescue of Jewish schoolchildren. Philip became the school's athletics champion and fastest runner over the half-mile. When he won his race, Lise herself had been a spectator.

And there was the Olympic torch itself! Because of his athletic prowess at school, said Philip, he was chosen to carry the torch from Slough to Maidenhead Bridge for the 1948 Olympic ceremony. And on his arrival at Maidenhead, the manager of the riverside Skindles Hotel ushered him and his father Walter inside for a slap-up meal: 'a rare treat in those days of rationing!'

A total of 1,688 torches were provided for the journey from the ancient site in Olympia, Greece, to Wembley Stadium, London. It was therefore only the flame that made the entire journey, and not the torch. And every runner was allowed to keep the torch which he or she had carried.

The ideal of the Olympic Movement is to promote peace and a sense of brotherhood and sisterhood throughout the world. I could not help but contrast this with the torchlight processions that the Nazis had held when Hitler had come to power, and which were a feature of the menacing and hate-filled Nuremberg rallies.

There was Otto Robert Frisch, playing the piano in Cambridge during his retirement. 'He dropped the "Otto" when he came to England.' Frisch also composed music. And there was Lise visiting the Meitners' farm, with Philip and Anne, and Walter playing chess with his father-in-law Wilhelm Graf, a Doctor of Law.

Anne showed me the ring that Hahn had given Lise prior to her escape from Nazi Germany. When Lise died it passed to Ulla Frisch, who gifted it to Anne. The ring was originally inset with a single diamond. Anne's engagement ring was set with a sapphire, and a relation had left her another diamond ring, so Anne had Hahn/Lise's ring altered to include the sapphire and the extra diamond. 'At the time, I had no idea of the significance of the ring,' she said. Anne now wears it on the ring finger of her left hand, next to her wedding ring.

Following the exodus of the Meitner family, there remained in Vienna Bertha Graf (born 1873), Lotte's mother, who was by now a widow. She left Vienna for the UK on the very last aeroplane to leave that city before war broke out on 3 September 1939. She arrived at Croydon airport, where she was met by Walter and his family, with whom she lived thereafter.

On the 1939 National Register, Walter, his wife Lotte, and Lotte's mother, Bertha, are recorded as residing at 85 West Hill, Putney, London.

At the outbreak of war, some 70,000 Germans and Austrians who were resident in the UK were classed as enemy aliens and divided into three categories: A, B, and C. Walter was in Category A, and was interned on the Isle of Man, according to a 'Report of Internment', issued by the Manchester Police on 21 June 1940. 'He didn't resent it at all,' said Philip. In fact, there he met many other gifted émigrés, scientists included. On 7 November 1940, however, through the intervention of his nephew Otto Robert Frisch, Walter was released.[15]

Although classed as a 'Female Enemy Alien', the decision of the tribunal was that Bertha, described as 'housewife', should be 'Exempt from Internment'.[16] The same also applied to Lotte.

Chapter 35

Later Years

In Cambridge, despite her retirement, Lise continued to give lectures, both here and abroad, and also to visit her beloved Austria and its mountains.

In late August 1960, Hahn's son Hanno, an art historian who was Lise's godson, and Hanno's wife Ilse (née Pletz), died as the result of a road traffic accident in France.

In 1962, Werner Heisenberg spoke of Hahn's energy, industry, and conscientiousness. But he was even more generous in his praise of Lise.

> Lise Meitner's relation to science was somewhat different. She not only asked 'What' but also 'Why'. She wanted to understand … she wanted to trace the laws of nature that were at work in that new field. Consequently, her strength lay in the asking of questions and the interpretation of experiment.[1]

This was praise indeed for Lise, from the distinguished German physicist and Nobel Laureate!

In some ways, Hahn may be likened to a workman on an archaeological dig, groping around in the desert sand and occasionally finding some artefact or other, which he recognised to be of value yet had little or no idea of what it was, or of how it came to be there – until the archaeologist and site director – i.e. Lise – arrived on the scene and explained it to him.

Had it not been for Lise, it might never have occurred to Hahn to create a team, the purpose of which being to experiment with uranium and bombard it with neutrons; to realise that what he had discovered as a fission product was barium and not radium; to look for krypton as the second fission product. And, of course, it was Lise and Frisch who interpreted these results in terms of theoretical physics, and thus realised the implications, namely that nuclear fission releases vast amounts of energy.

It would be half a century before the Nobel deliberations on the awarding of the 1944 Nobel Prize to Hahn would be made public.

In 1998, Max Perutz, who was awarded the Nobel Prize for Chemistry in 1962, stated as follows.

> Having been locked up in the Nobel Committees files these fifty years, the documents leading to this unjust award now reveal that the protracted deliberations by the Nobel jury were hampered by lack of appreciation both of the joint work that had proceeded the discovery, and of Meitner's written and verbal contributions after her flight from Berlin.[2]

On 19 May 1963, Lise attended an exhibition entitled 'Atoms at Work' in Vienna. Here she was reunited with her friend and former colleague, Sigvard Eklund, now Director General of the Swedish Atomic Energy Agency.[3]

In 1966, Lise, together with Hahn and Strassmann, were jointly awarded the US Atomic Energy Commission's Enrico Fermi Prize, 'for their independent and collaborative contributions' to the discovery of fission. Hahn, typically, had proposed Strassmann alone for the Fermi prize, and not Lise, but he was overruled.[4] Whereas in Germany Hahn had a captive audience longing to shower him with adulation, in the USA and elsewhere there was no doubt as to the vital part that Lise played in the discovery of nuclear fission.

Said Perutz,

> In 1964 the US Atomic Energy Commission invited me to nominate a candidate for the prestigious Enrico Fermi Prize. I nominated Lise Meitner who was by then living in Cambridge. When the news of her prize arrived, she was 87 and too frail to travel to Washington to receive it. Instead, the physicist and Nobel Laureate, Glen Seaborg travelled to Cambridge, and on October 23, 1966, presented the prize to her on behalf of the Atomic Energy Commission at my wife's and my home.[5]

In their later years, Lise and Hahn exchanged complimentary letters with each other, but they both refrained from mentioning the subject of nuclear fission!

In his autobiography, Hahn explained the process of uranium fission, and how he had been unable to believe that he and Strassman had achieved it, until its theoretical basis had been explained to him by

Lise the physicist, who had reached her conclusions after discussing the matter with her nephew Otto Frisch. Now, in a rare moment of humility, Hahn explained how his failure to understand the physics involved, had led him to make erroneous calculations with spurious results.

> Earlier on, instead of subtracting the nuclear charge [i.e. atomic number], I had made the mistake of subtracting the atomic weight of barium from the atomic weight of uranium, thus being led to assume the presence of other fission products besides the barium that was definitely established as present. Meitner and Frisch explained the process by what is known as a droplet model of the atomic nucleus, a model proposed by Niels Bohr. The process that I had called 'bursting' they called 'fission', which became the generally recognized term.[6]

However, in his autobiography, Hahn stated that the Nobel Prize 'had been given to me for the work I had done either alone or with my colleague Fritz Strassmann'.[7] This was arguably Hahn's greatest lie of all.

Lise, who was familiar with the works of William Shakespeare, might have recalled the words of Duncan, in the play *Macbeth*:

> There's no art
> To find the mind's construction in the face;
> He was a gentleman on whom I built
> An absolute trust.

Or the words of Macbeth himself:

> Oftentimes, to win us to our harm,
> The instruments of darkness tell us truths;
> Win us with honest trifles, to betray's [us]
> In deepest consequence.

And yet despite Hahn's increasingly shabby treatment of Lise, which sometimes amounted to frank hostility, she retained a deep affection for him. Perhaps it was a delusion on *her* part to believe that her feelings were reciprocated. Lise's family recognised this, and when Hahn died on 28 July 1968, they kept the news secret from her for fear of upsetting her.

Chapter 36

Lise's Dear Friend Elisabeth Schiemann

As already mentioned, Lise was a student at the Friedrich Wilhelm University when she first met Elisabeth. They developed a deep bond of friendship, but it was not without its ups and downs!

Elisabeth Schiemann was born on 15 August 1881 in Fellin, Livonia (in present-day Latvia). Her father Theodor was a professor of history, married to Emilie (née von Mulert). Her younger sister was Gertrud (born 1883). Neither sister married.

From 1907 to 1912, Elisabeth studied Life Sciences at the Friedrich Wilhelm University, Berlin. This is where she met Lise. Elisabeth became a plant geneticist and Assistant Professor of Hereditary Research at Berlin's Agricultural College. In 1931, she became Visiting Research Fellow at the Botanical Museum in Berlin-Dahlem.

In 1943, Elisabeth became Head of Department of the newly founded KWI for Plant Research in Tuttenhof on the northern outskirts of Vienna. In 1948, the Institute was incorporated into the Max Planck Society.

Elisabeth retired in 1956. Her legacy included genetically improving cereals such as wheat, barley, and rye, thereby increasing crop yields.

Elisabeth died in Berlin on 3 January 1972. She is buried in the churchyard of the village church of St Anne, Dahlem, of which she had been a parishioner.[1] On her grave, the pastor planted a strawberry plant from her former breeding garden.

If friendship is to be measured by the number of letters written, then Elisabeth Schiemann must be counted amongst Lise's dearest friends. For, between 1911 and 1959, in excess of 300 letters and postcards were sent by Lise to her friend. These letters were catalogued and paraphrased by Jost W.B. Lemmerich, who noted that from 1939 to 1945 (i.e. during the Second World War) they were 'often written in a sort of code to prevent the Gestapo understanding them'.[2]

In the following correspondence with Elisabeth (and with Elisabeth's sister, Gertrud), paraphrased by Jost W.B. Lemmerich,[3] Lise revealed her deepest thoughts, fears, and emotions. She also revealed that she had time for other interests, which dispels the notion that she spent *all* of her life in the laboratory! Her letters and postcards also indicate which places she visited, either to attend symposia, to give lectures, to take her holidays, or for occasional periods of convalescence from illness – usually brought about by overwork!

On 9 August 1911 from Vienna, Lise thanked Elisabeth for her postcard and demonstrated her sense of humour by confessing that she herself, was 'lazy with great success and has put on weight, so her career as a jockey is in danger'!

26 August 1912. Lise lamented 'the difficulties' that she and Elisabeth had 'in understanding each other' and explained that 'her pessimistic mood is an expression of her disappointed idealism'.

From Munich on Christmas Day, 25 December 1912, Lise thanked Elisabeth for her Christmas present 'which she has only just unwrapped. She has been with her sister in Dachau and tomorrow she will travel to Garmisch where they will stay for a week. She loves the mountains and especially with snow'. The name 'Dachau' would have entirely different connotations in the years to come.

29 December 1912, Innsbruck. Lise revealed her love of walking in beautiful places. She told Elisabeth that she and her sister and brother-in-law had 'walked a great part of the way from Garmisch to Innsbruck'.

11 April 1914, Erfurt, Germany. Lise indicated to her friend that she would have loved to have had her company, and 'regrets that Elisabeth is not with them because walking is wonderful'.

On 28 July 1914, the First World War broke out. Writing from Vienna on 1 August 1914, Lise told Elisabeth that her younger brother Walter had been called up for military service.

11 August 1914. Lise said that 'her mother's flat is near the railway station and she can observe the departure of the soldiers and their incredible enthusiasm. There is a very great trust in the German fighters. This makes her glad because with a not too small part of her heart she belongs to the Germans'. Lise would not always feel this way.

9 September 1914. Lise wrote in a more sober tone. 'She has seen injured soldiers and she has seen things which she will not forget.'

On 9 August 1915, Lise told Elisabeth that she had decided to work 'as an x-ray nurse'. She described her journey by train from Vienna to Lemberg, where there was a large Austro-Hungarian military garrison 'with 220 crew 50 nurses and ca. [circa] 10 doctors'.

22 August 1915, Lemberg, Poland. Lise described working in the operating theatre where 'their professor is an expert for operations. They have numerous injured Russians and prisoners as staff'.

On that same day, in the post, Lise received a proposal of marriage. The letter read, 'I would like to have the honour of marrying you. I admire you and the other Germans and your wonderful country. I hope you take my offer of marriage seriously. Also, I would like your photograph.' The proposal came from Nikolaos J. Hatzidakis (1872–1942), Professor of Higher Mathematics at the University of Athens, who was also a dedicated Greek patriot and poet. It is not known if Lise replied.[4]

Hatzidakis had married Henriette Olsen from Copenhagen in 1904 and she had borne him two children.[5] During the German occupation of Greece he refused to cooperate with the occupying powers and, in consequence, died of starvation in Athens in the Great Famine on 25 January 1942.

24–26 September 1915. Lise described the difficulties in communicating 'because she and most of the nurses cannot speak Hungarian. The great problem is the bed sores of the wounded soldiers, very often they die in spite of all their care'. For the 36-year-old Lise, this was surely a 'baptism of fire'!

18 October 1915. Lise told Elisabeth that she 'has already made more than 200 x-ray photographs but this is rather an impersonal occupation and she is glad to work in the operating theatre as well. Her professor told her that one of her x-ray photographs had saved a soldier's life because her diagnosis had helped him to perform the correct operation'.

22 December 1915. Lise described 'the fate of a seriously-wounded Bosnian soldier and her feelings about the finality of death'.

28 January 1916. Lise told Elisabeth that her professor had 'proposed her to the rank of a "gagistin".' (German for female form of 'gagist' – a professional soldier.) She will now be 'on the same level of the doctors' with a wage of '600k per month. She dislikes getting paid for her work'. Finally, 'she asks whether Elisabeth is angry with her because she has not written'. This was a constant theme running through Lise's letters. She was always anxious not to offend her friend Elisabeth in any way and thereby jeopardise their friendship.

1 July 1916, Trient, Austria. Lise 'is now sitting in a little forest and could have a feeling of deepest peace if she had not heard the noise of the artillery.' She described 'the wonderful houses and gardens with beautiful trees and flowers', thus revealing her love for nature.

8 August 1916. Lise stated that she 'was in Prague in a Czech hospital for a short time which was very unpleasant for her because everyone spoke Czech, which she cannot understand'.

24 August 1917, Berlin. Lise described to Elisabeth how 'like a child, she longs for a forest and sometimes imagines when walking along a street that at the next turn she will be in a forest'. Surely here Lise was fondly recalling childhood walks with her family in the Austrian Alps.

5 September 1917, Sauerbrunn, Austria. Lise was with her nephew, Otto Robert Frisch. 'She is writing while sitting in the forest among the trees and a little stream is nearby.' One day in the distant future, Lise and Frisch would walk together through a forest in the snow and make a discovery that would change the world.

5 October 1918. Said Lise, 'the end of the war may be near and shall demand heavy sacrifices from Germany and Austria. But she believes that the German culture, the truest and deepest German individuality, is indestructible'.

12 November 1918, Berlin. Lise revealed that she was 'in disagreement' with Elisabeth's parents. However, 'she hopes her friendship with Elisabeth will not be affected by such differences because then she will no longer have a friend'. Although she was never afraid to express herself, Lise valued friendships above almost all else.

17 September 1919. In a postcard to Elisabeth, Lise declared that 'she has had a wonderful holiday' in Sweden, at Sorvik and Fiskebackskil, and had 'extended it as long as possible'.

A year later, on 25 August 1920, Lise described 'a lazy holiday in Hinterstein, Germany, which has a nice landscape with mountains and forests. She refers to the walk she took and the places she had passed. This experience of free nature helps her against the ghosts of the past and the future'. In other words, when she communed with nature, this was a solace for her.

Meanwhile, Lise's career was progressing well. On 27 April 1921, from Lund in Sweden, she described how she had dined with Manne Siegbahn, who had 'given her a room in the institute' where she would deliver a lecture. Siegbahn would one day play an important part in Lise's life.

3 August 1922, Berlin. Lise informed Elisabeth that 'the faculty had given her the *venia legendi*' – the right to give lectures at Berlin's Friedrich Wilhelm University.

14 February 1923. Lise stated that 'the last days were tiring for her because she was at the institute every night'. By her own admission, Lise was a 'workaholic'!

12 August 1923, Füssen, Germany. This 'is a nice town and she had gone for long walks. She visited [King] Ludwig II castle [Schloss] Hohenschwangau and had enjoyed the tour very much. On her way back she saw the "Zugspitze" which reminded her of their walk'. Lise was constantly reminiscing about the pleasures she derived from previous walks in the company of Elisabeth.

9 April 1926, Bozen, Italy. Lise described 'a very cheerful time' spent in her hometown of Vienna, where 'the weather was very fine, many flowers were in blossom and the trees were bright green'.

24 August 1930, Pertisau, Austria. 'During the first week her brother [Walter] was with her. They had taken long walks together.'

10 August 1934, Pinzgau, Austria. Lise, with her excellent memory and always with her pocket diary and notebook to fall back on, recalled that 'she and Elisabeth were at that place 21 years ago'.

13 August 1935, Marebbe, Italy. Lise sent Elisabeth 'a bunch of flowers for her birthday which she had picked herself. She had done a three day hike up the mountains with Dr Esch'.[6] Lise was not only a mental powerhouse, but also a physical one!

28 August 1936, Berlin. Lise had visited Elisabeth's mother 'yesterday evening and Mrs Schiemann was much better than the last time she had seen her. This afternoon Mrs Schiemann, Edith [Hahn] and Gertrud [Elisabeth's sister] met in her garden'.

29 October 1938. Having recently arrived in Stockholm, Lise stated that 'she is still living in a hotel which is better for her because without her furniture she has no option. She must have a room for herself. In the institute people are coming and going in and out of her room which makes it impossible to think'. So much for the 'open plan' offices of today! 'She has to write her notes in Latin which is uncomfortable for her. The Swedish cannot read her Gothic writing. Her Swedish improves slowly, and she can read the newspapers, but speaking and following a conversation is difficult for her.'

27 September 1940. 'It was a special delight for her that Elisabeth had written to her on the 15th. She reminisces about Elisabeth's birthday in 1913 which they had spent together in a forest house at Vorder-Graseck' in Bavaria. Elizabeth was born on 15 August 1881 and was now 59 years of age. Once again, here was Lise revealing just how essential friends were in her life.

9 August 1941. Lise told Elisabeth that 'she returned from her holiday in Dalarna yesterday', and that this 'was her first holiday for three years. It is a nice quiet place and good for walking. The area is full of wild flowers and she missed Elisabeth's expertise. Walking and being alone was good for her'. Elisabeth, as already mentioned, was a botanist.

7 August 1942. Lise asked Elisabeth why she 'has not written to her and is saying that this is not a cheer up for her. She sends her birthday greetings and sends a parcel'. For the sake of her emotional well-being, Lise would prefer Elisabeth to communicate with her frequently and regularly.

16 October 1942, Stockholm. In respect of scientific conferences, said Lise, there was 'nothing of that kind in Stockholm'. There was 'no possibility of discussing scientific problems with colleagues, in any aspects of her subject'.

20 December 1942. A despairing Lise told Elisabeth that she had 'lost all interest in her former profession'.

8 August 1943, Hjortuäs, Dalarna, Sweden. Lise declared that once again she was enjoying the delights of the countryside, which reminded her of her native land. 'The landscape is similar to the Salzkammergut. The forest is full of raspberries, blueberries and cranberries and one can collect them easily.'

25 October 1943, Stockholm. Following a visit by Otto Hahn, said Lise, the two of them had 'said good-bye as better friends than they had ever been in the last years'.

On 21 November 1943, Lise said of Elisabeth and of her sister Gertrud, 'they help threatened friends'.[7] This was a reference to those persecuted by the Nazis. For example, during the course of the war, Elisabeth, an outspoken critic of the Nazi regime, and her sister Gertrud, a musician, hid the Jewish pianist Andrea Wolffenstein (born 1897 in Berlin) and her sister Valerie (born 1891 in Berlin) in their Berlin apartment. Andrea was subsequently concealed for several months by Fritz Strassmann and his wife Maria in their Berlin apartment. Both sisters survived the war. For this, both Elisabeth and Strassmann were recognised by the Yad Vashem Holocaust Memorial as 'Righteous Among the Nations'.

24 June 1944, Stockholm. Lise expressed concern for Hahn's son Hanno, who had had a 'serious operation'. She 'asks whether he is out of danger'.

4 November 1944. Lise stated that 'she has just finished a little (scientific) paper and needs a controlled experiment, but she has not been able to do one for the past three months because the cyclotron has either been in use for other experiments or out of use all together'. Her frustration is almost palpable!

18 March 1945. Lise again demonstrated her caring nature when she told Elisabeth that 'her ardent wish for Gertrud's birthday is that they come through all the air raids unscathed'.

22 May 1946, Washington DC, USA. Lise declared that 'the misfortune the Nazis brought on Germany and the whole world is terrible'.

3 November 1946, Stockholm. In respect of her Swedish scientist colleagues, none of them were 'considering boycotting Germans but often express regret that all they heard from their German colleagues were complaints, and never one word about the grief and misfortune brought upon millions of people all over the world by the Nazis. It makes no impact for all Germans to suddenly declare that they were not Nazis'.

Lise remained active in science, for example, working with project director, Sigvard Eklund, on Sweden's first experimental nuclear reactor, plans for which were approved in spring 1947.

In April 1947, whilst having lunch with Elisabeth Schiemann in London, the subject of anti-Semitism arose. Whereupon Elizabeth retorted that 'there was a great deal of anti-Semitism in England'.[8]

On 1 July 1947, Lise wrote to Gerta von Ubisch as follows.

> Earlier this year, I … met Elisabeth Schiemann in England; she has a post as an additional professor at the University in Berlin. English geneticists had given her an invitation to England for eight months so that she could study the necessary literature for a new edition of her book on the origin of crops ['The Origin of Cultivated Plants', 1932]; these sources were not available in Germany. She was very happy about this stay in England.[9]

On 4 August 1947, Lise told von Laue, in respect of the Hahns and Elisabeth Schiemann, that she was 'ready to consider any honest [i.e. honestly intended] viewpoint and if I cannot share it, that has nothing to do with my friendship'. However, she did not look at problems '*only* from the German point of view', and for this reason, her friendship with Hahn and Elisabeth appeared to be under strain. Nonetheless, she said, 'Please understand I do not wish to lose my friends because of the pressure on friendship brought about by the burdens of the day'.[10] This ability of Lise to compartmentalise, and to remain friends with those whose core beliefs were diametrically and indeed violently opposed to her owns, is difficult to understand. Perhaps a dread of losing friends lay at the back of her mind.

11 August 1947, Hjortuäs, Dalarna. The indefatigable Lise informed Elizabeth that in April she had been to London, Liverpool, Manchester, Cambridge, and Harwell in the UK to visit Institutes and to talk to English colleagues. At the beginning of May she was in Finland to lecture in Abo and Helsingfors. At the end of May she was in Lund.

3 April 1948, Stockholm. Lise said poignantly that she knew 'quite well what scientific isolation is because she has lived with it for nearly ten years'.

On 20 October 1952, Lise stated that she had seen 'Gertrud and Elisabeth Schiemann at Innsbruck and they had a nice day together and had understood each other much better, as they used to'.[11] This probably meant that the three friends had not discussed the war; a subject about which they disagreed.

10 August 1953, Plansee, Germany. Lise 'has had unexpected visitors and they have made a tour by car to the area where she and Elisabeth walked nearly 40 years ago to the day. She sends her birthday greetings'. Lise rejoiced in keeping these precious memories of Elisabeth fresh in her mind.

17 April 1954, Stockholm. Lise told Elisabeth that 'she reads a weekly English paper and a monthly German one as well as the Swedish ones'. She had already learned Latin, as previously mentioned.

28 February 1956. Lise recalled how 'in the old days she used to learn things about biology and botany from Elisabeth'.

10 August 1956. Lise expressed concern for her former colleague Strassmann. She had 'talked with Strassmann at length. She is not certain if he is totally happy in Mainz'.

23 October 1956. Lisa wondered 'why Elizabeth believes she [Lise] is – or was – angry with her', and she assured her friend that 'She never

was. She is only sometimes sorry that the distance between them in both place and time [is so great]'.

23 December 1956. A doleful Lise told Elisabeth that 'she will spend Christmas evening alone with only her Swedish maid, but without her family. It will be the first time since 1939'.

24 February 1957. Lise declared that 'the loyalty among the scientists is very bad', by which she meant that they all tend to stick together.

> The Swedish have a saying 'royal Swedish jealously' but this makes nothing better. If she has a question, she asks Otto Robert [Frisch]. She has a comfortable room at the institute, and there is a good library. Dr Eklund is very helpful but she has no chance to discuss scientific problems. It is an institute with a [atomic] reactor and she is not interested in the technical problems.

On 30 July 1957, from Bezau, Austria. Her brother Walter was with her 'and they are sitting on the grass'.

On 9 January 1959, from London. Lise had visited her nephew Frisch, his wife Ulla and the children, Monica and Tony. 'They are charming.'

On 20 July 1959, from Kitzbühel, Austria. Lise described her trip to the USA, and how she had spent time with the Franck family at Durham, North Carolina and it was 'a great pleasure which she always feels [when] in contact with Franck's wonderful personality'.

Summary

These letters give a unique insight into Lise's personality and dispel the notion that she was permanently incarcerated in her scientific laboratory. They show the joie de vivre that she experiences, especially when in communication with her dear friend Elisabeth Schiemann.

The letters also say a great deal about Lise's musical tastes – not surprisingly Austrian composers are well represented – and literary tastes. On 29 December 1938 from Kungälv, Sweden, she told Elisabeth that 'to her, music is the comfort of undestroyable value'. And she described attending 'a performance of Brahms's Quintet for Clarinet'.

On 12 March 1944 from Stockholm, Lise sent Elisabeth birthday greetings with a delightful reminiscence. She 'remembers the time 30 years ago when – on Mrs Schiemann's birthday – they did a performance of Haydn's Children's Symphony in children's clothes, and flowers in their hair'. She had been to a concert 'to hear the Amadeus Quartet'.

21 March 1956. Lise 'listens to a lot of good music, especially chamber music. Yesterday, Don Giovanni was on the radio from Glyndebourne under the [German] conductor, Fritz Busch: a performance from 1936'.

29 October 1957. Lise had attended 'a nice concert given by the Quartetto di Roma'. However, 'she had seen a performance of Iphigenie which was very bad'. Lise, as a musician herself, was not uncritical of musical performances.

On 24 March 1958, Lise told Elisabeth's sister Gertrud Schiemann that she had 'sent her a book about Kathleen Ferrier as a birthday present. For her it was always a special experience to listen when Mrs Ferrier was singing'. (Kathleen Ferrier (1912–1953) was an English contralto.)

Lise's letters to Elisabeth indicate that she read widely. On 28 December 1913, from Vienna, she declared that she was 'alone and was reading a novel by Lagerlöf and it takes her back 8-10 years'.

On 22 December 1915, 'she mentions a fairy-tale by Grimm, how a doctor outwitted death'.

On 1 July 1937, she told Gertrud that she was 'reading a book by Albert Schweitzer about culture and ethics, but she is not quite satisfied with his views'. Here again, we see Lise exercising her critical faculties, and in no way in awe of the great man!

On 21 February 1941, Lise quoted a profound verse by German writer and statesman Johann W. von Goethe which, when translated, reads 'Inventing yourself is beautiful; but happy to have recognised something found by others, do you call it less yours?'

24 June 1941. Lise told Elisabeth that she had read Austrian prehistorian Professor Oswald Menghin's 'book about the Stone Age'.

On 21 March 1956, from Stockholm, Lise sent birthday greetings to Gertrud and quoted 'a sentence by Goethe to an old man' which reads in translation, 'I have enough, it remains an idea and love'.

Chapter 37

The Death of Lise

Lise died on 27 October 1968 in a Cambridge nursing home, aged 89. Despite being a cigarette smoker, and one who was exposed to radiation for many years, she had outlived the following persons: Enrico Fermi (died 1954); Albert Einstein (died 1955); Irène Curie (died 1956); Max von Laue (died 1960); her beloved younger brother, Walter (died 1963); Niels Bohr (died 1962); and James Franck (died 1964).

Lise is buried in the churchyard of the Church of St James, Bramley, Hampshire. Only family members were in attendance. There were no eulogies – presumably at her request.

On her tombstone are inscribed the words:

LISE MEITNER

1878–1968
A physicist
who never lost
her humanity

They were composed by her nephew, Otto Frisch.

Epilogue

Lise's life and work are not defined by the failure of the Nobel Foundation to award her a Nobel Prize, or by this gross miscarriage of justice. After all, there have been many such similar lamentable omissions in the past. What does define her, apart from her consummate ability and many noteworthy scientific accomplishments, is her gracious behaviour, humanity, and compassion: always striving to see the best in people, and to offer practical help and advice to those in need, on many occasions despite her own reduced circumstances.

In any event, Lise received numerous other awards and honorary doctorates from more enlightened institutions. So, when the history books are written, and Hahn and Strassmann are mere footnotes, Lise (and Frisch) will be remembered as being the brains behind the discovery of nuclear fission.

Lise was respected not only for her scientific brilliance – by Einstein, Planck, Bohr, and all the great physicists of the day – but also as someone who cared deeply for others and for the state of the world. Consequently, she inspired such love and devotion from friends and colleagues that they were willing to risk their own lives to save her in her time of crisis.

In 1970, an impact crater on the moon was named the 'Meitner Crater'. This was on the far side of the moon and therefore out of sight from Earth. The irony of this would not have been lost on Lise, that Hahn, once he had made full use of her, would have preferred her to become invisible.

In 1982, a new element (Z=109) was created at the GSI Helmholtz Centre for Heavy Ion Research at Darmstadt, Germany. It was named 'Meitnerium'. Its discoverer, German physicist Peter Armbruster, named it for Lise Meitner, as a form of restitution for the injustice that she had experienced in Germany.

On 17 December 1956, 'at the behest of Max von Laue', a plaque by German artist and sculptor, Richard Scheibe was placed on the first floor of the Otto Hahn Building (formerly the KWIC) of the Free University of Berlin. The plaque reads '"In this building, formerly the Kaiser Wilhelm Institute for Chemistry, Otto Hahn and Fritz Strassmann discovered nuclear fission in December 1938". This discovery opened new paths for the study of material and space and placed the energy of the atom's nucleus in the hands of mankind'.

'In 1997 the Institute for Biochemistry at the Free University added the following plaque beside the outside one, "Lise Meitner, co-discoverer of nuclear fission, worked in this building from 1913–1938, as did Max Delbrück, one of the pioneers of molecular genetics, assistant to Ms. Meitner from 1932–1937"'. Justice, to some extent, had been done.

'The Otto Hahn Building also houses a bust of Lise by German sculptor Emy Röder, which is located on the fourth floor next to the auditorium bearing Lise's name'.[1]

Appendix 1

Relevant Nobel Prize Winners

The Nobel Prize in Physics 1954

Divided equally between Max Born 'for his fundamental research in quantum mechanics, especially for his statistical interpretation of the wavefunction' and Walther Bothe, 'for the coincidence method and his discoveries made therewith'.

The Nobel Prize in Physics 1951

Awarded jointly to Sir John Douglas Cockcroft and Ernest Thomas Sinton Walton, 'For their pioneer work on the transmutation of atomic nuclei by artificially accelerated atomic particles.'

The Nobel Prize in Chemistry 1951

Awarded jointly to Edwin Mattison McMillan and Glenn Theodore Seaborg, 'for their discoveries in the chemistry of the transuranium elements'.

The Nobel Prize in Physics 1948

To Patrick Maynard Stuart Blackett, 'for his development of the Wilson cloud chamber method, and his discoveries therewith in the fields of nuclear physics and cosmic radiation'.

The Nobel Prize in Chemistry 1944

To Otto Hahn, 'for his discovery of the fission of heavy nuclei'.

The Nobel Prize in Chemistry 1943

To George de Hevesy, 'for his work on the use of isotopes as tracers in the study of chemical processes'.

The Nobel Prize in Physics 1938

To Enrico Fermi, 'for his demonstrations of the existence of new radioactive elements produced by neutron irradiation, and for his related discovery of nuclear reactions brought about by slow neutrons'.

The Nobel Prize in Chemistry 1936

To Petrus (Peter) Josephus Wilhelmus Debye, 'for his contributions to our knowledge of molecular structure through his investigations on dipole moments and on the diffraction of X-rays and electrons in gases'.

The Nobel Prize in Physics 1935

To James Chadwick, 'for the discovery of the neutron'.

The Nobel Prize in Chemistry 1935

Awarded jointly to Frédéric Joliot and Irène Joliot-Curie, 'in recognition of their synthesis of new radioactive elements'.

The Nobel Prize in Physics 1933

Erwin Schrödinger and Paul Adrien Maurice Dirac, 'for the discovery of new productive forms of atomic theory'.

The Nobel Prize in Physics 1932

Werner Karl Heisenberg, 'for the creation of quantum mechanics, the application of which has, inter alia, led to the discovery of the allotropic forms of hydrogen'.

The Nobel Prize in Chemistry 1931

Awarded jointly to Carl Bosch and Friedrich Bergius, 'in recognition of their contributions to the invention and development of chemical high pressure methods'.

The Nobel Prize in Physics 1929

To Prince Louis-Victor Pierre Raymond de Broglie, 'for his discovery of the wave nature of electrons'.

The Nobel Prize in Chemistry 1929

Jointly to Arthur Harden and Hans Karl August Simon von Euler-Chelpin, 'for their investigations on the fermentation of sugar and fermentative enzymes'.

The Nobel Prize in Chemistry 1926

To Thé Svedberg, 'for his work on disperse systems'.

The Nobel Prize in Physics 1925

Awarded jointly to James Franck and Gustav Ludwig Hertz, 'for their discovery of the laws governing the impact of an electron upon an atom'.

The Nobel Prize in Physics 1924

To Karl Manne Georg Siegbahn, 'for his discoveries and research in the field of X-ray spectroscopy'.

The Nobel Prize in Physics 1923

To Robert Andrews Millikan, 'for his work on the elementary charge of electricity and on the photoelectric effect'.

The Nobel Prize in Physics 1922

To Niels Henrik David Bohr, 'for his services in the investigation of the structure of atoms and of the radiation emanating from them'.

The Nobel Prize in Chemistry 1922

To Francis William Aston, 'for his discovery, by means of his mass spectrograph, of isotopes, in a large number of non-radioactive elements, and for his enunciation of the whole-number rule'.

The Nobel Prize in Physics 1921

To Albert Einstein, 'for his services to Theoretical Physics, and especially for his discovery of the law of the photoelectric effect'.

The Nobel Prize in Chemistry 1921

To Frederick Soddy, 'for his contributions to our knowledge of the chemistry of radioactive substances, and his investigations into the origin and nature of isotopes'.

The Nobel Prize in Physics 1918

To Max Karl Ernst Ludwig Planck, 'in recognition of the services he rendered to the advancement of Physics by his discovery of energy quanta'.

The Nobel Prize in Chemistry 1918

To Fritz Haber, 'for the synthesis of ammonia from its elements'.

The Nobel Prize in Physics 1915

Awarded jointly to Sir William Henry Bragg and William Lawrence Bragg, 'for their services in the analysis of crystal structure by means of X-rays'.

The Nobel Prize in Physics 1914

To Max von Laue, 'for his discovery of the diffraction of X-rays by crystals'.

The Nobel Prize in Chemistry 1914

To Theodore William Richards, 'in recognition of his accurate determinations of the atomic weight of a large number of chemical elements'.

The Nobel Prize in Chemistry 1911

To Marie Curie, née Sklodowska, 'in recognition of her services to the advancement of chemistry by the discovery of the elements radium and polonium, by the isolation of radium and the study of the nature and compounds of this remarkable element'.

The Nobel Prize in Chemistry 1908

To Ernest Rutherford, 'for his investigations into the disintegration of the elements, and the chemistry of radioactive substances'.

The Nobel Prize in Physics 1906

To Joseph John Thomson, 'in recognition of the great merits of his theoretical and experimental investigations on the conduction of electricity by gases'.

The Nobel Prize in Physics 1904

To Lord Rayleigh (John William Strutt), 'for his investigations of the densities of the most important gases and for his discovery of argon in connection with these studies'.

The Nobel Prize in Chemistry 1904

To Sir William Ramsay, 'in recognition of his services in the discovery of the inert gaseous elements in air, and his determination of their place in the periodic system'.

The Nobel Prize in Physics 1903

Divided, one half awarded to Antoine Henri Becquerel, 'in recognition of the extraordinary services he has rendered by his discovery of spontaneous radioactivity'; the other half jointly to Pierre Curie and Marie Curie, née Sklodowska, 'in recognition of the extraordinary services they have rendered by their joint researches on the radiation phenomena discovered by Professor Henri Becquerel'.

The Nobel Prize in Chemistry 1903

To Svante August Arrhenius, 'in recognition of the extraordinary services he has rendered to the advancement of chemistry by his electrolytic theory of dissociation'.

The Nobel Prize in Chemistry 1902

To Hermann Emil Fischer, 'in recognition of the extraordinary services he has rendered by his work on sugar and purine syntheses'.

The Nobel Prize in Physics 1901

To Wilhelm Conrad Röntgen, 'in recognition of the extraordinary services he has rendered by the discovery of the remarkable rays subsequently named after him'.

Appendix 2

Places From Which Lise Sent Letters or Postcards, 1907–1959

This indicates how widely Lise travelled. (Derived from Detailed Catalogue of Lise Meitner's Papers, compiled by Jost W.B. Lemmerich, courtesy of Churchill College, Cambridge. With thanks to Bernard C. Burgess.)

1912	Jan	Vienna (Austria)
	Aug	Berlin (Germany)
	Aug	Vienna
	Dec	Landshut (Austria)
	Dec	Munich (Germany)
	Dec	Innsbruck (Austria)
1913	Jan	Bad Aussee (Austria)
	Mar	Vienna
	Apr	Vienna
	Dec	Vienna
1914	Jan	Berlin
	Mar	Ingolstadt (Germany)
	Apr	Essen (Germany)
	Apr	Erfurt (Germany)
	Jul	Passau (Germany)
	Aug	Vienna
	Dec	Vienna
1915	Apr	Vienna
	Aug	Lemberg (Poland)
	Nov	Vienna
	Nov	Lemberg (Poland)
1916	Mar	Berlin
	Apr	Vienna
	Jun	Trient (Austria)

	Jul	Innsbruck
	Jul	Vienna
	Aug	Lublin (Poland)
1917	Apr	Vienna
	Aug	Berlin
	Sep	Sauerbrunn (Austria)
	Sep	Vienna
	Dec	Vienna
1918	Aug	Vienna
	Aug	Eggenburg bei Graz (Austria)
	Sep	Berlin
	Dec	Vienna
1919	May	Vienna
	Aug	Fiskebackskil (Sweden)
	Aug	Sorvik (Sweden)
	Sep	Berlin
	Dec	Vienna
1920	Aug	Hinterstein (Germany)
	Dec	Vienna
1921	May	Lund (Sweden)
	Sep	Weimar, Jena (Germany)
1922	Apr	Weserbergland (Germany)
	Jul	Berlin
	Aug	Bavaria
	Sep	Hindelang (Germany)
	Dec	Vienna (Austria), Bruenn (Brno) (Czechoslovakia)
1923	Jan	Berlin
	Aug	Füssen (Germany)
	Aug	Semmering (Austria)
1924	Apr	Vienna
	Aug	Baden bei Wien (Austria)
	Sep	Mittenwald (Germany)
	Dec	Vienna
1925	Jun	Vienna
	Aug	Seeboden (Austria)
1926	Apr	Bozen (Italy)
	Aug	Grins (Austria)
1927	Aug	Augsburg (Germany)

	Aug	Tscheppasee (Switzerland)
	Sep	Silvanaplana (Switzerland)
	Oct	Berlin
1928	Apr	Heppenheim (Germany)
	Jul	Cambridge/London (UK)
	Aug	Douglashuette (Austria)
1929	Jan	Breitenstein am See (Switzerland)
	Apr	Bozen
	Aug	Semmering (Austria)
	Sep	Como (Italy)
1930	Aug	Pertisau (Austria)
1931	Sep	Vienna
	Oct	Rome, Venice, Bologna, Naples, Sorrento (Italy)
1932	Jun	Laengenfeld, Obergurgl (Austria)
	Jul	Edinburgh (UK)
	Sep	Berlin
1933	Jun	Vienna
	Jun	Zürich (Switzerland)
	Aug	Hamburg (Germany)
	Aug	Gothenburg (Sweden), Copenhagen (Denmark)
	Sep	Merkstrand (Sweden)
	Dec	Vienna
1934	Aug	Wald im Pinzgau (Austria)
	Sep	Leningrad, Moscow (USSR), with Hahn
1935	Jan	Vienna
	Jul	Marebbe (Italy)
	Jul	Vienna
	Aug	Salzburg (Austria)
	Dec	Vienna
1936	Aug	Vienna
	Aug	Gardena (Italy)
	Aug	Berlin
	Dec	Vienna
1937	Aug	Sulden (Italy)
	Sep	Copenhagen
	Dec	Vienna
1938	Aug	Kungälv (Sweden)
	Oct	Stockholm

	Nov	Gothenberg (Sweden), Copenhagen (Denmark)
	Dec	Kungälv
1939	Mar	Copenhagen
	Apr	Stockholm
	Jun	Stockholm
	Jul	Cambridge/London
	Aug	Stockholm
	Dec	Copenhagen
1940	Mar	Stockholm
	Sep	Stockholm

1941 to 1944 there are regular letters of a personal nature from Stockholm to Elisabeth Schiemann.

1946	May	Washington DC (USA)
	Nov	Stockholm
1947	Feb	Stockholm
	April	London, Liverpool, Manchester, Cambridge, Harwell (UK)
	May	Finland
	May	Lund
1948	Mar	Switzerland
	Mar	Trondheim (Norway)
	Apr	Brussels (Belgium) for Solvay Conference
	May	Göttingen (Germany)
	July	Storlien (Sweden)
1949	Jan	London, Harwell, Birmingham, Bristol, Oxford, and Brussels
	Mar	Stockholm
	Aug	Basel (Switzerland), Como (Italy), Bonn, Silvaplana (Germany)
1950	Mar	Stockholm
	Jun	Stockholm
	Jul	Hintertux (Austria)
	Dec	London
1951	Mar	Stockholm
	May	Stockholm
	Jul	Gries (Austria)

	Sep	Stockholm
	Nov	Stockholm
	Dec	London
1952	Mar	Stockholm
	Jul	Stockholm
	Aug	Seefeld (Austria)
	Oct	Stockholm
	Dec	England
1953	May	Berlin
	May	Stockholm
	Aug	Plansee (Germany)
	Nov	Stockholm (75th birthday)
1954	Jan	Cambridge
	Feb	Stockholm
	July	Lech (Austria), Florence, Perugia, Assisi (Italy)
	Dec	Stockholm
1955	Mar	Stockholm
	Jun	London, Cambridge (UK), Chartres (France), Frankfurt, Marburg (Germany), Fiskaebackskil (Sweden)
	Aug	Stockholm
	Nov	Stockholm, Lund
1956	Feb	Stockholm
	Mar	Stockholm
	Aug	Berlin, Cologne (Germany)
	Oct	Stockholm
	Oct	Cambridge, London
	Dec	Stockholm
1957	Feb	Stockholm
	Mar	Stockholm
	Apr	Bozen
	Jul	Bezau (Austria)
	Aug	Lindfield (UK)
	Sep	Amsterdam (Holland)
	Dec	London
1958	May	Badenweiler (Germany)
	Jun	Stockholm
	Jul	London

	Aug	Baden (Germany)
	Dec	Stockholm
1959	Jan	London, Cambridge
	Feb	Stockholm
	Mar	Berlin, Göttingen
	Apr	Ardmore, Washington, DC, New York, Durham, Chicago (USA)
	Jul	Kitzbühel (Austria), Zürich (Switzerland)
	Sep	Stockholm
	Oct	Berlin
	Oct	Stockholm

Appendix 3

Lise Meitner's Berlin Abodes

1908 Kochstrasse 74, SW 68
1909 Kantstrasse 19, Charlottenburg
1911 Kantstrasse 141, Charlottenburg
1912 Dahlmannstrasse 15, Charlottenburg
1914 Mommsenstrasse 22, Charlottenburg
1921 Zietenstrasse 15, Lichterfelde
1926 Gosslerstrasse 29, Dahlem
1932 Zietenstrasse 2, Lichterfelde
1938 Thielalle 67, Dahlem

The last address, Thielalle 67, was the house of the Director of the KWI, the use of which Otto Hahn had given up. Lise Meitner dwelt there in a spacious apartment on the first floor.

Based on Keiser, Vera, *Radiochemie, Fleiss und Intuition: Neue Forschungen zu Otto Hahn* (Radiochemistry, Diligence and Intuition: New Research on Otto Hahn), GNT-Verlag, Diepholz and Berlin, 2018.

Appendix 4

The Kaiser Wilhelm Institutes

By the year 1938, nine Kaiser Wilhelm Institutes had been created in Dahlem (and others elsewhere). Specialities included Experimental Therapy, Biology, Fibre Chemistry, Metals Research, Entomology, Silicate Research, Comparative Public Law and International Law, Human Genetics and Eugenics, Cell Physiology.

Notes

Abbreviations

BSC Bohr Scientific Correspondence, Niels Bohr Archive, Copenhagen.

FP James Franck Papers, Joseph Regenstein Library, University of Chicago.

MC Meitner Collection, Churchill College Archives Centre, Cambridge.

OHN Otto Hahn Nachluss, Archiv zur Geschichte der Max-Planck-Gessellschaft, Berlin.

Introduction

1. Rossiter, Margaret W., 'The Matilda Effect' (*Science*, 1 May 1993).
2. Gage, Matilda Joslyn, 'Woman as an Inventor' (*North American Review*, Volume 136, Number 318, May 1883), pp. 478–489.

Chapter 2: Early Years in Vienna

1. Rife, Patricia, *Lise Meitner and the Dawn of the Nuclear Age*, p. 6.

Chapter 3: Lise's Correspondence: An Invaluable Resource

1. In this narrative, some of Lemmerich's translations of Lise Meitner's correspondence have been slightly altered, but only for clarity.
2. Lemmerich, Jost W.B., Detailed Catalogue of Lise Meitner's Papers at Churchill Archive Centre, Volume I: 'Correspondence with Colleagues and Friends 1907–1956'.
3. Ibid., p. vi.

Chapter 4: The University of Vienna

1. Frisch, Otto, 'Lise Meitner, 1878–1968', Biographical Memoirs of Fellows of the Royal Society, London 16 (1970), p. 406.
2. Meitner, Lise, 'Heat Conduction in an Inhomogenous Body', Physical Institute of Vienna, IIa, Bd. 115, February 1906, pp. 125–137.

Chapter 5: The Friedrich Wilhelm University, Berlin

1. Meitner, Lise, 'Max Planck als Mensch', *Naturwissenschaften*, Volume 45, 1958, pp. 406–407.
2. Reed, Terence James ('Jim'), formerly Taylor Professor of the German Language and Literature at Queen's College, Oxford to Bernard Burgess, 1 May 2020.
3. Meitner to Gerta von Ubisch, 1 July 1947 (MC).
4. Gerta von Ubisch to Meitner, 28 February 1947.
5. Meitner, Lise, 'Lise Meitner Looks Back', *IAEA Bulletin*, Volume 6 (1), pp. 4–12.

Chapter 6: Atomic Theory: Elements, Atoms, Radioactivity

1. Helmenstine, Anne Marie, PhD, 'List of Naturally Occurring Elements', ThoughtCo, Feb. 11, 2020, thoughtco.com/how-many-elements-found-in-nature-606635.
2. Rife, Patricia, *Lise Meitner and the Dawn of the Nuclear Age*, p. 28.
3. Stevenson, A., and Waite, M., *Concise Oxford English Dictionary*.
4. Ibid.

Chapter 7: The Collaboration Between Otto Hahn and Lise Meitner

1. Rife, Patricia, *Lise Meitner and the Dawn of the Nuclear Age*, pp. 381–387.
2. Hahn, Otto, *My Life*, p. 202.
3. Hoffmann, Klaus, *Otto Hahn: Achievement and Responsibility*, p. 35.
4. Hahn, Otto, *My Life*, pp. 64–65.
5. Hoffmann, Klaus, op. cit., p. 35.
6. Hahn, Otto, *My Life*, p. 202.
7. Meitner, Lise, 'Lise Meitner Looks Back', *IAEA Bulletin*, Volume 6 (1), p. 5.
8. Rife, Patricia, op. cit., p. 38.

Chapter 8: The Kaiser Wilhelm Institute for Chemistry, Berlin

1. Sime, Ruth Lewin, *Lise Meitner: A Life in Physics*, p. 144.
2. Rife, Patricia, *Lise Meitner and the Dawn of the Nuclear Age*, p. 37.
3. Frank, Philipp, *Einstein: His Life and Times*, p. 139.
4. Hahn, Otto, *My Life*, p. 88.
5. Ibid., p. 89.

Chapter 9: War and After

1. Hahn, Otto, *My Life*, p. 122.
2. Meitner to Hahn, 14 March 1915 (OHN).
3. In Krafft, Fritz, 'Lise Meitner: Her Life and Times', *Zeitschrift für Angewandte Chemie*, International Edition, Volume 17, November 1978, p. 830.

Chapter 10: The Years 1920 to 1934

1. Lemmerich, Jost W.B., Volume I: 'Correspondence with Colleagues and Friends 1907–1956', p. 350.
2. Weart, Spencer, 'The Discovery of Fission and a Nuclear Physics Paradigm', in William Shea (editor), *Otto Hahn and the Rise of Nuclear Physics* (Dordrecht and Boston, Reidel, 1983), p. 102.

Chapter 11: Radioactivity: Tools Available to Lise and the Berlin Team in Their Investigation of Uranium

1. Madsen, Michael, 'Pioneering Nuclear Science: The Discovery of Nuclear Fission', IAEA, 20 December 2013.
2. Woodford, Chris (2009/2019) Geiger counters. https://www.explainthatstuff.com/how-geiger counters-work.html.
3. Tritton, Roger (Managing Editor), *The Hutchinson Encyclopaedia*.

Chapter 12: Enrico Fermi and Uranium

1. Bernstein, Jeremy, *Hitler's Uranium Club*, pp. 7–8.
2. Fermi, Enrico, 'Artificial Radioactivity produced by Neutron Bombardment', Nobel lecture, 12 December 1938.
3. Watson, Peter, *Fallout*, p. 27.

4. Fermi, Enrico, 'Artificial Radioactivity produced by Neutron Bombardment', Nobel lecture, 12 December 1938.
5. Fermi, E, 'Possible Production of Elements of Atomic Number Higher than 92', *Nature*, 133, pp. 898–899 (1934).
6. Lise Meitner, Physical Institute, Royal Academy of Sciences, Stockholm and O.R. Frisch, Institute of Theoretical Physics, University Copenhagen, 16 January 1939, published in *Nature*, 11 February 1939. O.R. Frisch to Editor of *Nature*, 11 February 1939, Volume 143, pp. 239–240.
7. Galison, Paul, 'Author of Error', Social Research, Volume 72, Number 1, Spring 2005.
8. Hoffmann, Klaus, *Otto Hahn: Achievement and Responsibility*, p. 256.

Chapter 13: A Word of Caution From Ida Noddack

1. Noddack, Ida, 'On Element 93', *Zeitschrift fur Angewarde Chemie*, Volume 47, p. 653, September 1934.

Chapter 14: Lise is Fascinated by Fermi's Findings

1. Meitner, Lise, 'Right and Wrong Roads to the Discovery of Nuclear Energy', *Naturwissenschaftlichen Rundschau*, 1963.
2. Meitner to Max von Laue, 4 September 1944 (MC).
3. Meitner, Lise, 'Right and Wrong Roads to the Discovery of Nuclear Energy', *Naturwissenschaftlichen Rundschau*, 1963.
4. Ibid.
5. Fermi, E. 'Possible Production of Elements of Atomic Number Higher Than 92', *Nature*, Volume 133, 1936. pp. 898–899.
6. Sime, Ruth Lewin, *Lise Meitner: A Life in Physics*, p. 168.
7. Hahn, Otto, Lise Meitner, and Fritz Strassmann, 'New Conversion Processes in the case of Irradiation of Uranium: Elements Beyond Uranium', *Berichte der Deutsche Chemische Gesellschaft*, Volume 69, 1936. pp. 905–919.
8. Strassmann, Friedrich Wilhelm, *Complete Dictionary of Scientific Biography*.
9. Meitner, Lise, and Max Delbrück, *Der Aufbau der Atomkerne: Natürliche und Künstliche Kernunwandlungen*.
10. Hahn, Otto, Lise Meitner, and Fritz Strassmann, 'New Conversion Processes in the case of Irradiation of Uranium: Elements Beyond

Uranium', *Berichte der Deutsche Chemische Gesellschaft*, Volume 69, 1936, pp. 905–919.

11. Krafft, Fritz, 'Lise Meitner: Her Life and Times', *Zeitschrift für Angewandte Chemie*, International Edition, Volume 17, November 1978, p. 834.
12. Aritra, G., 'What is Bohr's Theory of the Compound Nucleus?', Socratic Q&A online, 1 March 2008.
13. Lemmerich, Jost W.B., Volume I: 'Correspondence with Colleagues and Friends 1907–1956', p. 380.
14. L. Meitner, O. Hahn, and F. Strassmann, 'About the Transformation of Uranium by Neutron Irradiation', *Zeitschrift für Physik,* Volume 106, 1937, pp. 249–270.
15. O. Hahn, L. Meitner, and F. Strassmann, 'About the Transuranes and their Chemical Behaviour', *Berichte der Deutsche Chemische Gesellschaft,* 70, p. 1374, 1937 (submitted 15 May 1937).
16. Irene Curie and Pavel Savitch, 'On the Nature of Radioelement 3.5 Hours formed in the Irradiation of Uranium by Neutrons', *Comptes Rendus*, 206, 1938, pp. 1643–1644.
17. Meitner, Lise, *Diary*, 9 May 1938 (MC).
18. Sime, Ruth Lewin, *Lise Meitner: A Life in Physics*, p. 190.
19. Pearson, J. Michael, 'On the Belated Discovery of Fission', *Physics Today*, 68(6), June 2015, p. 41.
20. Frisch, Otto, *What Little I Remember*, pp. 114–115.

Chapter 15: The Nazi Menace

1. Norman, Andrew, *Adolf Hitler: Dictator or Puppet?*, Pen & Sword Military, 2020.
2. Edith Hahn to James and Ingrid Franck, 22 April 1933, in Lemmerich, Jost, 'Max Born, James Franck, Physiker in ihrer Zeit: Der Luxus des Gewissens', Berlin: Staatsbibliotek Preussicher Kulturbesitz, Ausstellungskatalogue 17, 1982, p. 115.
3. Hahn to Ministerialrat Achelis, 27 July 1933, in Herbert Steiner, 'Lise Meitners Entlassung', *Österreich in Geschichte und Literatur*, p. 463.
4. I. Curie and F. Joliot, 'Un Nouveau Type de Radioactivité', *Comptes Rendus* 198, 1934, pp. 254–256.
5. Yad Vashem: The World Holocaust Remembrance Center.
6. Jewish Virtual Library.

7. Norman, Andrew, *Adolf Hitler: Dictator or Puppet?*.
8. Meitner to Max Born, 22 October 1944 (MC).
9. *Wikipedia*: The History of the Jews in Austria.
10. Ibid.
11. Ibid.
12. Ibid.
13. Ibid.
14. Yad Vashem: The World Holocaust Remembrance Center.

Chapter 16: Lise Escapes the Clutches of the Nazis

1. Sime, Ruth Lewin, *Lise Meitner: A Life in Physics*, p. 187.
2. Ibid., p. 192.
3. Ibid., p. 190.
4. Ibid., p. 186.
5. Rife, Patricia, *Lise Meitner and the Dawn of the Nuclear Age*, p. 164.
6. Sime, Ruth Lewin, *Lise Meitner: A Life in Physics*, p. 189.
7. Hahn, Dietrich (editor), *Otto Hahn: Erlebnisse und Erkenntnisee*, p. 54.
8. Sime, Ruth Lewin, op. cit., p. 193.
9. Rife, Patricia, op. cit., p. 169.
10. Sime, Ruth Lewin, op. cit., p. 195.
11. Ibid., p. 193.
12. Debye to Bohr, 16 June 1938 (MB).
13. Bohr to Fokker, 21 June 1938 (MB) Adriaan Fokker Papers, Rijksmuseum Boerhaave, Leiden, Netherlands.
14. Sime, Ruth Lewin, op. cit., p. 196.
15. Ibid., pp. 197–198.
16. Ibid., p. 201.
17. Rife, Patricia, op. cit., p. 170.
18. Meitner, Lise, *Diary*, 4 July 1938.
19. Meitner to Werner Heisenberg, 3 March 1954, in Lemmerich, Jost W.B., Volume I: 'Correspondence with Colleagues and Friends 1907–1956', p. 145.
20. Debye to Coster, 6 July 1938 (MB).
21. Rife, Patricia, op. cit., p. 171.
22. Sime, Ruth Lewin, op. cit., p. 203.
23. Rife, Patricia, op. cit., p. 171.
24. Information kindly supplied by Ruth Lewin Sime.

25. Coster to Fokker, 11 June 1938, Rijksmuseum Boerhaave Museum Archives, Leiden, Netherlands.
26. Coster to Fokker, 16 June 1938, Rijksmuseum Boerhaave Museum Archives, Leiden, Netherlands.
27. Information kindly supplied to the author by Arina R. Klokke.
28. Coster to Goudsmit, 12 July 1938, by kind permission of Anthea J. Coster.
29. Hahn, Otto, *My Life*, p. 149.
30. Ibid., p. 149.
31. Hahn to Meitner, 19 December 1938 (MC).
32. Kramish, Arnold, *The Griffin*, p. 49.
33. Hans Coster, personal communication, 1 February 1986, in Ruth Lewin Sime, *Lise Meitner: A Life in Physics*, p. 204.
34. Meitner, Lise, *Diary*, 13 July 1938.
35. Meitner, Lise, *Notebook*, 13 July 1938.
36. Information kindly supplied by Bernard C. Burgess, 27 April 2020.
37. Meitner to Gerta von Ubisch, 1 July 1947 (MC).
38. Sime, Ruth Lewin, *Lise Meitner: A Life in Physics*, p. 445.
39. Hahn to Coster, 15 July 1938 (MC).
40. Anthea J. Coster, Principal Research Scientist, MIT Haystack Observatory.
41. Sime, Ruth Lewin, op. cit., p. 205.
42. Coster, Anthea (presenter), 'Lise Meitner: Her Discovery of Fission and Dramatic Escape from Nazi Germany', University of Calgary, 9 April 2015.

Chapter 17: Into Exile

1. Fokker to Bohr, 16 July 1938, Rijksmuseum Boerhaave Museum Archives, Leiden, Netherlands.
2. Miep Coster to Fokker, date uncertain but probably 18 July 1938, Rijksmuseum Boerhaave Museum Archives, Leiden, Netherlands.
3. Sime, Ruth Lewin, *Lise Meitner: A Life in Physics*, pp. 206–207.
4. Ibid., p. 207.
5. Rife, Patricia, *Lise Meitner and the Dawn of the Nuclear Age*, p. 174.
6. Meitner to Gerta von Ubisch, 1 July 1947 (MC).
7. J.D. Cockcroft to Frisch, 30 August 1938 (MC).
8. Rife, Patricia, op. cit., pp. 389–390.
9. Sime, Ruth Lewin, op. cit., pp. 446–454.

10. Bryher, *The Heart to Artemis,* p. 278.
11. Ibid., p. 277.
12. Hahn, Otto, *My Life*, p. 162.
13. Yad Vashem: The World Holocaust Remembrance Center.
14. Arnold Berliner to Meitner, 1 November 1938 (MC).
15. Hahn to Meitner, 2 November 1938 (MC).
16. Meitner to Hahn, 4 November 1938 (MC).
17. O. Hahn and F. Strassmann, 'About the Formation of Radium Isotopes from Uranium which has been Irradiated with Fast Neutrons and with Slow Neutrons', *Naturwissenschaften*, Volume 26, 1938, pp. 755–756.
18. Stevenson, A., and Waite, M., *Concise Oxford English Dictionary.*
19. Yad Vashem: The World Holocaust Remembrance Center.
20. United States Holocaust Memorial Museum.
21. Sime, Ruth Lewin, *Lise Meitner: A Life in Physics*, p. 227.
22. Bryher, op. cit., p. 278.
23. Stevenson, A., and Waite, M., op. cit.
24. *Wikipedia*: Jews escaping from German-occupied Europe to the United Kingdom.
25. Sime, Ruth Lewin, op. cit., p. 228.
26. Ibid., p. 228.
27. Strassmann, Fritz, *Kernspaltung*, Berlin, December 1938.
28. Hahn, Otto, *My Life*, p. 162.
29. Hahn to Meitner, 19 December 1938 (MC).
30. Sime, Ruth Lewin, op. cit., p. 169.
31. Hahn to Meitner, 21 December 1938 (MC).
32. Hahn, O., and F. Strassmann, 'On the Detection and Behaviour of Alkaline Earth Metals produced by Neutron Irradiation of Uranium', *Die Naturwissenschaften*, Volume 27, pp. 11–15, January 1939.
33. Meitner to Hahn, 21 December 1938 (MC).
34. Meitner to Hahn, 21 December 1938 (MC).

Chapter 18: Eureka! Lise and Her Nephew Otto Frisch Strike Gold!

1. Stevenson, A., and Waite, M., *Concise Oxford English Dictionary.*
2. Otto Frisch, interviewed by Charles Weiner, 3 May 1967 at the American Institute of Physics, New York City.

3. Ibid.
4. Frisch, Otto, *What Little I Remember*, pp. 115–116.
5. Ibid., p. 116.
6. Ibid., pp. 116–117.

Chapter 19: Aftermath

1. Hahn to Meitner, 28 December 1938 (MC).
2. Meitner to Hahn, 29 December 1938 (MC).
3. Meitner to Hahn, 1 January 1939 (MC).
4. Stevenson, A., and Waite, M., *Concise Oxford English Dictionary*.
5. Meitner to Hahn, 3 January 1939 (MC).
6. Frisch to Meitner, 3 January 1939 (MC).
7. Hahn to Meitner, 7 January 1939 (MC).
8. Meitner to Frisch, undated letter (MC).
9. Frisch to Meitner, 8 January 1939 (MC).
10. Meitner to Hahn, 14 January 1939 (MC).
11. Sime, Ruth Lewin, *Lise Meitner: A Life in Physics*, p. 248.
12. Meitner, Lise, and Otto R. Frisch, 'Disintegration of Uranium by Neutrons: A New Type of Nuclear Reaction'. *Nature*, Volume 143, pp. 239–240 (11 February 1939).
13. Frisch, O.R., 'Physical Evidence for the Division of Heavy Nuclei under Neutron Bombardment', *Nature* (London), 1939, Volume 143, p. 276.
14. Meitner to Hahn, 18 January 1939 (MC).
15. Hahn to Meitner, 24 January 1939 (MC).
16. Sime, Ruth Lewin, op. cit., p. 264.
17. Hahn to Meitner, 25 January 1938 (MC).
18. Meitner to Hahn, 26 January 1939 (MC).
19. Hahn, Otto and Fritz Strassmann, 'Proof of the Formation of Active Isotopes of Barium from Uranium and Thorium Irradiated with Neutrons: Proof of the Existence of More Active Fragments Produced by Uranium Fission', *Die Naturwissenschaften*, Volume 27, Number 6, pp. 89–95, 10 February 1939.
20. Eva von Bahr-Bergius to Carl W. Oseen, 31 January 1939. Information kindly supplied by Professor Karl Grandin, Director, Centre for the History of Science, Royal Swedish Academy of Sciences, Stockholm, Sweden.

21. Eva von Bahr-Bergius to Carl W. Oseen, 31 January 1939. Information kindly supplied by Professor Karl Grandin.
22. Information kindly supplied by Professor Karl Grandin.
23. Carl W. Oseen to Eva von Bahr-Bergius, 2 February 1939. Information kindly supplied by Professor Karl Grandin.
24. Meitner to Hahn, 5 February 1939 (MC).
25. Sime, Ruth Lewin, op. cit., p. 255.
26. Meitner to Walter Meitner, 6 February 1939 (MC).
27. Hahn to Meitner, 7 February 1939 (MC).
28. Meitner, Lise, and Otto R. Frisch, 'Disintegration of Uranium by Neutrons: A New Type of Nuclear Reaction'. *Nature*, Volume 143, pp. 239–240 (11 February 1939).
29. Hahn to Meitner, 3 March 1939 (MC).
30. Meitner to Hahn, 6 March 1939 (MC).
31. Meitner to Hahn, 10 March 1939 (MC).
32. Hahn to Meitner, 13 March 1939 (MC).
33. Meitner to Bohr, 24 March 1939 (MC).
34. Hahn to Meitner, 20 March 1939 (MC).
35. Meitner to Rosbaud (draft), 1939 (MC).
36. Meitner to Hahn, 13 May 1939 (MC).
37. Sime, Ruth Lewin, op. cit., p. 275.
38. Meitner to Hahn, 15 July 1939 (MC).
39. Meitner to Hahn, 15 July 1939 (MC).
40. Information kindly supplied by Ruth Lewin Sime.
41. Herneck, Friedrich, *Bahnbrecher des Atomzeitalters*, p. 454.
42. Ibid., p. 454.
43. Ibid., p. 455.
44. Meitner, Lise, *Diary*, 18 July 1939.
45. Meitner, Lise, *Diary*, 3 August 1939.

Chapter 20: Another War

1. *Wikipedia*: The history of the Jews in Austria.
2. Ibid.
3. Ibid.
4. Bryher, *The Heart to Artemis,* p. 277.
5. Meitner to Hahn, 12 November 1939 (MC).
6. Sime, Ruth Lewin, *Lise Meitner: A Life in Physics*, p. 299.
7. Ibid., p. 299.

8. Lemmerich, Jost W.B., Volume I: 'Correspondence with Colleagues and Friends 1907–1956', p. 96.
9. Lemmerich, Jost W.B., Volume III, 'Correspondence with Max and Magda von Laue', p. 7.
10. Ibid., p. 8.
11. Lemmerich, Jost W.B., Volume I: 'Correspondence with Colleagues and Friends 1907–1956', p. 278.
12. Lemmerich, Jost W.B., Volume III, 'Correspondence with Max and Magda von Laue', p. 10.
13. Lemmerich, Jost W.B., Volume I: 'Correspondence with Colleagues and Friends 1907–1956', p. 360.
14. Lemmerich, Jost W.B., Volume III, 'Correspondence with Max and Magda von Laue', p. 10.
15. Sime, Ruth Lewin, op. cit., pp. 301–302.
16. Meitner to von Laue, 20 April 1942 (MC).
17. Lemmerich, Jost W.B., Volume I: 'Correspondence with Colleagues and Friends 1907–1956', p. 268.
18. Lemmerich, Jost W.B., Volume III, 'Correspondence with Max and Magda von Laue', p. 13.
19. Frisch, Otto, *What Little I Remember*, p. 118.
20. Ibid., p. 119.
21. Ibid., p. 15.
22. Roth, Jay, 'Unsolvable Problems and the Role of Polarity Thinking in Schools', online.
23. Lemmerich, Jost W.B., Volume I: 'Correspondence with Colleagues and Friends 1907–1956', p. 97.
24. Lemmerich, Jost W.B., Volume III, 'Correspondence with Max and Magda von Laue', p. 16.
25. Ibid., p. 18.
26. Meitner to Hahn, 15 April 1943 (MC).
27. Lemmerich, Jost W.B., Volume III, 'Correspondence with Max and Magda von Laue', p. 20.
28. Lemmerich, Jost W.B., Volume I: 'Correspondence with Colleagues and Friends 1907–1956', p. 306.
29. Frisch, O.R., 'Lise Meitner, 1878–1968', Biographical Memoirs of Fellows of the Royal Society, London 16 (1970) p. 414.
30. Bernstein, Jeremy, *Hitler's Uranium Club*, p. xxv.
31. Lemmerich, Jost W.B., Volume III, 'Correspondence with Max and Magda von Laue', p. 23.

32. Ibid., p. 24.
33. Lemmerich, Jost W.B., Volume I: 'Correspondence with Colleagues and Friends 1907–1956', p. 339.
34. Meitner to von Laue, 4 September 1946 (MC).
35. Meitner to Eva von Bahr-Bergius, 21 June 1944 (MC).
36. Meitner to Pettersson, 26 October 1944 (MC).
37. Lemmerich, Jost W.B., Volume I, 'Correspondence with Colleagues and Friends 1907–1956', p. 33.
38. Lemmerich, Jost W.B., Volume III, 'Correspondence with Max and Magda von Laue'.
39. Ibid., p. 13.
40. Ibid., p. 22.
41. Ibid., p. 27.
42. Ibid., p. 30.
43. Lemmerich, Jost W.B., Volume I: 'Correspondence with Colleagues and Friends 1907–1956', p. 274.
44. Ibid., p. 304.

Chapter 21: Farm Hall

1. Bernstein, Jeremy, *Hitler's Uranium Club*, pp. 55–56.
2. Ibid., pp. 119–120.
3. Ibid., pp. 356–357.
4. Bernstein, Jeremy, op. cit., p. 122.
5. Ibid., p. 358.
6. Frank, Sir Charles, *Operation Epsilon: The Farm Hall Transcripts*, pp. 102–103.
7. Sime, Ruth Lewin, *Lise Meitner: A Life in Physics*, p. 364.
8. Von Laue to Paul Rosbaud, 4 April 1959, in Bernstein, Jeremy, *Hitler's Uranium Club*, p. 369.
9. Bernstein, Jeremy, *Hitler's Uranium Club*, p. 255.
10. Ibid., p. 251.
11. Ibid., p. 255.
12. Meitner to Hahn 3 May 1933 (OHN).
13. Bernstein, Jeremy, op. cit., pp. 254, 377.
14. Ibid., pp. 359–360. It is known for a fact that Siegbahn, for one, did attend the conference.
15. Bernstein, Jeremy, op. cit., p. 320.
16. Ibid., p. 361.

17. Hahn, Otto, *My Life*, p. 185.
18. Bernstein, Jeremy, op. cit., p. xvii.
19. Meitner to Hahn, 27 June 1945 (MC).
20. Sime, Ruth Lewin, op. cit., p. 311.
21. Meitner to Max Born, 22 October 1944 (MC).
22. Hentschel, Klaus, 'Max Planck: My Audience with Adolf Hitler', *Physics and National Socialism*, Birkhäuser Basel, 1947, pp.359–361.
23. Meitner, Lise, *Diary*, 7 August 1945 (MC).

Chapter 22: Paul Rosbaud: Was Lise a Spy?

1. Kramish, Arnold, *The Griffin*, p. 12.
2. Ibid., p. 224.
3. Ibid., pp. 216–222.
4. O'Neil, Robin, *The Mahler Family in the Rise and Fall of the Third Reich*, p. 60.
5. Kramish, Arnold, op. cit., p. 54.
6. Ibid., p. 112.
7. Arnold Berliner to Meitner, 27 February 1940 (MC).
8. Von Laue to Meitner, 2 March 1940 (MC).
9. Stevenson, A., and Waite, M., *Concise Oxford English Dictionary*.
10. Berliner to Meitner, 21 November 1940 (MC).
11. Kramish, Arnold, op. cit., p. 219.
12. Ibid., pp. 263–264.
13. Ibid., pp. 224–227.
14. Ibid., p. 235.
15. Ibid., p. 191.
16. Ibid., p. 227.

Chapter 24: The War Ends

1. Rosbaud to Meitner, 25 October 1945 (MC).
2. Saad, Lydia, 'Gallup Vault: Americas' Mindset After Hiroshima', 26 May 2016.
3. Max von Laue to Theodor von Laue, 7 August 1945 (LP).
4. Lemmerich, Jost W.B., Volume I: 'Correspondence with Colleagues and Friends 1907–1956', p. 36.
5. Birgit Broomé Aminoff to Meitner, 16 November 1945 (MC).
6. Meitner to Birgit Aminoff, 20 November 1945.

7. Meitner to Eva von Bahr-Bergius, 5 December 1945 (MC).
8. Sime, Ruth Lewin, *Lise Meitner: A Life in Physics*, pp. 327–328.
9. Klein to Bohr, 17 November 1945 (BSC).
10. Lemmerich, Jost W.B., Volume I: 'Correspondence with Colleagues and Friends 1907–1956', p. 236.
11. Ibid., p. 239.
12. Ibid., p. 353.
13. Ibid., p. 97.
14. Meitner to Franck, 16 January 1946 (MC).
15. Lemmerich, Jost W.B., Volume I: 'Correspondence with Colleagues and Friends 1907–1956', Meitner to Egil A. Hylleraas, 18 January 1946, p. 174.
16. Ibid., p. 147.
17. Axelsson, George, 'Is the Atom Terror Exaggerated', *The Saturday Evening Post*, August 1946, pp. 34–47.
18. Ibid., pp. 34–47.
19. Lemmerich, Jost W.B., Volume I: 'Correspondence with Colleagues and Friends 1907–1956', p. 86.
20. Ibid., p. 4.
21. Hahn to Meitner, 17 September 1946 (MC).
22. Meitner to Lola Allers, 27 October 1946.
23. Meitner to von Laue, 12 November 1946 (MC).
24. Meitner to Hahn, 15 November 1946 (MC), p. 339.
25. Lemmerich, Jost W.B., Volume I: 'Correspondence with Colleagues and Friends 1907–1956', p. 128.
26. Ibid., p. 128.
27. Meitner to Margrethe Bohr, 22 November 1946.

Chapter 25: How Hahn and Not Lise Became Sole Contender For a Nobel Prize

1. Information kindly supplied by Professor Karl Grandin.
2. Hahn, Otto, 'New Atoms', Elsevier, New York, 1950, p. 42.
3. '25 Jahre Uranspaltung', *Urania*, Berlin, DDR, Volume 1, p. 8.
4. Today, the membership of the Royal Swedish Academy of Science's Assembly and Committees is far more broadly based. For example, of the 625 members of the Academy, 175 are foreign members.
5. Rife, Patricia, *Lise Meitner and the Dawn of the Nuclear Age*, p. 389.

Chapter 26: Nobel Nominations and Deliberations: Reason and Unreason

1. Swedish Academy of Sciences Nobel Archives, nomination letter and report to the Committee for Chemistry, 31 March 1939.
2. Crawford, Elisabeth, Ruth Lewin Sime, and Mark Walker, 'A Nobel tale of Wartime Injustice', *Nature*, Volume 382, 1 August 1996.
3. Crawford, Elisabeth, Ruth Lewin Sime, and Mark Walker, op. cit., *Nature*, Volume 382, 1 August 1996.
4. Grandin, Karl, email to the author, 5 February 2020.
5. Crawford, Elisabeth, Ruth Lewin Sime, and Mark Walker, 'A Nobel tale of Wartime Injustice', *Nature*, Volume 382, 1 August 1996.
6. Erik Hulthén's 'Special Report', 9 June 1945. Courtesy Karl Grandin and translated by him.
7. Otto Frisch, interviewed by Charles Weiner, 3 May 1967 at the American Institute of Physics, New York City.
8. Niels Bohr to Oskar Klein, 11 September 1945. Information kindly supplied by Professor Karl Grandin.
9. Oskar Klein to Niels Bohr, 17 November 1945. Information kindly supplied by Professor Karl Grandin.
10. Crawford, Elisabeth, Ruth Lewin Sime, and Mark Walker, op. cit., *Nature*, Volume 382, 1 August 1996.
11. Ibid., p. 231.
12. Günnar Hägg, Arne Westgren obituary, online.

Chapter 28: The Alleged Nazi Bomb

1. 'German Nuclear Weapons Program', *Wikipedia*.
2. Ibid.
3. Heisenberg, Werner: 'Max-Planck-Institut für Physik und Astrophysik in München'. In Max-Planck-Gesellschaft, Jahrbuch 1961, T. 2, S. pp. 632–643.
4. Henning, Eckart and Marion Kazemi, 'Dahlem: Domain of Science', p. 125.
5. Stevenson, A., and Waite, M., *Concise Oxford English Dictionary*.
6. 'Science and the Swastika', Episode 3: 'The Good German', Darlow Smithson Productions, 2001.
7. Walker, Mark, *German Natnal Socialism and the Quest for Nuclear Power 1939–1949*, p. 55.

8. Bernstein, Jeremy, *Hitler's Uranium Club*, p. xxiii.
9. Op. cit., p. 122.
10. Meitner to Max Born, 20 September 1942 (MC).
11. Speer, Albert, *Inside the Third Reich*, p. 226.
12. Ibid., p. 227.
13. Ibid., p. 226.
14. Ibid., p. 227.
15. Eckart, Henning, and Marion Kazemi, 'Dahlem: Domain of Science', p. 125.
16. Stevenson, A., and Waite, M., op. cit.
17. 'German Nuclear Weapons Program', *Wikipedia*.
18. Heisenberg, Werner, op. cit., Max-Planck-Institut für Physik und Astrophysik in München. In Max-Planck-Gesellschaft, Jahrbuch 1961, T. 2, S. pp. 632–643, and Eckart Henning, and Marion Kazemi, 'Dahlem: Domain of Science', p. 125.
19. Eckart, Henning, and Marion Kazemi, op. cit., p. 125.
20. Heisenberg, Werner, op. cit., in Max-Planck-Gesellschaft, Jahrbuch 1961, T. 2, S. pp. 632–643. Eckart, Henning, and Marion Kazemi, 'Dahlem: Domain of Science', p. 125.
21. 'Science and the Swastika', op. cit.

Chapter 29: Niels Bohr: The Truth at Last!

1. Niels Bohr Archive, Blegdamsvej 17, DK-2100, Copenhagen, Denmark.

Chapter 30: Manne Siegbahn: A Thorn in Lise's Side

1. Ross, Rachel, 'What is X-ray Spectroscopy?', 5 December 2018, Life Science online.
2. Friedman, Robert Marc, *The Politics of Excellence*, pp. 151–152.
3. Ibid., p. 213.
4. Oskar Widman to Wilhelm Palmaer, 19 November 1926. Wilhelm Palmaer Papers, University Library, Stockholm.
5. Meitner to Hahn, 12 February 1939 (MC).
6. Meitner to Hahn, 4 March and 21 June 1944 (MC).
7. Hans Pettersson to Meitner, 16 November 1945 (MC).

8. Friedman, Robert Marc, 'Text, Context, and Quicksand: Method and Understanding in Studying the Nobel Science Prizes', *Historical Studies in the Physical Sciences*, 20, No. 1: 74, 1989.
9. Oskar Klein to Niels Bohr, 17 November 1945. Information kindly supplied by Professor Karl Grandin.

Chapter 31: Lise's Integrity and Hatred of Dishonesty

1. Ball, Philip, *Serving the Reich*, p. 227.
2. Hahn, Otto, *My Life*, p. 188.
3. Meitner to James Franck, 16 January 1947 (MC, wrongly dated 1946).

Chapter 32: Lise's Humanity

1. Meitner to von Laue, 12 November 1946 (MC).
2. Krafft, Fritz, 'Lise Meitner: Eine Biographe', speech delivered January 1988, Hahn-Meitner Institute, Berlin.

Chapter 33: The Peace

1. Meitner to Eva von Bahr-Bergius, 24 December 1946 (MC).
2. Meitner to Lola Allers, 29 December 1946 (MC).
3. Information kindly supplied by Professor Karl Grandin.
4. Information kindly supplied by Professor Karl Grandin.
5. Information kindly supplied by Professor Karl Grandin.
6. Meitner to Hahn, 30 March 1947 (MC).
7. Meitner to James Franck, 6 January 1947 (wrongly dated 1946) (MC).
8. Meitner to James Franck, 16 January 1947 (wrongly dated 1940) (MC).
9. Lemmerich, Jost W.B., Volume III, 'Correspondence with Max and Magda von Laue', p. 32.
10. Gerta von Ubisch to Meitner, 28 February 1947 (MC).
11. Meitner to von Laue, 12 November 1946 (MC).
12. Lemmerich, Jost W.B., Volume I: 'Correspondence with Colleagues and Friends 1907–1956', p. 374.
13. Meitner to Gerta von Ubisch, 1 July 1947 (MC).
14. Lemmerich, Jost W.B., Volume I: 'Correspondence with Colleagues and Friends 1907–1956', p. 219.

15. Meitner to von Laue, 4 August 1947 (MC).
16. Meitner to von Laue, 4 August 1947 (MC).
17. Lemmerich, Jost W.B., Volume I: 'Correspondence with Colleagues and Friends 1907–1956', p. 362.
18. Lemmerich, Jost W.B., Volume III, 'Correspondence with Max and Magda von Laue', p. 35.
19. Lemmerich, Jost W.B., Volume I: 'Correspondence with Colleagues and Friends 1907–1956', p. 241.
20. Ibid., p. 340.
21. Meitner to Eva von Bahr-Bergius, 10 January 1948 (MC).
22. Hahn, Dietrich (editor), *Otto Hahn, Begründer des Atomzeitalters: Eine Biographie in Bildern und Dokumenten.*
23. Lemmerich, Jost W.B., Volume I: 'Correspondence with Colleagues and Friends 1907–1956', pp. 124–125.
24. Ibid., p. 347.
25. Ibid., p. 369.
26. Ibid., p. 34.
27. Meitner to Hahn, 6 June 1948.
28. Meitner to Hahn, 6 June 1948 (MC).
29. Hahn to Meitner, 16 June 1948.
30. Lemmerich, Jost W.B., Volume I, 'Correspondence with Colleagues and Friends 1907–1956', p. 99.
31. Meitner to von Laue 7 September 1948 (MC).
32. Lemmerich, Jost W.B., Volume I: 'Correspondence with Colleagues and Friends 1907–1956', p. 252.
33. Lemmerich, Jost W.B., Volume III, 'Correspondence with Max and Magda von Laue', p. 38.
34. Lemmerich, Jost W.B., Volume I: 'Correspondence with Colleagues and Friends 1907–1956', p. 258.
35. Ibid., p. 317.
36. Ibid., p. 395.
37. Ibid., p. 342.
38. Ibid., p. 364.
39. Lise Meitner lecture, Austrian UNESCO Commission, 30 March 1953, in *Atomenergie und Frieden: Lise Meitner und Otto Hahn* (Vienna, Wilhelm Frick-Verlag, 1954), pp. 23–24.
40. Meitner to Hahn, 22 June 1953.
41. Sime, Ruth Lewin, *Lise Meitner: A Life in Physics*, p. 371.

42. Sime, Ruth Lewin, 'An Inconvenient History: The Nuclear-Fission Display in the Deutsches Museum', *Physics in Perspective*, Birkhäuser, Basel, Switzerland, Volume 12, 2010, pp. 190–218.
43. Meitner to Hahn, 15 November 1953 (MC).
44. Lemmerich, Jost W.B., Volume I: 'Correspondence with Colleagues and Friends 1907–1956', p. 103.
45. Ibid., p. 2.
46. Ibid., p. 103.
47. Ibid., p. 341.
48. Czarny, Ryszard, *Sweden: From Neutrality to International Solidarity*, p. 66.
49. Lemmerich, Jost W.B., Volume III, 'Correspondence with Max and Magda von Laue', p. 46.
50. Lemmerich, Jost W.B., Volume I: 'Correspondence with Colleagues and Friends 1907–1956', p. 358.
51. Ibid., p. 248.
52. Lemmerich, Jost W.B., Volume III, 'Correspondence with Max and Magda von Laue', p. 47.
53. Meitner to James Franck, 8 September 1955 (FP).
54. Lemmerich, Jost W.B., Volume I: 'Correspondence with Colleagues and Friends 1907–1956', p. 132.
55. Ibid., p. 104.
56. Ibid., p. 377.
57. Sime, Ruth Lewin, *Lise Meitner: A Life in Physics*, p. 376.
58. Lemmerich, Jost W.B., Volume I: 'Correspondence with Colleagues and Friends 1907–1956', p. 265.
59. Ibid., p. 10.

Chapter 34: Walter Meitner, Lise's Beloved Youngest Sibling, and His Family

1. Information kindly provided by Anne and Philip Meitner.
2. Tom Topol, author of *Let Pass or Die: Passport History*.
3. Fry, Helen, *Spymaster: The Secret Life of Kendrick*, p. 154.
4. British Foreign Office files, Series FO 371.
5. Information kindly supplied to the author by Helen Fry, 29 March 2020.
6. Information kindly supplied to the author by Tom Topol.

7. Fry, Helen, op. cit., Helen Fry, interview with Prudence Holmes, daughter of Clara Holmes. Information kindly supplied to the author by Helen Fry on 29 March 2020.
8. Ibid., p. 40.
9. Ibid., p. 43.
10. Ibid., p. 127.
11. Ibid., p. 128.
12. Ibid., p. 155.
13. Ibid., p. 171.
14. Information kindly supplied by Tony Barrett, Lotte Meitner-Graf Archive.
15. *Ancestry*.
16. *Ancestry*.

Chapter 35: Later Years

1. Werner Heisenberg, 'Gedenkworte für Otto Hahn un Lise Meitner', *Order pour le Mérite für Wissenschaften und Künste: Reden und Gedenkworte* 9 (1968–1969).
2. Perutz, Max, *I Wished I'd Made You Angrier Earlier*.
3. Information kindly supplied by Professor Karl Grandin.
4. M.-L. Rehder, Göttingen, personal communication, 30 June 1985, in Ruth Lewin Sime, *Lise Meitner: A Life in Physics*, p. 379.
5. Smith, Mark E., reply by M. F. Perutz, Lise Meitner's Genius, New York Review of Books, 3 February 1994.
6. Hahn, Otto, *My Life*, pp. 152–153.
7. Ibid., p. 199.

Chapter 36: Lise's Dear Friend Elisabeth Schiemann

1. Kilian, Benjamin, Helmut Knüpffer and Karl Hammer, 'Elisabeth Schiemann (1881–1972): A Pioneer of Crop Plant Research, with Special Reference to Cereal Phylogeny', *Genetic Resources and Crop Evolution*, January 2013.
2. Lemmerich, Jost W.B., Volume II: 'Correspondence with Elisabeth and Gertrud Schiemann'.
3. Ibid.
4. Professor Hatzidakis to Meitner, Piraeus, 1915 (MC).

5. The date of Henriette's death is not known, but it presumably occurred sometime after the birth of her second child Ioannis on 12 December 1913.
6. Possibly a reference to Dr Udo Esch the physician, who married Marie L. von Kluge, daughter of Field Marshal Günter von Kluge in 1938.
7. Lemmerich, Jost W.B., Volume I, 'Correspondence with Colleagues and Friends 1907–1956', p. 9.
8. Meitner, Lise, *Diary*, 24 April 1947 (MC).
9. Meitner to Gerta von Ubisch, 1 July 1947 (MC).
10. Meitner to von Laue, 4 August 1947 (MC).
11. Lemmerich, Jost W.B., Volume I, 'Correspondence with Colleagues and Friends 1907–1956', p. 211.

Epilogue

1. Eckart, Henning, and Marion Kazemi, 'Dahlem: Domain of Science', *Berlin*, 2009. p. 125.

Bibliography

Ball, Philip, *Serving the Reich* (University of Chicago Press, Chicago, 2014)

Bernstein, Jeremy, *Hitler's Uranium Club* (introduction by David Cassidy) (AIP Press, New York, 1996)

Bryher, *The Heart to Artemis* (Collins, London, 1963)

Crawford, Elisabeth, *The Beginnings of the Nobel Institution* (Cambridge University Press, Cambridge, UK, 1984)

Czamy, Ryszard, *Sweden: From Neutrality to International Solidarity* (Springer, Cham, Switzerland, 2018)

Frank, Sir Charles, *Operation Epsilon: The Farm Hall Transcripts* (University of California Press, Berkeley, California, USA and Institute of Physics, Bristol, UK, 1993)

Frank, Philipp, *Einstein: His Life and Times* (Jonathan Cape, London, 1949)

Friedman, Robert Marc, *The Politics of Excellence* (Henry Holt, New York, 2001)

Frisch, Otto, *What Little I Remember* (Cambridge University Press, Cambridge, UK, 1980)

Fry, Helen, *Spymaster: The Secret Life of Kendrick* (Marranos Press, London, 2014)

Hahn, Dietrich (editor), *Otto Hahn, Begründer des Atomzeitalters: Eine Biographie in Bildern und Dokumenten* (München, List Verlag, 1979)

Hahn, Dietrich (editor), *Otto Hahn: Erlebnisse und Erkenntnisee* (Econ Verlag, Dusseldorf, 1975)

Hahn, Otto, *My Life* (MacDonald, London, 1970)

Hargittai, István, *The Road to Stockholm* (Oxford University Press, Oxford, UK, 2002)

Herneck, Friedrich, *Bahnbrecher des Atomzeitalters* (Buchverlag der Morgen, Berlin, 1965)

Hoffmann, Klaus, *Otto Hahn: Achievement and Responsibility* (Springer, New York, Berlin, Heidelberg, 2001)

Kramish, Arnold, *The Griffin* (Macmillan, London, 1986)

Lemmerich, Jost W.B., Detailed Catalogue of Lise Meitner's Papers at Churchill Archive Centre, Volume I, 'Correspondence with Colleagues and Friends 1907–1956'

Lemmerich, Jost W.B., Detailed Catalogue of Lise Meitner's Papers at Churchill Archive Centre, Volume II: 'Correspondence with Elisabeth and Gertrud Schiemann'

Lemmerich, Jost W.B., Detailed Catalogue of Lise Meitner's Papers at Churchill Archive Centre, Volume III, 'Correspondence with Max and Magda von Laue'

Meitner, Lise, *Diary* (Churchill Archives Centre, MTNR 3/20)

Meitner, Lise, *Notebook* (Churchill Archives Centre, MTNR 2/15)

Norman, Andrew, *Hitler: Dictator or Puppet?* (Pen & Sword Military, Barnsley, UK, 2020)

O'Neil, Robin, *The Mahler Family in the Rise and Fall of the Third Reich* (Memoirs, London, 2015)

Pearson, J. Michael, 'On the Belated Discovery of Fission', *Physics Today*, 68(6), June 2015, pp. 40–45

Perutz, Max, *I Wished I'd Made You Angrier Earlier* (Oxford University Press, Oxford, 1998)

Rennert, David, and Tanje Traxler, *Lise Meitner: Pioneer of the Atomic Age* (Residenz Verlag, Salzburg, Austria, 2018)

Rife, Patricia, *Lise Meitner and the Dawn of the Nuclear Age* (Birkhäuser, Boston, Basel, Berlin, 1999)

Sime, Ruth Lewin, *Lise Meitner: A Life in Physics* (University of California Press, Berkeley, 1996)

Stevenson, A., and Waite, M., *Concise Oxford English Dictionary* (Oxford University Press, Oxford and New York, 2011)

Walker, Mark, *German National Socialism and the Quest for Nuclear Power 1939–1949* (Cambridge University Press, 1989)

Watson, Peter, *Fallout* (Simon & Schuster, London, New York, Sydney, Toronto, New Delhi, 1988)

Index